THE
ELIZABETHAN DRAMATISTS
AS
CRITICS

The Elizabethan

DRAMATISTS
AS CRITICS

By David Klein, Ph. D.
Professor Emeritus of English,
City College of New York

PHILOSOPHICAL LIBRARY
New York

Library of Congress Catalog Card Number: 62-18540

Printed in the United States of America

TO THE MEMORY

OF MY WIFE

HANNAH

AND OUR DAUGHTER

RUTH

CONTENTS

PREFACE

The great romantic drama of the Elizabethan Age did not have its Aristotle to formulate its theory. As ANGLIA put it, *Die theorie und kritic des englischen dramas des 16. jahrhunderts kann nur aus gelegentlichen äusserungen damaligen dramatiker richtig erkannt werden*. Accordingly, in 1910, I published a volume entitled *Literary Criticism from the Elizabethan Dramatists*, in which I aimed to make accessible, and to organize, the *gelegentlichen äusserungen*, those scattered utterances of the Elizabethan dramatists which constitute their published reflections upon their own art. Its usefulness was widely acknowledged, which fact induces me to present this volume, in which I have incorporated the numerous items that have come to my attention in the intervening years—so numerous, indeed, as to make it thrice the size of its predecessor.

The need for a work of this kind is made manifest by a remark from one of the best beloved of our Shakespeare scholars: ". . . literature rarely talked about itself. In literature the Elizabethans seem to have had relatively little self-consciousness along with their almost incredible activity." The repertory which I here present is evidence that their consciousness of what they were doing was by no means as little as has been generally supposed. The material here collected constitutes the contemporary literary exposition of the romantic drama.

I take this opportunity to express my gratitude to Professor Thomas Whitfield Baldwin and Professor Marvin Rosenberg, for their active interest in my project; to my wife Kate, without whose devoted assistance and gentle encouragement this book would still have reposed in the limbo of things to come; to the personnel of the Philosophical Library, for their patient solicitude in the face of the unusual difficulties inherent in the printing of a work of this kind, even when not compounded by the human factor.

THE
ELIZABETHAN DRAMATISTS
AS
CRITICS

I. APPLIED CRITICISM

Of literary criticism in the narrow sense, what the Elizabethans termed *censure*, and what I have here called *applied criticism*, namely, the application of aesthetic theory to accomplished work, the Elizabethans have given us little of consequence. Discussion of contemporary books and plays there certainly was—evidently violent discussion. Doesn't Shakespeare tell us so?

The play, I remember, pleas'd not the million; 'twas caviary to the general. But it was (as I receiv'd it, and others, whose judgment in such matters cried in the top of mine) an excellent play, well digested in the scenes, set down with as much modesty as cunning. I remember, one said there were no sallets in the lines to make the matter savory, nor no matter in the phrase that might indict the author of affectation; but call'd it an honest method, as wholesome as sweet, and by very much more handsome than fine.

It is safe to assume that Jonson transplants his own environment to ancient Rome when he tells us (*Discoveries*, ed. Schelling, p. 80) that Horace

could not be ignorant of the judgment of the times in which he lived, especially being a man so conversant and inwardly familiar with the censures of great men that did discourse of these things daily amongst themselves.

And from him we learn that the playwrights took part in the discussion (*Every Man in His Humor*, I iv):

Bobadill. I would fain see all the poets of these times pen such another play as that [*Spanish Tragedy*] was! They'll prate and swagger, and keep a stir of art and devices, when, as I am a gentle-

1

man, read 'hem, they are the most shallow, pitiful, barren, fellows that live upon the face of the earth.

A distinct echo of the prating and swaggering has reached us from the Mermaid Tavern; and engraved in marble over the chimney in Jonson's club room, the Apollo, in the Old Devil Tavern at Temple Bar, were Jonson's *Leges Convivales. Rules for the Tavern Academy: or, Laws for the Beaux Esprits.* They numbered twenty-four, number twelve of which reads: *At Fabulis magis quam Vino velitatio fiat*; which Jonson Englished: "Let the contests be rather of books than of wine."

Michael Drayton, in his *Epistle to Reynolds,* indulges in reminiscences of wintry evenings spent in "some well chosen place," where, "with moderate meat and wine and fire," they would discuss poetry and "stage pieces famous long before, . . . as well as those of these latter times."

And the discussions were not confined to the taverns. There were drawing-room assemblages of the kind we associate with Paris in the days of Louis XIV, if we are to judge by the following passage in Chapman's *Monsieur D'Olive* (I i 302):

> *D'Olive.* I will have my chamber the rendezvous of all good wits, the shop of good words, the mine of good jests, an ordinary of fine discourse; critics, essayists, linguists, poets, and other professors of that faculty of wit, shall at certain hours i' the day resort thither; it shall be a second Sorbonne, where all doubts or differences of learning, honor, duellism, and poetry, shall be disputed.

The "critics" are included. These had become an established nuisance. Witness the following passages.

Tomkis, *Lingua*, II iv:

> *Memory.* The most customers I remember myself to have are . . . scholars, and nowadays the most of them are become critics, bringing me home such paltry things to lay up for them, that I can hardly find them again.
> *Phantastes.* Jupiter, Jupiter! I had thought these flies had bit none but myself.

Ibid. V ix:

> *Appetitus.* Nay, if you begin to critic once, we shall never have done.

2

Marston, *What You Will*, Prol.:

> ... nor pursues the love
> Of the nice critics of this squeamish age,
> Nor strives he to bear up with every sail
> Of floating censure.

Middleton, *Mad World*, V i:

> *Semus.* There are certain players come to town, sir, and desire
> to interlude before your worship.
> *Sir Bounteous.* Players! By the mass, they are welcome. They
> will grace my entertainment well. But for *certain* players, there
> thou liest, boy—they were never more uncertain in their lives; now
> up, and now down; they know not when to play, where to play, nor
> what to play: nor when to play, for fearful fools; where to play,
> for puritan fools; nor what to play, for critical fools.

Jonson's opinion of them is thus characteristically expressed
(*Magnetic Lady*, Interlude II):

> *Boy.* They are no other but narrow and shrunk natures;
> shrivell'd up; poor things, that cannot think well of themselves,
> who dare to detract others. That signature is upon them, and it
> will last; a half-witted barbarism, which no barber's art, or his balls,
> will ever expunge or take out!

and with equal scorn in verses addressed to Master Joseph Rutter:

> I was scarce allowed
> By those deep grounded, understanding men,
> That sit to censure plays, yet know not when,
> Or why, to like.[1]

But his most vituperative portrait of them is found in his address
to the reader of *Sejanus*, where he speaks of them as

> those common torturers that bring all wit to the rack; whose noses
> are ever like swine spoiling and rooting up the Muse's gardens;
> and their whole bodies like moles, as blindly working, under earth,
> to cast any, the least, hills upon virtue.

---

[1] How this reminds one of the amusing epilogue to a work by a
kindred spirit: Shaw's *Fanny's First Play*!

3

D'avenant, *Platonic Lovers*. Ded.:

> If it shall gain your liking, the severe rulers of the stage will be much mended in opinion.

That the activities of the critic and the consequent resentment on the part of the playwrights began early in the history of the Elizabethan drama is indicated by the fact that the prologue to *Common Conditions*, a play dated 1570, begs the audience not to judge rashly, and without seeing the whole play through; yet the author is resigned to the fact that no matter how good the play may be, there will be some determined to criticise adversely, and he assumes a defiant attitude toward them. This attitude of defiance is the common one assumed. A good example is presented by the prologue to *Wily Beguiled* (attributed to Peele):

> Let Momus' mates judge how they list,
> We fear not what they babble;
> Nor any paltry poet's pen
> Amongst that rascal rabble.

Similarly the epilogue to Marston's *Faun*:

>   . . . all the sting,
> All the vain foam of all those snakes that ring
> Minerva's glassful shield, can never taint,
> Poison, or pierce. Firm art disdains to faint.

And in the prologue to *The Dutch Courtezan*, he says the same thing:

>   . . . know, firm art cannot fear
> Vain rage.

But the opinions of such self-appointed arbiters who arraigned plays daily had to go with the wind; there were no media, journalistic or other, to perpetuate them.

Sometimes a playwright, in the course of his play, would indulge in fairly specific criticism of a contemporary, as when Ben Jonson, in the Induction to *Bartholomew Fair*, glances at Shakespeare's *Tempest*, or when he makes Marston vomit up his pet vocabulary in *The Poetaster*; or in *Every Man in His Humor*, ironically extols the absurdities in the *Spanish Tragedy*; or when Shakespeare, too, in the *Midsummer Night's Dream*, holds up to ridicule the rhetorical devices of Kyd, or in *Love's Labor's Lost*, the three-piled hyperbolic style of Lyly; or when Chapman does the same in *All Fools* (III i 205).

Sometimes, too, a playwright would give us a thumbnail sketch of a contemporary writer—Peele, Drayton, Jonson, and the author of the *Parnassus* plays each composed a series of them. But usually these are only expressions of attitude, without critical substance. I quote a few that have a measure of concreteness.

Chapman on Marlowe (*Hero and Leander* III 183):

Then ho, thou most strangely intellectual fire,
That proper to my soul hast power to inspire
Her burning faculties, and with the wings
Of thy unsphered flame visitst the springs
Of spirits immortal, now (as swift as time
Doth follow motion) find the eternal clime
Of his free soul whose living subject stood
Up to the chin in the Pierian flood
And drunk to me half this Musaean story
Inscribing it to deathless memory.

Peele on Marlowe (*Honor of the Garter*, Prol.):

Marley, the Muses' darling for thy verse,
Fit to write passions for the souls below,
If any wretched souls in passion speak.

Drayton on Marlow (*Elegies of Poets and Poesy*) :

Neat Marlow, bathed in the Thespian springs,
Had in him those brave translunary things
That the first poets had; his raptures were
All air and fire, which made his verses clear;
For that fine madness still he did retain,
Which rightly should possess a poet's brain.

How limited Drayton's appreciation of Shakespeare! (*Elegies of Poets and Poesy*):

> . . . be it said of thee,
> Shakespeare, thou hadst as smooth a comic vein,
> Fitting the sock, and in thy natural brain
> As strong conception, and as clear a rage,
> As anyone that traffick'd with the stage.

Spenser (who finds his way into this treatise by virtue of his nine lost comedies of which Harvey thought more highly than of the *Fairy Queen*) had a truer estimate of Shakespeare's greatness (*Colin Clout's Come Home Again*) :

> And thou, though last, not least, in Aetion,
> A gentler shepherd may nowhere be found:
> Whose muse, full of high thoughts' invention,
> Doth, like himself, heroically sound.

If Sonnet VIII of *The Passionate Pilgrim* can be accepted as Shakespeare's the admiration was mutual:

> Dowland to thee is dear, whose heavenly touch
> Upon the lute doth ravish human sense;
> Spenser to me, whose deep conceit is such
> As, passing all conceit, needs no defense.
> Thou lov'st to hear the sweet melodious sound
> That Phoebus' lute, the queen of music, makes;
> And I in deep delight am chiefly drown'd
> Whenas himself to singing he betakes.
> One god is god of both, as poets feign.

From the second part of *The Return from Parnassus* we glean quite an assortment. Out of a long list of authors commented on, Spenser alone receives unqualified approval:

> A sweeter swan than ever sung in Po,
> A shriller nightingale than ever blest
> The prouder groves of self-admiring Rome.
> Blither was each valley, and each shepherd proud,
> While he did chant his rural minstrelsy.
> Attentive was full many a dainty ear;
> Nay, hearers hung upon his melting tongue
> While sweetly of his Fairy Queen he sung;
> While to the water's fall he tuned for fame,
> And in each bark engrav'd Eliza's name.

6

Sweet honey dropping Daniel doth wage
War with the proudest big Italian
That melts his heart in sugar'd sonnetting.
Only let him more sparingly make use
Of other's wit, and use his own the more,
That well may scorn base imitation.

What is said of Marston is very much like Jonson's arraignment of him in *The Poetaster*, performed earlier in the same year (1601):

Methinks he is a ruffian in his style;
Withouten bands of garter's ornament
He quaffs a cup of Frenchman's Helicon.
Then, royster doyster, in his oily terms,
Cuts, thrusts, and foins at whomsoe'er he meets,
And strews about Ram-Alley meditations.
Tut, what cares he for most modest close couched terms,
Cleanly to gird our looser libertines?
Give him plain naked words stript from their shirts,
That might beseem plain dealing Aretine.
Ay, there is one that backs a paper steed
And manageth a pen-knife gallantly;
Strikes his poniardo at a button's breadth,
Brings the great battering-ram of terms to town,
And at first volley of his cannon-shot
Batters the walls of the old fusty world.

Marlowe was happy in his buskin'd muse,
Alas, unhappy in his life and end.
Pity it is that wit so ill should dwell,
Wit lent from heaven, but vices sent from hell.
Our theater hath lost, Pluto hath got,
A tragic penman for a dreary plot.

Thomas Nash. Ay, here is a fellow that carried the deadly Stoccado in his pen, whose muse was armed with a gagtooth, And his pen possessed with Hercules' furies.
Let his faults sleep with his mournful chest,
And there forever with his ashes rest.
His style was witty, though it had some gall,
Some things he might have mended—so may all.

The aristocratic bias[1] of the Cambridge author comes painfully to the fore in his estimate of Ben Jonson. To be sure, Jonson had a Cambridge degree, but this was admittedly only by courtesy; his provenance was simply not to be swallowed.

> The wittiest fellow of a bricklayer in England. A mere empyric; one that gets what he hath by observation, and makes only nature privy to what he indites; so slow an inventor that he were better betake himself to his old trade of bricklaying; a bold whoreson, as confident now in making a book as he was in times past in laying of a brick.

And concerning Shakespeare this is all he has to say:

> Who loves not Adon's love, or Lucrece's rape?
> His sweeter verse contains heart-throbbing lines;
> Could but a graver subject him content,
> Without love's foolish lazy languishment.

In his appreciation he refuses to go even as far as his fellow Cantabrian, Drayton. A similar failure to comprehend the greatness of Shakespeare is evinced in Webster's brief appraisal of half a dozen of his contemporaries, addressed to the reader of *The White Devil*:

> Detraction is the sworn friend of ignorance. For mine own part, I have very truly cherished my good opinion of other men's worthy labors; especially of that full and heightened style of Master Chapman, the labor'd and understanding works of Master Jonson, the no less worthy composures of the both worthily excellent Master Beaumont and Master Fletcher, and lastly (without wrong last to be named) the right happy and copious industry of Master Shakespeare, Master Dekker, and Master Heywood.

Depreciation of Shakespeare of a more positive kind is offered by William Cartwright in a verse addressed to Fletcher in the folio of 1647:

---

[1] This bias is revealed in the Cambridge play, *Albumazar,* by Tomkis: the prologue apologizes for the employment of English as the medium for the play.

Shakespeare to thee was dull, where best jest lies
I' the ladies' questions and the fool's replies;
Old-fashioned wit, which walked from town to town
In turn'd hose, which our fathers called the clown;
Whose wit our nice times would obsceneness call,
And which made bawdry pass for comical.
Nature was all his art; thy vein was free
As his, but without his scurrility.

We must admit that Cartwright touched Shakespeare in a vulnerable spot when he alluded to "the ladies' questions and the fool's replies." The pity of it was that he saw in these a sample of Shakespeare's "best jest." Regrettably, Cartwright's opinion seems to have been the prevailing one at the time. In the same volume John Berkenhead speaks of Shakespeare's "trunk-hose wit." How precipitately Shakespeare's star was setting is forcefully demonstrated by Pepys, who found *Othello* to be "a mean thing" compared with Samuel Tuke's *The Adventures of Five Hours*.

Davenant, too, in the prologue to *The Unfortunate Lovers* (1643) impresses upon his audience how far superior the contemporary plays were to those of the previous generation. One is reminded of the way Bach's son apologized for the shortcomings of his father. These instances illustrate forcibly what Professor Schücking says about the sociology of taste.

Cartwright is more sensible in what he says in the same poem about Jonson's love scenes:

Jonson had writ things lasting and divine;
Yet his love scenes, Fletcher, compared to thine,
Are cold and frosty, and express love so,
As heat with ice, or warm fires mixed with snow.

Richard Flecknoe was a late arrival among the Elizabethans, so he was in a position to pass judgment upon his distinguished predecessors. This he does in his *Discourse of the English Stage*:

To compare our English dramatic poets together (without taxing them) Shakspear excelled in a natural vein, Fletcher in wit, and Johnson in gravity and ponderousness of style; whose only fault was, he was too elaborate; and had he mixt less erudition with his plays, they had been more pleasant and delightful than they are.

Comparing him with Shakespear, you shall see the difference betwixt nature and art; and with Fletcher, the difference betwixt wit and judgment; wit being an exuberant thing, like Nilus, never more commendable then when it overflows; but judgment a staid and reposed thing, always containing itself within its bounds and limits.

Beaumont and Fletcher were excellent in their kind, but they often err'd against decorum, seldom representing a valiant man without somewhat of the braggadocio, nor an honorable woman without somewhat of Doll Common in her; to say nothing of their irreverent representing kings' persons on the stage, who shu'd never be represented but with reverence. Besides, Fletcher was the first who introduc'd that witty obscenity in his plays, which, like poison infused in pleasant liquor, is always the more dangerous the more delightful.

Playwrights frequently penned laudatory poems like Cartwright's to one another. But their purpose being mere praise (usually to enhance the sale of a book) their content was of the most general kind. They are therefore barren for our purpose. The sentiments expressed in them were probably not to be taken too seriously. Jonson as much as admits this when he declares, in his address to the reader of *Catiline*, that "the most commend out of affection, self-tickling, an easiness, or imitation." A striking illustration is Jonson's well-known eulogy on Shakespeare prefixed to the First Folio. Compare this memorable effusion with the sober prose of *Timber* (incidentally affording another instance of literary dispute):

I remember the players have often mentioned it as an honor to Shakespeare, that in his writing, whatsoever he penned, he never blotted a line. My answer hath been, "Would he had blotted a thousand," which they thought a malevolent speech. I had not told posterity this but for their ignorance who chose that circumstance to commend their friend by wherein he most faulted; and to justify mine own candor; for I loved the man, and do honor his memory on this side idolatry as much as any. He was, indeed, honest, and of an open and free nature; had an excellent fancy, brave notions, and gentle expressions, wherein he flowed with that facility that sometimes it was necessary he should be stopped. *"Sufflaminandus erat,"* as Augustus said of Haterius. His wit was in his power; would the rule of it had been so too. Many times he fell into those things could not escape laughter, as when he said in the person of Caesar, one speaking to him: "Caesar, thou dost me wrong." He replied: "Caesar did never wrong but with just cause": and such like, which were ridiculous. But he redeemed his vices with his virtues. There was ever more in him to be praised than to be pardoned.

This flatly contradicts some of the important statements in the other, proving that they, however true and self-evident they appear to us, were to him a sample of the conventional adulation appropriate to that species of writing. The same holds true of what he says in the same poem of "Marlowe's mighty line." His real opinion is thus expressed in *Timber*:

The true artificer will not run away from nature as he were afraid of her; or depart from life, or the likeness of truth; but speak to the capacity of his hearers. And though his language differs from the vulgar somewhat, it will not fly from all humanity, with all the Tamerlanes and Tamer-chams of the late age, which had nothing in them but the scenical strutting and furious vociferation to warrant them to the ignorant gapers.

A whimsical piece of contemporary criticism is Thomas Middleton's swift review of the trend of the Elizabethan drama from Marlowe to the time of his writing (1611), found in his address to the reader of *The Roaring Girl*:

The fashion of playmaking I can properly compare to nothing so naturally as the alteration in apparel; for in the time of the great crop-doublet your huge bombastic plays, quilted with mighty words to lean purpose, was only then in fashion; and as the doublet fell, neater inventions began to set up. Now, in the time of spruceness, our plays follow the niceness of our garments: single plots, quaint conceits, lecherous jests, dressed up in hanging sleeves—and those are fit for the times.

The following, written about the same time (1610), is a bitter tirade by Marston on the low level reached by the contemporary theater. (*Histriomastix* III 189):

Chrisoganus.   Write on, cry on, yawl to the common sort
Of thick-skinned auditors such rotten stuffs,
More fit to fill the paunch of Esquiline
Than feed the hearings of judicial ears ...
O age, when every scrivener's boy shall dip
Profaning quills into Thessalia's spring;
When every artist prentice that hath read
The pleasant pantry of conceits, shall dare
To write as confident as Hercules;
When every ballad-monger boldly writes,
And windy froth of bottle-ale doth fill
Their purest organ of invention—
Yet, all applauded, and puffed up with pride,
Swell in conceit, and load the stage with stuff
Raked from the rotten embers of stale jests;
Which basest lines best please the vulgar sense,
Make truest rapture lose pre-eminence.

But this kind of complaint is probably chronic in all ages.
Spenser indulges in it as far back as 1591. In *Tears of the Muses*,
193, Thalia complains:

All places they with folly have possessed,
And with vain toys the vulgar entertain,

having banished

Fine counterfesance and unhurtful sport,
Delight and laughter decked in seemly sort.
All these, and all that else the comic stage
With seasoned wit and godly pleasance graced,
By which man's life in his likest image
Was limned forth, are wholly now defaced,
And those sweet wits which wont the like to frame
Are now despised, and made a laughing game. . . .
Instead thereof scoffing scurrility
And scornful folly with contempt is crept,
Rolling in rimes of shameless ribaudry,
Without regard or due decorum kept.
Each idle wit at will presumes to make,
And doth the learned's task upon him take.

Polyhymnia, speaking for non-dramatic poetry, contributes to the complaint, 547:

> For the sweet numbers and melodious measures
> With which I wont the winged words to tie,
> And make a tuneful diapase of pleasures,
> Now being let to run at liberty
> By those which have no skill to rule them right,
> Have now quite lost their natural delight.
> Heaps of huge words uphoarded hideously,
> With horrid sound, though having litle sense,
> They think to be chief praise of poetry.

As against this lament Daniel, only two years later, in the dedication of his *Cleopatra*, had the courage to boast:

> O that the ocean did not bound our style
> Within those strict and narrow limits so;
> But that the melody of our sweet isle
> Might now be heard to Tiber, Arne, and Po;
>   That they might know how far Thames doth outgo
>   The music of declined Italy.

And a quarter of a century after Marston's wail Heywood, in the prologue to *Challenge for Beauty*, affirms the superiority of the English drama over all others:

> The Roman and Athenian drama far
> Differ from us, and those that are
> In Italy and France, even in these days,
> Compared with ours, are rather jigs than plays.
> Like of the Spanish may be said, and Dutch . . .
> None versed in language but confess them such.

It may be interesting to call attention to the way an author pronounces a favorable judgment upon his work. In *Histrio-mastix,* at the end of Act II, when Landulpho, the visiting Italian lord, declares that the song sung by Posthast is "base trash," Philarchus remarks, "The Italian lord is an ass; the song is a good song." It is.

Richard Flecknoe, in his *Discourse of the English Stage*, written shortly after the Restoration, comments on some playwrights of bygone days:

> In this time were poets and actors in the greatest flourish: Johnson, Shakespear, with Beaumont and Fletcher their poets, and Field and Burbidge their actors. For plays, Shakespear was one of the first who inverted the dramatic style from dull history to quick comedy, upon whom Johnson refin'd, as Beaumont and Fletcher first writ in the heroic way, upon whom Suckling and others endeavored to refine again; one saying wittily of his *Aglaura* that 'twas full of fine flowers, but they seem'd rather stuck than growing there, as another of Shakespear's writings, that 'twas a fine farden, but it wanted weeding.

The critical utterances that remain to be cited would probably be considered the most important of all. The first is Chapman's dedication of *Achilles' Shield*, a translation of the Eighteenth Book of the Iliad (1598). The whole of this dedication constitutes an important piece of criticism, including a noteworthy comparison between Virgil and Homer. As it is easily accessible I shall quote only Chapman's vigorous attack on Scaliger, that giant of continental criticism. (Incidentally, we should need no further evidence how well acquainted the English dramatists were with the continental criticism):

> But thou soul-blind Scaliger, that never had anything but place, time, and terms to paint thy proficiency in learning, nor ever writtest anything of thine own impotent brain but thy only impalsied diminution of Homer (which I may swear was the absolute inspiration of thine own ridiculous genius), never didst thou more palpably damn thy drossy spirit in all thy all-countries-exploded filcheries, which are so grossly illiterate that no man will vouchsafe their refutation, than in thy senseless reprehensions of Homer, whose spirit flew as much above thy groveling capacity as Heaven moves above Barathrum.

So violent was Chapman's reaction to the stupidity of the continental criticism of Homer that he even made it serve the purpose of a farfetched analogy in *The Revenge of Bussy* (IV v 33ff.):

Clermont.   And as of Homer's verses many cities
On those stand of which Time's old moth hath eaten
The first or last feet, and the perfect parts
Of his unmatched poem sink beneath,
With upright gasping and sloth dull as death:
So the unprofitable things of life,
And those we cannot compass, we affect,
All that doth profit and we have, neglect.

Alongside of this is to be placed Ben Jonson's detailed and glowing estimate of Virgil in the last act of *The Poetaster*.

The accessibility of the remaining entries under this head does not justify reprinting here.

The most extensive piece of criticism of contemporary literature, dramatic and non-dramatic, is provided by Nash in his preface to Greene's *Menaphon*, and his pamphlet entitled *The Anatomy of Absurdity*. In *Summer's Last Will and Testament* (1592) (Hazlitt's Dodsley, VIII, p. 71) he puts into the mouth of Winter a hypothetical invective against all writing as a conveyor of sin, arraigning a list of important authors. Summer's retort is:

Winter, with patience unto my grief
I have attended thy invective tale.
So much untruth wit never shadowed:
'Gainst her own bowels thou art's weapons turn'st.
Let none believe thee that will ever thrive.

Thomas Carew's *Elegy on the Death of Dr. Donne* is a detailed and penetrating analysis of the greatness of that poet.

Finally, there is Shirley's preface to the Beaumont and Fletcher Folio. It is a warm and thoughtful appreciation.

But if examples of the application of aesthetic theory by Elizabethan dramatists are scanty, expressions of aesthetic theory itself are surprisingly plentiful; so plentiful, indeed, that they can be woven into a substantial pattern. None of the continental theaters offers a real parallel to the English phenomenon; the reason probably being that most of them submitted too readily to the dictates of classical criticism. The fact that the English theater did not submit is evidence of the intelligent awareness with which the English playwrights entertained their own, the new, ideas on dramatic composition. To them the subject was a live one, and they had to do a lot of hard thinking about it; to which they would be challenged, if by nothing else, by the presence on the continent of a vast body of literary criticism, and, more closely, Sidney's widely read *Apology*.[1] The written record of their thinking, as found in their plays and elsewhere, is surely an extension of the discussion and debate already alluded to, carried on in the taverns and elsewhere. That record is found largely, as one would expect, in prologues and epilogues. What is more notable, however, is that it also appears in the dialogue of the plays. Such a thing would be gravely inappropriate in plays controlled by classical canons which imposed a narrowly limited conception of unity, and restricted the supply of material out of which plays could be made. It would be foreign even to the Spanish drama, because, even though it resisted the pressure of classical criticism, it yet never became the mirror of the whole life of man, as the English drama did. In most continental plays, therefore, a passage, for instance, like that giving us Hamlet's views on acting would stick out, like an intrusion. On the other hand, the rich variety of the stuff that went into the typical Elizabethan play, could tolerate the presence of what were really digressions, without a resultant emphasis on their essential irrelevance.

The advanced state of the critical consciousness among the Elizabethan dramatists is further emphasized by the fact that several of them were the authors of expository works in the field of literary criticism. Indeed, the very first product of this kind produced by the age was *Certain Notes of Instruction Concerning the Making of Verse or Rhyme in English*, 1575, by George Gascoigne, author of *The Supposes*, the earliest extant English comedy in prose, and of *Jocasta*, the second earliest English tragedy in blank verse. Sometime before 1579 Spenser wrote *The English Poet*. When in 1579 Stephen Gosson, a former playwright, published his *School of Abuse*, Thomas Lodge, a prospective playwright, promptly replied with *A Defense of Poetry, Music,*

---

[1] Shirley. *Love in a Maze.* I ii:

Caperwit. . . . I hope you will excuse these fancies of mine . . . if now and then my brains do sparkle I cannot help it; raptures will out. . . . The midwife wrapt my head up in a sheet of Sir Philip Sidney. That inspired me.

and Stage Plays. In the following year Anthony Munday, another repentant playwright, published *A Third Blast of Retreat from Plays and Theaters*. (Not long after, however, he returned to play writing.) In 1592, Thomas Nash published an extensive defense of the theater in his *Pierce Penniless*. In 1602, Samuel Daniel, prompted by the appearance of Thomas Campion's *Observations in the Art of English Poesie*, published *A Defense of Rhyme*, and called upon his fellow craftsmen to join him in the defense. Ten years later appeared Thomas Heywood's *Apology for Actors*. Ben Jonson's *Timber* is a commonplace book, considerable portions of which are devoted to literary theory. More significant, undoubtedly, than any of the expositions mentioned must have been Jonson's commentary on Horace's *Ars Poetica*, the manuscript of which was burned in a fire that consumed Jonson's library and much of his work.[1]

In the authorship of the utterances in which playwrights revealed a critical consciousness, quantitatively speaking, Ben Jonson, as one would naturally expect, comes first, and Shakespeare next. No other writer is a close third. Accordingly, Shakespeare and Jonson will be singled out for individual treatment. The arrangement of the extracts under each heading will in the main be chronological. However, the advisability to keep the statements of a given author close together, or some other practical reason, may sometimes recommend a departure from this order.

---

[1] To this list must now be added the name of Richard Puttenham, author of the play, *Ginecocratia*, to whom (as I have just learned) and not to *George* Puttenham, is attributed *The Art of English Poesy* by G. C. Moore and E. K. Chambers.

II. EXCLUSIVE OF SHAKESPEARE AND JONSON

THEORY OF POETIC CREATION

The Renaissance exemplified two trends in art criticism: the romantic, which gave precedence to imagination and freedom in art production, stemming from Plato, and the classic, which insisted on the dominance of reason and control, stemming from Aristotle; but neither was completely disengaged from the other. Most of the Elizabethan dramatists followed the romantic trend; the classic trend was championed chiefly by Ben Jonson.

The romantic idea that the poet was divinely inspired was derived from Plato, and came to the Elizabethans by way of Boccaccio, Skelton, and Sidney, the last of whom put it this way: ". . . .they [poets] are so beloved of the gods that whatever they write proceeds of a divine fury."

Sometime before 1579 Spenser wrote an expository work entitled *The English Poet*. E. K., editor of *The Shepherd's Calendar*, in the Argument to the October Eclogue, describes poetry as

> . . . a divine gift and heavenly instinct not to be gotten by labor and learning, but adorned with both; and poured into the wit by a certain 'Ενθουσιασμος and celestial inspiration, as the author hereof elsewhere at large discourseth in his book *The English Poet*.

We can all join in William Webbe's forlorn wish: "I would wish to have the sight of his *English Poet*, which his friend E. K. did once promise to publish."

Lodge. *Defence of Poetry* (1579):

> Who doth not wonder at poetry? Who thinketh not that it proceded from above? . . . It is a pretty sentence, yet not so pretty as pithy, *poeta nascitur, non fit*: as who should say, poetry cometh from above, from a heavenly seat of a glorious God, unto an

excellent creature, man . . . it cometh not by labor, neither that night watchings bringeth it . . . it cometh not by exercise of play-making, neither insertion of gawds, but from nature, and from above . . . and whereas the poets were said to call for the Muses' help, their meaning was no other but to call for heavenly inspiration from above to direct their endeavors.

Daniel. *Philotas* (1605). Dedication:

'Tis not in the power of kings to raise
A spirit for verse that is not born thereto;
For late Eliza's reign gave birth to more
Than all the kings of England did before.

Dekker, Webster. *Northward Ho!* (1605). IV i:

Captain Jenkins.   You are a poet, sir, are you?
Bellamont. I'm haunted with a fury, sir.

Chapman. *Seven Books of the Iliad.* Dedication:

For as number, sound, and rhyme can challenge no inclusion of the soul without divine invention, no more can the soul expect eternity on earth without such eternal writing.

Chapman, in the preface to the *Masque of the Middle Temple and Lincoln's Inn* (1613) thus accounts for the difference between the poet and the poetaster:

The hill of the Muses (which all men must climb in the regular way to truth) is said of old to be forked. And the two points of it, parting at the top, are *insania* and *divinus furor*. Insania is that which every rank-brained writer and judge of poetical writing is rapt withal when he presumes either to write or censure the height of poesy, and that transports him with humor, vainglory, and pride, most profane and sacrilegious: when *divinus furor* makes gentle and noble the never-so-truly inspired writer. And the mild beams of the most holy inflamer easily and sweetly enter, with all understanding sharpness, the soft and sincerely humane; but with no time, no study, no means under heaven, any arrogant all-occupation devourer (that will, chandler-like, set up with all wares, selling poesy's nectar and ambrosia as well as mustard and vinegar) the chaste and restrained beams of humble truth will never enter, but only graze and glance at them, and the further fly them.

For inspiration to enable him to complete Marlowe's *Hero and Leander*, Chapman calls upon this "holy inflamer," describing it (significantly for Chapman) as a "strangely-intellectual fire" (*Hero and Leander*, Third Sestiad, 11. 183ff.) :

> Then ho, most strangely-intellectual fire,
> That, proper to my soul, hast power t' inspire
> Her burning faculties, and with the wings
> Of thy unsphered flame visit'st the springs
> Of spirits immortal! Now (as swift as Time
> Doth follow Motion) find th' eternal clime
> Of his free soul, whose living subject stood
> Up to the chin in the Pierian flood,
> And drunk to me half this Musæan story,
> Inscribing it to deathless memory:
> Confer with it, and make my pledge as deep,
> That neither's draught be consecrate to sleep.
> Tell it how much his late desires I tender
> (If yet he know not), and to light surrender
> My soul's dark offering.

William Alexander. *Anacrisis* (1634):

Every author has his own genius, directing him by a secret Inspiration to that wherein he may most excel.

Heywood. *Love's Mistress* (1634). I i:

> Not only whatsoever 's mine,
> But all true poets' raptures are divine.

Milton. *Reason of Church Government* (1641). Bohn ed., Vol. II, p. 479:

These abilities [poetic], wheresoever they be found, are the inspired gift of God, rarely bestowed, but yet to some in every nation.

William Habington. *On Master John Fletcher's Dramatic Poems* (1647) :

Though vulgar poets scorn or hate,
Man may beget, a poet can create.

Associated with the idea of divine inspiration was the notion
that the poet was afflicted with a sort of madness.
Dekker, Webster. *Northward Ho!* (1605) IV iii:

> *Bellamont.* . . . your best poets, indeed, are mad for the most
> part.

Drayton. *Elegies of Poets and Poesy* (1627):

Next Marlowe, bathed in the Thespian springs,
Had in him those brave translunary things
That the first poets had; his raptures were
All air and fire, which made his verses clear;
For that fine madness still he did retain,
Which rightly should possess a poet's brain.

Obviously, if the poet is divinely inspired he cannot choose
but write.

Beaumont. *On the Faithful Shepherdess* (1610):

I know too well that, no more than the man
That travels through the burning desert can,
When he is beaten with the raging sun,
Half smother'd in the dust, have power to run
From a cool river, which himself doth find,
Ere he be slak'd; no more can he whose mind
Joys in the Muses hold from that delight,
When nature and his full thoughts bid him write.

The main difference between the romantic and the classic view
on the question of poetic creation was that the former accepted
the idea of inspiration, while the latter merely recognized a
superior talent that had to be fostered by training. But the talent
was a prerequisite. Cheke and Bacon put the matter in a common
sense way. Ascham reports that Cheke told him (*Schoolmaster—*
Smith, I p. 40) that

in Sallust writing is more art than nature, and more labor than art: and in his labor also too much toil, as it were, with an uncontented care to write better than he could. . . . And therefore he doth not express the matter lively and naturally with common speech.

And Bacon puts it this way (Essay 43):

Not but I think a painter can make a better face than ever was; but he must do it by a kind of felicity (as a musician that maketh an excellent air in music) and not by rule.

Sidney, in the first sonnet of *Astrophel and Stella* goes so far as to affirm that study hinders talent:

Invention, Nature's child, fled step-dame Study's blows.

According to Nash (Preface to *Menaphon*) practice is more important than following the rules, important as this is:

Endeavor to add unto art experience. Experience is more profitable void of art than art which hath not experience. Of itself art is unprofitable without experience, and experience rash without art.

To ridicule the idea that a poem is an inspired creation for which the poet is not responsible, Shirley makes the foolish lord, Depazzi, advance it, in the *Humorous Courtier* (1631) II i:

Madam, while you live,
Your dreaming poets are the best, and have
Distilled raptures, spirits that converse with them,
And teach them what to write.

Of course none of the Elizabethan playwrights entertained such an extreme notion. This volume owes its existence to the fact that they were conscious theorists. The plays of William Cartwright belonged to the romantic category, yet he considered himself a "son of Ben." Commending Fletcher (another romantic dramatist) in verses contributed to the Beaumont and Fletcher Folio, he puts the case neatly this way;

For that thou couldst thine own free fancy bind
In stricter numbers, and run so confin'd
As to observe the rules of art, which sway
In the contrivance of a true-born play,
Those works proclaim which thou wrote retir'd
From Beaumont, by none but thyself inspir'd;
Where we see that 'twas not chance that made them hit,
Nor were thy plays the lotteries of wit;
But, like to Dürer's pencil, which first knew
The laws of faces, and then faces drew,
Thou knew'st the air, the color, and the place,
The symmetry which gives a poem grace.
Parts are so fitted into parts, as do
Show thou hadst wit, and mathematics too;
Knew'st where by line to spare, where to dispense,
And didst beget just comedies from thence.

To the requisites implied in this statement none of the playwrights of the time would have hesitated to subscribe. "Free
fancy" reminds one of "sweetest Shakespeare, fancy's child." The
difference between the two schools boils down to one of emphasis.
The case is further illustrated by similar verses contributed by
John Denham and Richard Brome to the same volume:

Denham. *On Master Fletcher's Works*:

When Jonson, Shakspere, and thyself did sit,
And sway'd in the triumvirate of wit,
Yet what from Jonson's oil and sweat did flow,
Or what more easy nature did bestow
On Shakspere's gentler muse, in these full grown
Their graces both appear.

Brome. To the Memory of Mr. John Fletcher:

He did not pump, nor drudge,
To beget wit, or manage it; or trudge
To wit conventions with note-book, to glean,
Or steal, some jests to foist upon a scene;
He scorned those shifts. . . .
His *scenes* were *acts,* and every *act* a *play.*

I knew him in his strength; even then when he
That was the master of his art and me,
Most knowing Jonson (proud to call him son),
In friendly envy swore he had outdone
His very self.

The last assertion must not be overlooked: Jonson too approved of Fletcher's work. And Beaumont, Fletcher's collaborator, in his glowing comment on Shakespeare, stresses the marvel of Shakespeare's achievement, accomplished merely by the *dim* light of nature, without the aid of what was termed "art:"

                    . . . here I would let slip
    (If I had any in me) scholarship,
    And from all learning keep these lines as clear
    As Shakspere's best are, which our heirs shall hear
    Preachers apt to their auditors to show
    How far sometimes mortal man may go
    By the dim light of nature.

The basic classic view is succinctly advanced by John Day in the address *To the Impartial Reader,* prefixed to the *Parliament of Bees*:

Old father Seton told me long ago that *Inventium et Judicium* were the main grounds logic was built upon; and sure I am that they are the two feet that poetry walks on.

Seton was a logician, whose popular *Dialectics* was published in 1572. The sixteenth century produced numerous books on logic and rhetoric, which formed an integral part of the educational system of the time, and in which Shakespeare and his fellows were thoroughly grounded and which, besides, largely determined the ideas embodied in academic criticism. In this passage, *judicium* means disposition or arrangement of material according to the rules. With equal succinctness, in the address to the reader, Day puts the matter more specifically:

Smooth-socked Thalia takes delight to dance
I' the schools of art.

In the same play he bestows, in a humorous vein, another rap at the romantic view of inspiration. Character V:

> *Iltriste.*   How might I do to hit the master vein of poesy?
> *Poetaster.*   I descend from Persius.
> He taught his pupils to breed poets thus:
> . . . to steal juice from Hebe's cup
> . . . pilfer clouds
> From off Parnassus top. . . .
> Then drink nine healths of sacred Hippocrene
> To the Muses. This, says Persius,
> Will make a poet. I think cheaper this: —
> Gold, music, wine, tobacco, and good cheer
> Make poets soar aloft and sing out clear.
> *Iltriste.*   Are you born poets?
> *Poetaster.*   Yes.

In the second act of *The Pilgrimage to Parnassus* (1598), possibly by the same author, Madido expatiates on the proposition that "Parnassus and Helicon are but the fables of the poets: there is no true Parnassus but the third loft in a wine tavern, no true Helicon but a cup of brown bastard." When he is through, Philomusus' rejoinder is:

> Nay then, I see thy wit in drink is drowned;
> Wine doth the best part of thy soul confound.

A similar view is expressed in I ii of *2 Return from Parnassus* (1602). No less a poet than Spenser, in the October Eclogue of the *Shepherd's Calendar* (1579), lent his authority to the notion that wine stimulates poetic creation:

> Whoever casts to compass weighty prize,
> And thinks to throw out thundering words of threat,
> Let pour in lavish cups and thrifty bits of meat,
> For Bacchus' fruit is friend to Phoebus wise;
> And when with wine the brain begins to sweat,
> The numbers flow as fast as spring doth rise.
> Thou knowest not, Percie, how the vine should rage.
> Oh! if my temples were distain'd with wine,

And girt in girlands of wild ivy twine,
How I could rear the muse in stately stage,
And teach her tread aloft in buskin fine,
With quaint Bellona in her equipage!

In Nash's *Will Summer's Last Will and Testament* (1592)
Bacchus himself proclaims the inspiring potency of his beverage:

Give a scholar wine going to his book, or being about to invent,
it sets a new point on his wit; it glazeth it, it scours it, it gives him
acumen.

And he quotes Plato, Aristotle, and Horace to support him. But
we know that Nash is not to be taken seriously; he tells us so in
his preface to Greene's *Menaphon*:

Pardon me, gentlemen, though somewhat merrily I glance at their
immoderate folly who affirm that no man can write with conceit
except he takes counsel of the cup.

In the song at the end of Act II of *Histriomastix* (before 1599)
beer, as well as wine, is hailed as an inspirer of creation.

O delicate wine, with thy power so divine,
Full of ravishing sweet inspiration;
Yet a verse may run clear that is tapt out of beer,
    Especially in the vacation.
But when the term comes that with trumpet and drums
    Our playhouses ring in confusion,
Then Bacchus we murder.

This song is sung extempore on the theme, "Your poets and your
pots are knit in true-love knots."

In Shirley's *Love in a Maze* (1632) the poetaster Caperwit
pleads:

I want a little quickening; two or three
Infusions of sack will heighten me,
And make my genius dance.

and in the prologue to the same author's *Coronation* (1635) we find:

> . . . the genius of his play
> Doth prophecy the conduits may run wine
> When the day's triumph's ended, and divine
> Brisk nectar swell his temples to a rage,
> With something of more price t'invest the stage.

Of course, these writers were merely playing with a time-honored, and semi-serious, jest. "What, my little rogue, hast thou been at the wine-pot that thou dost rhyme already?" Grandgousier asks Gargantua.

Davenport in his lines addressed to Thomas Carew, adds love as an inspiration:

> Thy verses are smooth, and high
> As glory, love, or wine from wit can raise.

Arden of Feversham (c. 1590) I i 252:

> *Clarke.* For, as sharp-witted poets, whose sweet verse
> Make heavenly gods break off their nectar draughts
> And lay their ears down to the lowly earth,
> Use humble promise to their sacred Muse,
> So we, that are the poets' favorites,
> Must have a love: ay, love is the painter's muse,
> That makes him frame a speaking countenance,
> A weeping eye that witnesses heart's grief.

Fletcher. *Prophetess* (1622) V iii end:

> *Diocles.* And let 'em know, our true love breeds more stories
> And perfect joys than kings do, and their glories.

Massinger. *New Way* (1625) III i 81:

> *Lovell.* Love hath made you
> Poetical, Alworth.

Shirley treats the subject jocularly in *The Humorous Courtier* (1631) II ii. A silly lord is being cajoled:

Crispino. Your lordship's cloak discovers not sufficiently the riches of the inside.

Laura. An excellent poet!

Depazzi. I'll tell you, madam, a strange thing. You see these trifles; before I was in love, I could not have made an acrostic in a day — sometimes two.

Lau. Now you can make chronograms.

Dep. I think I can; and anagrams, for a need.

Lau. Signior, you are wonderfully improved;
Love has inspired you richly. I perceive
Cupid is a Muse too.

Dep. Oh, now I cannot sleep for the multitude
Of verses that are capering in my skull.

Experience and association may be the source of poetic stimulation.

Carew. Upon *The Heir*, by Thomas May (1622) :

A love so well express'd must be the same
The author felt himself for his fair flame.

Marmion, in *The Antiquary* (1636) III, suggests that environment can endow one with poetic skill:

Leonardo. Why, this has some taste in it! How should he arrive to this admirable invention?

Duke. Are you so preposterous in your opinion to think that wit and elegancy are only confined to stagers and bookworms? 'Twere a solecism to imagine that a young bravery, who lives in the perpetual sphere of humanity, where every waiting-woman speaks perfect Arcadia, and the ladies' lips distil with the very quintessence of conceit, should be so barren of apprehension as not to participate of their virtues.

Leonardo. Now I consider, they are great helps to a man.

Duke. But when he has travel'd and delibated the French and the Spanish; can lie abed and expound Astræa, and digest him into compliments; and when he is up accost his mistress with what he had read in the morning; now if such a one should rack up his imagination, and give wings to his muse, 'tis credible he should more catch your delicate court-ear than all your head-scratchers, thumb-biters, lamp-wasters of them all.

Whatever they believed concerning insipiration, the dramatists did not hesitate to admit that the writing of a play meant hard work, implicitly admitting that there was something to be said for the classical view.

Marston. *What You Will* (1601) Prol.:

To those who know the pangs of bringing forth
A perfect feature . . .

Ibid. *Dutch Courtezan* (1604) Epil.:

For he shall find that slights such trivial wit,
'Tis easier to reprove than better it.

Dekker. *The Devil Is in It* (1612) Epil.:

If for many moons and midnights spent
To reap three hours of mirth, our harvest seed
Lies still and rot, the devil's in it then indeed:
Much labor, art, and wit make up a play.

Webster. *White Devil* (1612) To the Reader:

To those who report I was a long time in finishing this tragedy, I confess I do not write with a goose-quill winged with two feathers; and if they will needs make it my fault, I must answer them with that of Euripides to Alcestides, a tragic writer. Alcestides objecting that Euripides had only, in three days, composed three verses, whereas himself had written three hundred, "Thou tellest truth," quoth he, "but here's the difference — thine only be read for three days, whereas mine shall continue three ages."

(Reminds one of Browning's retort when told that a certain poet—was it Alfred Austen?—opined that Browning's poetry was obscure: "Clear cackle is easily expressed.")

Massinger. *Believe as You List* (1630) Prol.:

He dares not boast
His pains and cares, or what books he has tost
And turn'd to make it up.

Shirley. Verses on Massinger's *Renegado* (1630)

And if there be
A tribe who in their wisdom do accuse
This offspring of thy Muse,
    Let them agree
Conspire one comedy, and they will say
'Tis easier to commend than make a play.

Ibid. *St. Patrick* (1639) Prol.

For your own sakes we wish all here today
Knew but the art and labor of a play;
Then you would value the true muse's pain,
The throes and travail of a teeming brain.

Dekker raises an intriguing question at the beginning of Act IV, in *Northward Ho!*:

Bellamont. Why should not I be an excellent statesman? I can in the writing of a tragedy make Caesar speak better than ever his ambition could; When I write of Pompey I have Pompey's soul within me; and when I personate a worthy poet I am then truly myself, a poor unpreferred scholar.

The idea, stemming from Strabo (cf. Spingarn, *Lit. Crit.*, p. 54), that a writer's product is linked to the personality of the writer, is likewise assumed in the idea that a poet must be a good man. Milton insists on this in his *Apology against a Pamphlet Call'd Smectymnuus*:

I was confirmed in this opinion, that he who would not be frustrate of his hope to write well hereafter in laudable things, ought himself to be a true poem; that is, a composition and pattern of the best and honorablest things; not presuming to sing high praise of heroic men or famous cities, unless he have in himself the experience and the practice of all that which is praiseworthy.

The subject is amply discussed by I. A. Richards, in his *Principles of Literary Criticism*, Chap. VIII, entitled "Art and Morals."
There is also the kindred notion that to be successful in his work the artist must not be encumbered with this world's goods.

Fletcher, Massinger. *Lovers' Progress* (1623) I i:

   Leon.   I have heard
You are poetical.
   Mallfort.   Something given that way;
Yet my works seldom thrive; and the main reason
The poets urge for't, because I am not
As poor as they are.

THE NATURE OF POETRY

Sir Philip Sidney, who summed up the best of Renaissance criticism in himself, and whose pervasive influence on the Elizabethan dramatists Professor Alwin Thaler has demonstrated, explained the nature of poetry thus:

Nature never set forth the earth in so rich tapestry as divers poets have done. . . . Her world is brazen; the poets only deliver a golden . . . Neither let it be deemed too saucy a comparison to balance the highest point of man's wit with the efficacy of nature: but rather give right honor to the heavenly Maker of that maker; who, having made man to his own likeness, set him beyond and over all the works of that second nature; which in nothing he showeth so much as in poetry, when with the force of a divine breath he bringeth things forth far surpassing her doings. . . . Poesy therefore is an art of imitation, for so Aristotle termeth it in his word *mimesis;* that is to say, a representing, counterfeiting, or figuring forth: to speak metaphorically, a speaking picture with this end: to teach and delight.

A clear statement and elaboration of the idea expressed by Sidney is provided by Francis Bacon in Book II of the *Advancement of Learning*. Since he had at least a tangential relation with the drama, its inclusion here is not out of place:

Poesy is a part of learning in measure of words for the most part restrained, but in all other points extremely licensed, and doth truly refer to the imagination, which, being not tied to the laws of matter, may at pleasure join that which nature hath served, and sever that which nature hath joined, and so make unlawful matches and divorces of things. . . . The use of this feigned history hath been to give some shadow of satisfaction to the mind of man in those points wherein the nature of things doth deny it, the world being in proportion inferior to the soul; by reason whereof there is agreeable to the spirit of man a more ample greatness, a more exact goodness, and a more absolute variety than can be found in the nature of things. Therefore, because the acts or events of true history have not that magnitude which satisfieth the mind of man, poesy feigneth acts and events more heroical; because true history propoundeth the successes and issues of actions not so agreeable to the merits of virtue and vice; therefore poesy feigns them more just in retribution and more according to revealed Providence; because true history represents actions and events more ordinary and less interchanged, therefore poesy endueth them with more rareness and more unexpected and alternative variations; so as it appeareth that poesy serveth and confereth to magnanimity, morality, and to delectation. And it was ever thought to have some participation of divineness, because it doth raise and erect the mind, whereas reason doth buckle and bow the mind unto the nature of things.

Nash, in *The Anatomy of Absurdity* (1589), describes poetry as

. . . a more hidden and divine kind of philosophy, enwrapped in blind fables and dark stories, wherein the principles of more excellent arts and moral precepts . . . are contained.

This contains the germ of the idea elaborated by Bacon; but Nash also attaches to poetry an allegorical function.

Chapman expresses Bacon's thought briefly thus, in *Chabot* (1613) III ii 10:

Proctor. . . . ποίειν, which is, to make, to create, to invent matter that was never extant in nature; from whence also is the name and dignity of *poeta*.

Nero (1623) III iii:

Petronius. The shows of things are better than themselves.
How doth it stir this airy part of us
To hear our poets tell imagined fights
And the strange blows that feigned courage gives!
When I Achilles hear upon the stage
Speak honor and the greatness of his soul,

Methinks I too could on a Phrygian spear
Run boldly and make tales for after times.

In a humorous vein things that poets feigned could be called
lies. *In Will Summer's Last Will and Testament* (1592), Nash
gives a mock history of poetic creation, according to which letters
were invented "to write lies withal. . . . Musaeus, Linus, Homer,
Orpheus, ... thereby won their fame."

Day. *Parliament of Bees.* Character V:

> *Iltriste.*   May not a woman be a poet?
> *Poetaster.*   Yes;
> And learn the art with far more easiness
> Than any man can do; for poesy
> Is but feigning, feigning is to lie,
> And women study that art more than men.

Shirley. *Honoria and Mammon* (1631) III i. Aurelia's response
to her suitor's speech:

> This language
> Doth taste too much of poetry; take heed, sir.

The relation between the material for art and the art product
is effectively presented by Chapman in a passage in which he gives
early expression to the accepted view that it is the human element
in art that attracts us. *Byron's Conspiracy* (1607) III i 49:

> *Byron.*   . . . but as the stuff
> Prepar'd for arras pictures is no picture
> Till it be form'd, and man has cast the beams
> Of his imaginous fancy through it,
> In forming ancient kings and conquerors
> As he conceives they look'd and were attir'd,
> Have all their price set down from man's conceits,
> Which make all terms and actions good or bad,
> And are but pliant and well-color'd threads
> Put into feigned images of truth.

Poetry will be related to the age in which it is produced, and
the age must be propitious for poetry to be produced at all. *Sir
Thomas More* (1590) III ii 229:

> *More.*   This is no age for poets; they should sing
> To the loud cannon *heroica facta*;
> *Qui faciunt reges heroica carmina laudant.*
> And as great subjects of their pen decay,
> Even so unphysicked they do melt away.

Chapman's dedication of the *Iliad* to Prince Henry contains an extended explanation and glorification of poetry as opposed to prose:

> Truth, with poesy grac'd, is fairer far,
> More proper, moving, chaste, and regular,
> Than when she runs away with untruss'd prose.
> Proportion, that doth orderly dispose
> Her virtuous treasure, and is queen of graces,
> In poesy, decking her with choicest phrases,
> Figures and numbers, when loose prose puts on
> Plain letter-habits; makes her trot upon
> Dull earthly business (she being more divine)
> Holds to homely cates, and harsh hedge-wine,
> That should drink poesy's nectar; every way
> One made for other, as the sun the day,
> Princes and virtues. And as in a spring
> The pliant water, moved with anything
> Let fall into it, puts her motion out
> In perfect circles, that move round about
> The gentle fountain, one another raising,
> So truth and poesy work; so poesy blazing
> All subjects fall'n in her exhaustless fount,
> Works most exactly; makes a true account
> Of all things to her high discharges given,
> Till all be circular, and round as heaven.

On the same theme Nash in *Pierce Penniless* (1592):

> Lay chronographers . . . want the wings of choice words to fly to heaven which we have. . . . Poetry is the honey of all flowers, the quintessence of all sciences, the marrow of wit, and the very phrase of angels.

Simplicity and sincerity are characteristics of good poetry, according to Fletcher. *Valentinian* (1617) V v:

Licipus.   By any means some songs: but very short ones,
And honest language, Paulus, without bursting:
The air will fall the sweeter.

A noble statement of the impossibility of giving adequate expression to the poet's ideal is the following by Marlowe. *1 Tamburlaine* (1587) V ii 97:

What is beauty? sayeth my sufferings then.
If all the pens that ever poets held
Had fed the feeling of their masters' thoughts
And every sweetness that inspir'd their hearts,
Their minds, and muses on admir'd themes;
If all the heavenly quintessence they still
From their immortal flowers of poesy,
Wherein, as in a mirror, we perceive
The highest reaches of a human wit;
If these had made one poem's period,
And all combin'd in beauty's worthiness,
Yet should there hover in their restless heads
One thought, one grace, one wonder, at the least,
Which into words no virtue can digest.

Chapman, repeating Marlowe's question, emphasizes the subjective element in beauty and truth, which Renaissance criticism tended to identify. *All Fools* (1599) I i 44:

Rinaldo.   And what is beauty? A mere quintessence,
Whose life is not in being, but in seeming;
And therefore is not to all eyes the same,
But, like a cozening picture, which one way
Shows like a crow, another like a swan.

In the following quotations he further stresses the relative nature of beauty. (May-Day [1601] III i 14) :

Angelo.   . . . as of Moors so of chimney-sweepers,
The blackest is most beautiful.

Masque of the Middle Temple (1613) Pref.:

Truth and worth have no faces to enamor the licentious. . . . The same body, the same beauty, a thousand men seeing, only the man whose blood is fitted has that which he calls his soul enamored. And this out of infallible cause . . . the cause of men's being enamored with truth, and of her slight respect in others, is the divine freedom, one touching with his apprehensive finger, the other passing.

He explains more simply in his verse on Fletcher's *Faithful Shepherdess* (1610) :

. . . scholars please

That are no poets, more than poets learn'd,
Since their art is solely by their souls discern'd;
The others' falls within the common sense.

Thinking along the same lines Spenser has this to say on the nature of beauty in his *Hymn in Honor of Beauty*, 64:

How vainly then do idle wits invent
That beauty is nought else but mixture made
Of colors fair, and goodly temp'rament
Of pure complexion. . . .
Or that it is but comely composition
Of parts well measur'd with meet disposition. . . .
Why do not then the blossoms of the field,
Which are array'd with much more orient hue,
And to the sense most dainty odors yield,
Work like impression in the looker's view?
Or why do not fair pictures like power show,
In which oft-times we nature see of art
Excel'd, in perfect limning every part?
But ah! believe me, there is more than so
That works such wonders in the minds of men.
I, that have prov'd, too well it know, . . .
That beauty is not, as fond men misdeem,
An outward show of things, that only seem.

DIGNITY OF THE POETIC ART

According to Spenser the poetic art was of such lofty dignity that its practice was to be denied the common people. In *The Tears of the Muses*, printed in 1591, but probably written much earlier, Polyhymnia complains:

> Whilom in ages past none might profess
> But princes and high priests that secret skill . . .
> Then was she held in sovereign dignity,
> And made the nurseling of nobility.
> But now nor prince nor priest doth her maintain,
> But suffer her profaned for to be
> Of the base vulgar, that with hands unclean
> Dares to pollute her hidden mystery,
> And treadeth under foot her holy things,
> Which was the care of kesars and of kings.

The dramatists, generally, accorded it the loftiest dignity, naturally, since they preached its divine origin but they did not project so aristocratic a bias.

Nash. *The Unfortunate Traveller* (1593) (Percy Repr. p. 39):

Destiny never defames herself but when she lets excellent poet die. If there be any spark of Adam's paradised perfection yet embered up in the breasts of mortal men, certainly God hath bestowed that his perfectest image on poets. None come so near to God in wit. . . . Despised they are of the world, because they are not of the world; their thoughts are exalted above the world of ignorance and all earthly conceits. . . . Happy, thrice happy are they whom God hath doubled his spirits upon, and given double soul unto to be poets.

Drayton. *England's Heroical Epistles* (1597):

When heav'n would strive to do the best it can,
And put an angel's spirit into a man,
The utmost power it then doth spend,
When to the world a poet it doth send.

Chettle. Munday. *Death of Robert, Earl of Huntington* (1598)
II i:

    Hubert.   For poetry's high spirited sons will raise
True beauty to all wish'd eternity.

Pilgrimage to Parnassus (1598) V i:

    Philomusus.   O do not wrong this music of the soul,
The fairest child that e'er the soul brought forth;
Which none contemn but some rude foggy squires
That know not to esteem of wit or art.

Daniel. *Musophilus* (1599):

And as for poesy . . .
What shall I say? since it is well approved
The speech of heaven . . .
. . . weakness speaks in prose, but power in verse.

Another passage in the same poem, though it does not deal
exclusively with poetry, is nevertheless quoted here, because it
evidences an advanced critical comprehension of one of the main
functions of all literature.

O blessed letters, that combine in one
All ages past, and make one live in all!
By you do we confer with who are gone,
And the dead-living into council call.
By you the unborn shall have communion
Of what we feel and what doth us befall.

Tomkis. *Lingua* (1603) V xvi:

    Somnus.   Lo, then doth Somnus conquer all the world
With his most swift wand, and half the year
Reigns o'er the best and the proudest emperors.

Only the nurselings of the Sisters Nine
Rebel against me, scorning great command;
And when dark night from her bedewy wings
Drops sleepy silence to the eyes of all
They only wake, and with unwearied toil
Labor to find the *Via Lactea,*
That leads to the heaven of immortality;
And by the lofty towering of their minds,
Fledged with the feathers of a learned muse,
They raise themselves unto the highest pitch,
Marrying base earth and heaven in a thought.
But thus I punish their rebellion:
Their industry was never yet rewarded.

Chapman. Preface to the Reader of *Homer*:

. . . for the glory of God, and the singing of his glories, no man dares deny, man was chiefly made. And what art performs this chief end with so much excitation and expression as poesy?

Chapman proceeds in this vein at considerable length. Later in the *Masque of the Middle Temple* (1613), he calls poets "our chief men of wit."

Ibid. On Jonson's *Sejanus* (1605):

O would the world feel how sweet a touch
The knowledge hath which is in love with goodness,
(If poesy were not ravished so much,
And her compos'd rage held the simplest woodness,
Though of all heats that temper human brains,
Hers was most subtle, high, and holy,
First binding savage lives in civil chains,
Solely religious, and adored solely)
If men felt this, they would not think a love
That gives itself in her did vanities give.

Chapman here advances one of the stock claims of Renaissance criticism; namely, that poetry was the earliest civilizing influence, "the first light-giver to ignorance," in the words of Sidney.

Marston. *Histriomastix* (1610) II:

Chrisoganus. Proud lord, poor art shall wear a glorious crown,
When her despisers die to all renown.

In Act III he repeats the vaunt, at the same time deploring, like Spenser in the passage quoted above, the sad state into which poetry had fallen. When Spenser wrote there was justification for the lament; however when Marston wrote, it had become an absurd chronic convention.

Day. *Parliament of Bees* V:

> *Iltriste.*   How many sorts of poets are there?
> *Poetaster.*   Two; great poets and small poets.
> *Ilt.*   Great and small ones? So.
> Which do you call great, the fat ones?
> *Poet.*   No;
> But such as have great heads, which, emptied forth,
> Fill all the world with wonder at their worth. . . .
> The small ones call the shrimps of poesy.

In the same scene Day describes the ideal poet thus:

> . . . the true poet indeed doth scorn to gild
> A coward's tomb with glories, or to build
> A sumptuous pyramid of golden verse
> Over the ruins of an ignoble hearse.
> His lines, like his invention, are born free,
> And both live blameless to eternity.
> He holds his reputation so dear
> As neither flattering hope nor servile fear
> Can bribe his pen to temporize with kings.

And he ends his play with a glorification of all art:

> *Oberon.*   Art has banished ignorance,
> And chased all flies of rape and stealth
> From forth our winged commonwealth.

Suckling. To my friend Will Davenant:

> What mighty princes poets are! Those things
> The great ones stick at, and our very kings
> Lay down, they venture on; and with great ease
> Discover, conquer what and where they please.

In *Love's Mistress* (1634), after a procession of various kinds of asses, Heywood has Apuleius declare that there is no such creature as a Poet Ass.

The power of poetry is affirmed in the following citations, in the last one by implication.

Edward III (1590) II i 65:

> *King.* Now Lodowicke, invocate some golden Muse,
> To bring thee hither an inchanted pen,
> That may for sighs set down true sighs indeed;
> Talking of grief, to make thee ready groan;
> And when writest of tears, encouch the word
> Before and after with such sweet laments,
> That it may raise drops in a Tartar's eye,
> And make a flintheart Scythian pitiful;
> For so much moving hath a poet's pen.

In *Will Summer's Last Will and Testament* (1592) by Nash, Sol has been accused of a list of crimes by Autumn and Winter, including the charge that

> He terms himself the god of poetry,
> And setteth wanton songs unto the lute.

Sol defends himself:

> Music and poetry, my two last crimes,
> Are those two exercises of delight,
> Wherewith long labors I do weary out.
> The dying swan is not forbid to sing. . . .
> And as for poetry, words' eloquence . . .
> Not flint or rock, of icy cinders flam'd
> Deny the force of silver-falling streams.

Fletcher. *Elder Brother* (1626) II ii 31:

> *Eustace.*   Songs she
> May have, and read a little unbak'd poetry,
> Such as the dabblers of our time contrive;
> That has no weight or wheel to move the mind,
> Nor, indeed, nothing but an empty sound.

In the Induction to *The Malcontent* (c. 1600), Webster makes a plea for freedom of speech in poetry—and in the pulpit:

> *Burbage.* Sir, you are like a patron that, presenting a poor scholar to a benefice, enjoins him not to rail against anything that stands within compass of his patron's folly. Why should we not enjoy the ancient freedom of poesy?

This seems to be an elaboration of a thought Marston had expressed in the original prologue to the play:

> . . . once teach all old freedom of a pen,
> Which still must write of fools whiles 't writes of men.

The next quotation relates to poetry in general, but makes special references to the drama.

Marmion. *A Fine Companion* (1633). Prol.:

> *Critic.* For 'tis not every one that writes a verse
> Has washt his mouth in Helicon, or slept
> On the two-topt Parnassus. There's great difference
> Betwixt him that shall write a lawful poem,
> And one that makes a paper of loose verses
> To court his looser mistress; there's much air
> Requir'd to lift up the Dircaean swan,
> When he shall print his tracts among the clouds:
> Not as your ignorant poetasters use,
> In spite of Phoebus, without art or learning,
> To usurp the stage, and touch with impure hands
> The lofty buskin, and the comic style.

Milton. *Reason of Church Government* (1641). Bohn ed., Vol. II; p. 479:

> These abilities [poetic] . . . are of power, beside the office of a pulpit, to inbreed and cherish in a great people the seeds of virtue and public civility, to allay perturbations of the mind, and set the affections in right tune.

STATUS OF THE POET

The status of the poet himself was not commensurate with the dignity of his profession. As Somnus tells us above, in the quotation from *Lingua*, "their industry was never yet rewarded."

Richard Puttenham. *Art of English Poesie* (1589):

For as well poets as poesy are despised, and the name become of honorable, infamous, subject to scorn and derision.

Kyd. *Spanish Tragedy* (1583) IV i:

Hieronimo. When I was young I gave my mind
And plied myself to fruitless poetry,
Which, though it profit the professor nought,
Yet is it passing pleasing to the world.

The Pilgrimage to Parnassus (1598) dilates on the neglected condition of the scholar and the poet. Here is a small sample (622ff.):

Ingenioso. Why, our empty-handed satin suits do make more account of some foggy falconer than of a witty scholar, had rather reward a man for setting of a hair than a man of wit for making a poem. . . . Apollo is bankrupt.

Day. *Parliament of Bees* V:

Poet.   No bee
That frequents Hybla takes more pains than we
Do in our canzons; yet they live and thrive
Richly, when we want wax to store our hive.

Ibid. V:

> *Iltriste.*　A scholar to speak with me?
> *Gnatho.*　He says a poet.
> I think no less, for his apparel shows it.
> He's of some standing—his cloth coat is worn
> To a serge.

May-Day (1601) I ii:

> *Quintiliano.*　After dinner there will be a play, and if you would be counted complete, you must venture among them; for otherwise they will take you for a scholar or a poet, and so fall in contempt of you.

Dekker, Webster. *Northward Ho* (1605). IV i:

> *Bellamont.*　Why should not I be an excellent statesman? I can in the writing of a tragedy make Caesar speak better than ever his ambition could; when I write of Pompey, I have Pompey's soul within me; and when I personate a worthy poet, I am then truly myself, a poor unpreferred scholar.

Chapman, on *The Faithful Shepherdess* (1610):

> A poem and a play too! why, 'tis like
> A scholar that's a poet; their names strike
> Their pestilence inward, when they take the air,
> And kill outright; one cannot both fates bear.

Chapman, on *Sejanus*:

> 　　　　　　　　　　　. . . cheerful gold
> Was never found in the Pierian streams,
> But wants, and scorns, and shames for silver sold.

In Richard Brome's clever comedy entitled *The Antipodes* (1638), there are scenes supposed to be laid in a town called Antipodea London, which is the antipodes of London, not only geographically, but also in all other respects. In Act III, Scene i, the Londoners are astonished at the prosperity of the poets and Letoy explains:

Yes, poetry is good ware
In the Antipodes, though there be some ill payers,
As well as here; but the law there rights the poets.

In the first act of Brome's *Jovial Crew* (1641), the Second Beggar says:

He is a decay'd poet, newly fallen in among us; and begs as well as the best of us. He learnt it pretty well in his own profession before, and can the better practice it in ours now.

In the dedication of *The Unnatural Combat* (1639) Massinger indicates that those that make poetry a profession do so out of necessity, reminding us of the insinuation made by Thomas Randolph in *Hey for Honesty* I ii, that even Shakespeare wrote for the love of money.

Yet Killigrew, in *The Parson's Wedding* (1653) III i, has Wild declare:

I'll swear they say there are poets that have more men in liveries than books in their shelves.

ART AND NATURE

The term nature is here used in the sense in which it was used by the Renaissance critics; namely, that of native ability. Art is defined by Puttenham as "a certain order of rules prescribed by reason, and gathered by experience." On the relation between art and nature Marston has three statements.

Scourge of Villany (1559) Satire IX:

But art curbs nature, nature gildeth art.

In the following year, in the epilogue to *The Malcontent*, referring to Jonson, he says:

To whose desertful lamps pleased Fates impart
Art above nature, judgment above art.

the implied principle of which he elaborates in Satire V:

O that the beauties of invention,
For want of judgment's disposition,
Should all be soil'd; O that such treasury,
Such strains of well-conceited poesy,
Should molded be in such a shapeless form,
That want of art should make wit a scorn.

Marston's statement of the relation between art, nature, and judgment, evoked an emphatic contradiction from Chapman in *May-Day* (1601) I i 403: Quintiliano is talking to a fool, assuring him that possessing a quality is better than assuming one—which is true.

> *Quintiliano.*   . . . In a word, be impudent enough, for that's your chief virtue of society.
>
> *Innocentio.*   Is that? Faith, and I need not learn that; I have that by nature, thank God!
>
> *Quint.*   So much the better; for nature is far above art or judgment.

2 *Return from Parnassus* (1602) III i:

> *Recorder.*   Some art is requisite for the perfection of nature.

Daniel, in his *Defence of Rhyme* (1603), introduces another factor, custom, which, in addition to nature, he places above art:

> . . . rhyme, which both custom and nature doth most powerfully defend: custom, which is before all law, nature, which is above all art . . . the universality argues the general power of it; for if the barbarian use it, then it shows that it sways th' affection of the barbarian; if civil nations practice it, it proves that it works upon the hearts of civil nations; if all, then that it hath a power in nature on all. . . . "Ill customs are to be left." I grant it; but I see not how that can be taken for an ill custom, which nature hath thus ratified . . . as if art were ordained to afflict nature, and that we could not go but in fetters.

Yet he proceeds to indicate that nature is not enough:

> All excellence being sold us at the hard price of labor, it follows where we bestow most thereof we buy the best success: and rhyme, being far more laborious than loose measures, must needs, meeting with wit and industry, breed greater and worthier effects in our language.

Shirley in *Love in a Maze* (1631) IV ii, complaining about the decadence of the drama, recognizes the necessity of both nature and art, without suggesting precedence:

> *Caperwit.*   Your dance is the best language of some comedies,
> And footing runs away with all; a scene
> Expressed with life of art, and squared to nature,
> Is dull and phlegmatic poetry.

Likewise in his preface to the Beaumont and Fletcher Folio (1647):

Poetry is the child of nature, which, regulated and made beautiful by art, presenteth the most harmonious of all other compositions.

Milton. *Reason of Church Government* (1641). Bohn ed., Vol. II, p. 478:

. . . whether the rules of Aristotle herein are strictly to be kept, or nature to be followed, which in them that know art, and use judgment, is no transgression, but an enriching of art. . . .

Ibid.:

. . . if to the instinct of nature and the emboldening of art aught may be trusted, it would be no rashness [to use England's "ancient stories" for an epic].

In his essay on Beauty, the level-headed Bacon, by a simple analogy, makes clear the relation between native ability and study:

I think a painter may make a better face than ever was; but he must do it by a kind of felicity, as a musician who maketh an excellent air in music, and not by rule.

On the relation of art to nature in the sense in which both terms are used today, the Elizabethan dramatists do not seem to have got beyond a realistic conception, especially as applied to pictorial art. Apparently they would have joined with Meres, who, in his *Palladis Tamia* (1598), could find no better way of expressing his admiration for Zeuxis than by reporting that "he painted grapes so lively that birds did fly to eat them." This in spite of the fact that Sidney, in his *Apology*, had pointed out the possibility of a higher achievement. Between poets that treat of things realistic and "right poets," he tells us,

is such a kind of difference as betwixt the meaner sort of painters, who counterfeit only such faces as are set before them, and the more excellent, who, having no law but wit, bestow that in colors upon you which is fittest for the eye to see: as the constant, though lamenting, look of Lucretia, when she punished in herself another's fault. Wherein he painteth, not Lucretia, whom he never saw, but painteth the outward beauty of such a virtue.

(Precisely what the prior demanded of Fra Lippo, in Browning's poem.)

But in this respect England was no more backward than the rest of Europe. Witness what Boccaccio has to say about (of all men) Giotto:

[Giotto] had such a prodigious fancy that there was nothing in nature, the parent of all things, but he could imitate it so well, and draw it so like, as to deceive our very senses; making them imagine that to be the very thing itself which was only his painting.

The stark realism of *Arden of Feversham* (1591) was deliberately intended by the unknown author. Epilogue:

Gentlemen, we hope you'll pardon this naked tragedy,
Wherein no filed points are foisted in
To make it gracious to the ear or eye;
For simple truth is gracious enough,
And needs no other points of glosing stuff.

Tourneur. *Atheist's Tragedy* (1603) IV i:

Sebastian. What, moralizing upon this gentlewoman's needlework? Let me see.
Cataplasma. No, sir. Only examining whether it be done to the true nature and life o' the thing.
Sebas. Here y' have set a medlar with a bachelor's button o' one side and a snail o'the tother. The bachelor's button should have held his head up more pertly towards the medlar: the snail o' the tother side should ha' been wrought with an artificial laziness, doubling his tail and putting out his horn but half the length. And then the medlar falling (as it were) from the lazy snail and ending towards the pert bachelor's button, their branches spreading and winding one within another as if they did embrace.

Dekker. *1 Honest Whore* (1604) IV i 41:

Hippolito.   My Infelice's face, her brow, her eye,
The dimple on her cheek! and sweet skill
Hath from the cunning workman's pencil flown.
These lips look fresh and lively as her own,
Seeming to move and speak.

Massinger. *Picture* (1629) I i:

Baptista.   Take then this little model of Sophia,
With more than human skill limn'd to the life;
Each line and lineament of it, in the drawing,
So punctually observ'd, that, had it motion,
In so much 'twere herself.

Barry, in the prologue to *Ram Alley* (1609), indicates the same ideal applied to the histrionic art:

                    . . . to show
Things never done, with that true life
That thoughts and wits should stand at strife
Whether the things now shown be true,
Or whether we ourselves now do
The things we but present.

According to Fletcher, reality serves as a model for the production of effective art. *Lovers' Progress* (1623) IV iv:

Alcidon.   What a strange scene of sorrow is express'd
In different postures, in their looks and station!
A common painter, eyeing these to help
His dull invention, might draw to the life
The living sons of Priam, as they stood
On the pale walls of Troy, when Hector fell
Under Achilles' spear.

One man at least did not approve of pure realism. George Sandys, in the dedication of his translation of Grotius' *Christ's Passion* (1640):

There is a fault which painters call too much to the life. Quintilian censures one that he more affected similitude than beauty, who would have shown greater skill if less of resemblance. The same in poetry is condemned by Horace, of that art the great law-giver.

There is a significant observation on the nature of the kindred art, the dance, in Ford's *The Fancies Chaste and Noble* (1635), II ii. Troilo is watching a dance and is prompted to make this comment:

So, so, here's art in motion.

DICTION

All Europe was language conscious at this time, it being the tail-end of the formative period of the modern languages. In England this consciousness was not confined to those who occupationally were concerned with language, but permeated all classes of society. A number of playwrights supply us with evidence of this fact.

Richard Puttenham. *The Art of English Poesy* (1589). Bk.2, Ch. ix:

> . . . some words of exceeding great length, which have been fetched from the Latin inkhorn or borrowed of strangers, the use of them in rhyme is nothing pleasant, saving perchance to the common people, who rejoice much to be at plays and enterludes, and, besides their natural ignorance, have at all such times their ears so attentive to the matter, and their eyes upon the shows of the stage, that they take little heed to the cunning of the rhyme.

Nash. *Pierce Penniless* (1592):

> To those that demand what fruits the poets of our time bring forth, or wherein they are able to approve themselves necessary to the state, thus I answer: First and foremost, they have cleansed our language from barbarism, and made the vulgar sort here in London (which is the fountain whose rivers flow round about England) to aspire to a richer purity of speech than is communicated with the commonalty of any nation under heaven.

Greene (?), *Selimus* (1588) l. 1984, supplies a humorous illustration:

Bullithrumble [a clownish shepherd]. . . . we will have a hog's
cheek, and a dish of tripes, and a society of puddings, and to field—
a society of puddings? Did you mark that well-used metaphor?
Another would have said a company of puddings. If you dwell
with me long, sirs, I shall make you as eloquent as our parson
himself.

In *Locrine* (1586) I ii 18, Strumbo, in his prattle, stumbles on
the phrase, "not only, but also," and he stops to comment: "Oh
fine phrase," and presently he uses it in his letter to the girl he has
fallen in love with.

This universal interest accounts for the tremendous appeal
Shakespeare's poetry had for the masses. These in this respect resembled the modern American Negro who has a passion for the
beauty of words as such, and gives expression to that passion in his
daily speech—a fact that is commonly construed derogatorily.

Field. *Amends for Ladies* (1611) I i:

L. Feesimple. O mouth, full of agility! I would give twenty
marks now to any person that could teach me to convey my tongue
(sans stumbling) with such dexterity to such a period.

Glapthorne. *Lady's Privilege* (1640) III ii:

Adorni.   . . . why *Signor?*
*Mo*nsieur has a far more airy and harmonious sound;
There's music in the letters.

But England was behind the continent in literary and linguistic
development, which gave the English a feeling of inferiority.
(Meres did not include English among the "eight chief languages.") There is envy and longing in Lingua's lines in the
opening scene of Tomkis' university play, *Lingua* (1603):

The learned Greek, rich in fit epithets,
Blest in the lovely marriage of pure words.

This state of mind was to be expected, and the other European
nations must have gone through it. It is very apt to express itself

in vehement denial of inferiority. Listen to Rabelais' asseveration concerning the French vernacular; in the prologue to Book V.:

I see a swarm of our modern poets and orators, your Colinets, Marots, Herouets, Saint Gelais, Selels, Masuels, and many more, who have commenced masters in Apollo's academy on Mount Parnassus and drunk brimmers at the caballian fountain among the nine merry muses, have raised our vulgar tongue and made it a noble and everlasting structure. . . . I will prove, in the teeth of brokers and retailers of ancient rhapsodies, and such moldy trash, that our vulgar tongue is not so mean, silly, inept, poor, barren, and contemptible as they pretend.

This sounds like a fore-echo of the protestations that were forthcoming in England a generation later. Rabelais' statement preceded the fruitful activity of the Pléiade, which would have justified it. England supplies one that is considerably more anticipatory. As far back as 1520 John Rastell, in the prologue to his translation of Terence, declares that the vernacular had now been

amplified so
That we therin now translate as well may
As in eny other tongis other can do.

even boasting that

In englysh many wordys do habound
That no greke nor laten for them can be found.

And he gives "the cause that our tong is so plenteouse now:"

. . . we kepe our englysh contynually
And of the other tongis many wordis we borow
Which now for englysh we use & occupy.[1]

To Milton, the classical scholar, the employment of his mother tongue as a medium of literary expression was a dedication. In 1641 he spoke reminiscently of his early days as a writer (*Reason of Church Government*, Bohn ed., vol. II, p. 478):

I applied myself to that resolution which Ariosto followed against the persuasion of Bembo, to fix all the industry and art I could

---

[1]Quoted in E. J. Sweetings' *Early Tudor Criticism*

unite to the adorning of my native tongue; not to make verbal curiosities the end, but to be an interpreter and relator of the best and sagest things among mine own citizens throughout this island in the mother dialect. That what the greatest and choicest wits of Athens, Rome, or modern Italy, and those Hebrews of old did for their country, I, in proportion, might do for mine.

In his famous *Apology*, written about 1582, Sidney avers that for

uttering sweetly and properly the conceits of the mind . . . [English] hath it equally with any other tongue in the world.

Chapman, in his metrical address to the reader of the *Iliad*:

And for our tongue, that still is so impair'd
By traveling linguists, I can prove it clear
That no tongue hath the Muses' utterance heir'd
For verse, and that sweet music to the ear
Struck out of rhyme, so naturally as this.

Ibid., in the prose address:

. . . you shall in the next edition have . . . the due praise of your mother tongue above all others for poesy.

In the same year (1598) Chapman kept this promise in the dedication of *Achilles' Shield*, a translation of the Eighteenth Book of the Iliad:

. . . how full of height and roundness soever Greek be above English, yet is there no depth of concept triumphing in it but, as in a mere admirer it may be imagined, so in a sufficient translator it may be expressed . . . what curious, proud, and poor shamefastness should let an English muse to traduce him, when the language she works withal is more conformable, fluent, and expressive [than Italian, French, or Spanish].

Drayton. *England's Heroical Epistles* (1597). Surrey says:

Though to the Tuscan I the smoothness grant,
Our dialect no majesty doth want,

To set thy praises in as high a key
As France, or Spain, or Germany, or they.

Daniel has a thoughtful utterance. *Musophilus* (1599), 951:

Or should we careless come behind the rest
In power of words, that go before in worth,
Whenas our accents, equal to the best,
Is able greater wonders to bring forth:
When all that ever hotter spirits exprest,
Comes bettered by the patience of the north?
And who, in time, knows whither we may vent
T'enrich unknowing nations with our stores?

To appreciate the significance of Daniel's enthusiastic dream one must bear in mind that England had thitherto been at the receiving end of literary influences.

Awareness of inferiority impelled zealous efforts to remedy the situation, with results, as we know, that justified the claims just quoted; and among the workers were the dramatists, as maintained by Nash in the passage given above. Gabriel Harvey includes Daniel and Nash in the list of those whom he affectionately thanks "for their studious endeavors commendably employed in enriching and polishing their native tongue, never so furnished or embellished as of late."

Heywood, in *Apology for Actors* (1612), finds that the stage has been a main medium in the process of refining the English tongue:

... our English tongue, which hath been the most harsh, uneven, and broken language of the world, part Dutch, part Irish, Saxon, Scotch, Welsh, and indeed a gallimaufry of many, but perfect in none, is now by this secondary means of playing continually refined, every writer striving in himself to add a new flourish unto it; so that in process, from the rude and unpolished tongue, it is grown to a most perfect and composed language, and many excellent works and elaborate poems writ in the same, that many nations grow inamored of our tongue (before despised). ... Thus you see to what excellence our refined English is brought, that in these days we are ashamed of that euphony and eloquence which within these sixty years the best tongues in the land were proud to pronounce.

Heywood would lead us to believe that Daniel's dream of universal appreciation had already been realized. Our satisfaction, however, must be dampened when we read what Anston Cockayne says in his verses on Massinger's *Emperor of the East* nearly a score of years later:

> . . . live long
> To purify the slighted English tongue,
> That both the nymphs of Tagus and of Po
> May not henceforth despise our language so.
> Nor could they do it, if they e'er had seen
> The matchless features of the Fairy Queen;
> Read Jonson, Shakespeare, Beaumont, Fletcher, or
> Thy neat-limn'd pieces, skilful Massinger.

That the theater exerted an influence on the speech of the public is suggested by the following passage from the first scene of the second act of Tomkis' *Albumizar* (1614):

> *Trincalo.* . . . then will I confound her with compliments drawn from the plays I see at the Fortune and Red Bull, where I learn all the words I speak and understand not.

According to *The Actor's Remonstrance* (1643) the beneficent effect which the theater had on the development of the English language is one of its titles to favorable recognition:

> . . . plays, comedies and tragedies, being the lively representations of men's actions, in which vice is always sharply glanced at and punished, and virtue rewarded and encouraged, the most exact and natural eloquence of our English language expressed and daily amplified . . .

To return to Heywood. It is difficult to see what "euphony and eloquence" he can refer to as flourishing sixty years back. The terms would indicate that he was thinking of euphuism, since whose vogue hardly more than half that period had elapsed. Euphuism was the most popular of the attempts made to do something for the backward language; but its artificiality presently caused a vigorous reaction. Drayton, in his *Elegies of Poets and Poesy* (1627), gives Sidney the credit for leading the reaction:

The noble Sidney . . .
That hero for numbers, and for prose,
That throughly paced our language, as to show
The plenteous English hand in hand might go
With Greek and Latin, and did first reduce
Our tongue from Lyly's writing then in use,
Talking of stones, stars, plants, of fishes, flies;
Playing with words and idle similes. . . .
As the English apes and very zanies be
Of everything that they do hear and see,
So imitating his ridiculous tricks,
They spake and writ all like mere lunatics.

Nash, replying to Harvey, *Strange News* (1592) :

Is my style like Greene's or my jests like Tarlton's? This will I
proudly boast: that the vein which I have (be it a *median* vein or
a mad vein) is of my own begetting, and calls no man father in
England but myself; neither Euphues, nor Tarlton, nor Greene. . . .
Euphues I read when I was a little ape in Cambridge, and then I
thought it was *ipse ille*. It may be excellent good yet for aught I
know, for I lookt not on it this ten year; but to imitate it I abhor.

The various practices (adopting classic and Italian models,
inkhornisms, loan words, coinages etc.) resorted to in the endeavor to enrich the language could not escape being sometimes
applied with excessive zeal. In the inevitable discussion which
followed the playwrights joined.

In the prologue to *The Honor of the Garter* Peele has praise
for Harington,

That hath so purely naturaliz'd
Strange words, and made them all free denizens.

Chapman expresses himself positively. In the Epistle to the
Understander, prefixed to *Achilles' Shield* (1598) , he defends his
own coinage, and the enrichment of the language by borrowing:

For my variety of new words, I have no inkpot I am sure you know,
but such as I give passport with such authority, so significant and
not ill sounding, that if my country language were an usurer, or
a man of this age speaking it, he would thank me for enriching him.

> . . . All tongues have enriched themselves from their original with good neighborly borrowing, and as with infusion of fresh air and nourishment of new blood in their still growing bodies, and why may not ours? . . . Chaucer (by whom we will needs authorize our true English) hath more new words for his time than any man needs to devise now.

And in the same epistle he defends himself against the charge of obscurity and the employment of an un-English style:

> My epistle dedicatory before my *Seven Books* is accounted dark and too much labored . . . my far-fetcht and, as it were, my beyond-sea manner of writing, if they would take as much pains for their poor countryman as for a proud stranger, should be more gracious to their choice conceits than a discourse that falls naked before them, and hath nothing but what mixeth itself with ordinary table-talk.

But the majority of utterances are on the negative side, so that we find a contradiction between preaching and practice. Spenser pays tribute to Chaucer for his "English undefiled." What does he mean by that? As Chapman points out in the passage quoted above, "Chaucer hath more new words for his time than any man needs to devise now." Writers found themselves impelled by two opposing forces: patriotic conservatism, and the urgent need to enrich the language. Without their knowing it the latter proved the stronger; so much so that in their zeal they went to extremes, which they recognized as such in others, but not in themselves. Studying the available illustrations we find that it is the excesses that they really object to, and in the attack on these excesses Chapman too joined. Their attitude they acquired in their schooldays, under the influence of the rhetoricians Ascham, Cheke, and Wilson, who opposed foreign importations generally and particularly "set themselves against over-elaboration of style in this way or that," as Saintbury puts it.

Gascoigne. *Certain Notes of Instruction* (1575):

> . . . eschew strange words, or *obsoleta et inusitata,* unless the theme do give just occasion: marry, in some places a strange word doth draw attentive reading.

The opposition to foreignisms was not without an appreciation of the distinctive possession of the English language that gave it its peculiar character, and was the source of much of its poetic beauty; namely, the predominance of monosyllables. We quote Gascoigne again:

> the most ancient English words are of one syllable, so that the more monosyllables that you use the truer Englishman you shall seem, and the less you shall smell of the inkhorn.

In *The Steel Glass*, published the following year, he harps on the same subject:

> That Grammar grudge not at our English tongue,
> Because it stands by Monosyllables
> And cannot be declined as others are.

Chapman, (quoted by Collier, *Poetical Decameron*, I. 36):

> Our monosyllables so kindly fall
> And meet opposed in rhyme, as they did kiss.
> French and Italian, most immetrical,
> Their many syllables in harsh collision
> Fall as they brake their necks.

Singularly enough for so vigorous a writer, Nash did not see in these monosyllables an advantage. In picturesque fashion he states his position in the preface to *Christ's Tears* (1594):

> To the second rank of reprehenders, that complain of my bois-terous compound words, and ending my Italianate coined verbs all in *ize*, thus I reply: That no wind that blows strong but is boister-ous: no speech or words of any power or force to confute or persuade, but must be swelling and boisterous. For the compound-ing of my words, therein I imitate rich men, who having store of white single money together, convert a number of those small little cents into great pieces of gold, such as double pistoles and portu-gues. Our English tongue, of all languages, most swarmeth with the single money of monosyllables, which are the only scandal of it. Books written in them, and no other, seem like shopkeepers' boxes, that contain nothing else save half-pence, three-farthings, and two pences. Therefore what did me I, but, having a huge heap of

those worthless shreds of small English in my *pia mater's* purse, to make the royaler show with them to men's eyes, had them to the compounders immediately, and exchanged them four into one, and others into more, according to the Greek, French, Spanish, and Italian.

In his tart reply to Harvey in *Strange News* (1592), Nash lists a string of words and phrases used by Harvey, which he terms "inkhornisms." Many of them we should consider no more objectionable and no less useful than the term he uses to describe them: "absonism," and another unusual word he uses before he is through with the paragraph: "indesinence." In short, Nash unconsciously proclaims himself, with Harvey, a member of the sensitive generation that patriotically sought to nullify the shortcomings of its mother tongue. In fact, he concedes the right of some of the condemned terms to appear in verse, but not in prose, just as Gascoigne was willing to admit some of the "strange words" in particular connections. One wonders what would be the source of the vocabulary he boasts, in *Pierce Penniless,* to have within reach, to hurl at his enemies:

> . . . let him not measure the weight of my words by this book . . . .
> I have terms (if I be vext) laid in steep in *aqua fortis* and gunpowder, that shall rattle through the skies, and make an earthquake in a peasant's ears.

Daniel feels antagonistic toward the introduction of strange and foreign words, but is broad-minded about it. The last paragraph of his *Defence of Rhyme* reads:

> Next . . . stands our affectation, wherein we always bewray ourselves to be both unkind and unnatural to our own native language, in disguising or forging strange or unusual words, as if it were to make our verse seem another kind of speech, out of the course of our usual practice, displacing our words, or inventing new, only upon a singularity, when our own accustomed phrase, set in the due place, would express us more familiarly and to better delight than all this idle affectation of antiquity or novelty can ever do. And I cannot but wonder at the strange presumption of some men, that dare so audaciously adventure to introduce any whatsoever foreign words, be they never so strange, and of them-

selves, as it were, without a parliament, without any consent or allowance, establish them as free-denizens in our language.

He proceeds to concede, however, that such undesirable manifestations are an inevitable concomitant of the evolutionary process, thus acknowledging the need for change:

> But this is but a character of that perpetual revolution which we see to be in all things that never remain the same: and we must herein be content to submit ourselves to the law of time, which in few years will make all that for which we now contend *Nothing*.

It is clear from Daniel's sensible statement that what he really objected to was unnecessary innovation. He thus falls in line with his fellows who could not tolerate absurd excesses. Marston, for instance, shows that he is not in favor of hide-bound conservatism, by having an ignorant fool favor it. In Act II of *Histriomastix* (c. 1599) he has Gulch comment thus on an example of wretched stuff:

> *Gulch.* Well, fellows, I never heard happier stuff.
> Here's no new luxury or blandishment,
> But plenty of old England's mothers' words.

But in the same piece he has Landulpho comment this way on the prologue to the play within the play:

> Most ugly lines and base brown-paper-stuff,
> Thus to abuse our heavenly poesy,
> That sacred offspring from the brain of Jove,
> Thus to be mangled with profane absurds,
> Strangled and chok't with lawless bastard words.

Chapman. *Sir Giles Goosecap* (1601) IV ii:

> *Goosecap.* Then his fine words that he sets them in: "cancatical," "a fine anise-seed-wench-fool," "upon ticket," and so forth.
> *Furnifall.* Passing strange words, believe me!

By the same author, in the first scene of *The Gentleman Usher* (1602), the matter of "strange words" is presented from a curious and practical angle. A poem has been written by the pedant Sarpago:

Alphonso.　　　　. . . here is a poem that requires
Your worthy censures, offer'd, if it like,
To furnish our intended amorous show;
Read it, Vincentio. . . .
　　Vincentio (reads). 'The red-faced sun hath firk'd the flun-
　　　　dering shades,
And cast bright ammel on Aurora's brow.'
　　Alphonso.　High words and strange! Read on, Vincentio.
　　Vin.　'The busky groves that gag-tooth'd boars do shroud,
With cringle-crangle horns do ring aloud.'
　　Alph.　How likes Vincentio?
　　Vin.　　　　　　　　　　It is strangely good;
No inkhorn did ever bring forth the like;
And these brave prancing words with actor's spur
Be ridden throughly, and managed right,
'Twould fright the audience,—and perhaps delight.

In the same play, IV ii:

　　Bassiolo.　If there be not more choice words in that letter
Than in any three of Guevara's *Golden Epistles,*
I am a very ass.

And a little farther on:

　　Vin.　Here's enough in it to serve for my letters as long as I
live.

Munday. *Downfall of Huntington* (1598) Dodsley VIII. p. 135:

　　Ralph.　Ye protract, Master Friar. I obsecrate ye, with all cour-
tesy, omitting compliment, you would vouch or deign to proceed.
　　Friar.　Deign, vouch, protract, compliment, obsecrate?
Why, Goodman Tricks, who taught you thus to prate?

Chettle *et al. Patient Grizzel* (1598) II i:

　　Farneze.　. . . silk gallants who . . . speak no language but 'sweet
lady' and 'sweet signior' and chew between their teeth terrible
words, as though they would conjure, as 'compliment,' and 'projects,' and 'fastidious,' and 'capricious,' and 'misprision,' and 'the
sintheresis of the soul,' and such like raise-velvet terms.

64

Urenze.   What are the accoutrements of these gallants?
Far.   Indeed, that's one of their fustian, outlandish phrases, too.

In Tomkis' *Lingua* (1603) a speech by Lingua in which several foreign languages are impressed into service, evokes this interesting comment (III v):

Communis Sensus.   What's here? here's a gallimaufry of speech indeed.
Memory.   I remember, about the year 1602, many used this skew kind of language; which, in my opinion, is not much unlike the man Platony, the son of Lagus, King of Egypt, brought for a spectacle, half white, half black.
Com. Sen.   I am persuaded these same language-makers have the very quality of cold in their wit, that freezeth all heterogeneal languages together, congealing English tin, Grecian gold, Roman laten, all in a lump.
Phantastes.   Or rather, in my imagination, like your fantastical gull's apparel, wearing a Spanish felt, a French doublet, a Granado stocking, a Dutch slop, an Italian cloak, with a Welsh freeze jerkin.

Pedantic speech is satirized in the person of Phantasma in *2 Return from Parnassus* (1602), especially the use of Latin quotations. Other allusions to it follow. They point to a reaction against the formal rhetoric which had formed such an important part of their school curriculum.

Pilgrimage to Parnassus (1598) I i 27:

Plain dealing needs not rhetoric's tinkling bell.

Peele (?). *Wily Beguiled* (1595) Prol.:

What, Spectrum here again? Why, noble Cerberus,
nothing but patch-panel stuff, old gallimaufries, and cotton
candle eloquence?

Chapman. *Gentleman Usher* (1602) I ii 143:

Strozzo.   How did you like my speech?
Vincentio.   Oh fie upon it!
Your rhetoric was too fine.

Dekker. *Satiromastix* (1602) I ii:

Horace. . . . and then follow a troop of other rich and labor'd conceits: oh, the end will be admirable!

Heywood. *Rape of Lucrece* (1603) II v:

Collatine. My man's a rhetorician, I can tell you,
And his conceit is fluent.

Chapman. *Caesar and Pompey* (c. 1611) I ii 236:

Pompey. You speak well, and are learn'd; and golden speech
Did nature never give man but to gild
A copper soul in him; and all that learning
That heartily is spent in painting speech,
Is merely painted, and no solid knowledge.

Marston. *Histriomastix* (c. 1599) II:

Like over-nice portraying pictures,
We spoil the counterfeit in coloring.

Verbosity comes in for its share of condemnation.

Lyly. *Sapho and Phao* (1581) Epil.:

. . . neither can there anything breed such tediousness as hearing many words uttered in a small compass.

Webster. *White Devil* (1611) III i:

Vittoria. Surely, my lords, this lawyer hath swallowed
Some 'pothecaries' bills, or proclamations;
And now the hard and undigestible words
Come up, like stones we use to give hawks for physic.
Why, this is Welsh to Latin.
Lawyer. My lords, this woman
Knows not her tropes, nor figures, nor is perfect
In the academic derivation
Of grammatical elocution. . .

Francisco.   Put up your papers in your fustian bag,
Cry mercy, sir, 'tis buckram, and accept
My notion of your learned verbosity.
   Lawyer.   I most graduatically thank your lordship.

Outdated forms and trite phrases disapproved.
Gascoigne. *Certain Notes* (1575):

If I should undertake to write in praise of a gentlewoman, I
would neither praise her crystal eye, nor her cherry lips, . . .
For these things are *trita et obvia.*

Nash. *Summer's Last Will* (1592) Ind.:

   Will.   I'll show you what a scurvy prologue he hath made me,
in an old vein of similitudes.

He probably refers to Euphuism, regarding which he expressed
himself above.

Chapman. *Gentleman Usher* (1601) III ii 415:

   Bassiolo.   How do you
like the word *endear?*
   Margaret.   O fie upon it!
   Bas.   Nay, then, I see your judgment. What say you to *con-
dole?*
   Mar.   Worse and worse!
   Bas.   I hope you will take no exception to *believe it.*
   Mar.   Out upon 't! that phrase is so run out of breath in
trifles, that we shall have no belief at all in earnest shortly: 'believe
it, 'tis a pretty feather,' 'believe it, a dainty rush.' Believe it, an
excellent coxcomb.
   Bas.   So, so, so; your exceptions sort very collaterally.
   Mar.   Collaterally! There's a fine word now; wrest in that if
you can by any means.

Ibid. *M. D'Olive* (1605) IV ii 214:

   Roderigue.   And the more wise the more silent.
   Mugeron.   That's something common.

An especially attractive target was provided by the artificial devices and exaggerated patterns presented by the pioneers Kyd and Marlowe, which even the early Shakespeare could not escape, and which later could not escape the normally unsatiric Shakespeare. One of these patterns is bombast.

Greene. *Perimedes* (1588) To the Gentlemen Readers:

. . . lately two gentlemen poets made two madmen of Rome beat it out of their paper bucklers, and had it in derision for that I could not make my verses jet upon the stage in tragical buskins, every word filling the mouth like the faburden of Bow bell, daring God out of heaven with that atheist Tamberlaine, or blaspheming with the mad priest of the sun. But let me rather openly pocket up the ass at Diogenes' hand than wantonly set out such impious instances of intolerable poetry.

Nash. Preface to Greene's *Menaphon* (1589):

I am not ignorant how eloquent our gowned age has grown of late, so that every mechanical mate abhors the English he was born to, and plucks with a solemn periphrasis his *ut vales* from the ink-horn; which I impute not so much to the perfection of arts as to the servile imitation of vainglorious tragedians, who contend not so seriously to excite in action as to embowel the clouds in a speech of comparison. . . . But herein I cannot so fully bequeath them to folly, as their idiot art-masters, that intrude themselves to our ears as the alchemists of eloquence, who (mounted on the stage of arrogance) think to outbrave better pens with the swelling bombast of a bragging blank verse. Indeed, it may be the ingrafted overflow of some kill-cow conceit that . . . commits the digestion of their choleric incumbrances to the spacious volubility of a drumming decasyllabon.

In the same preface Nash ridicules Stanyhurst as having

revived by his ragged quill such carterly variety as no hodge plowman in a country but would have held as the extremity of clownery

and quotes as an example part of a description of a tempest:

Then did he make heaven's vault to rebound, with rounce
     robble hobble
Of ruff raff roaring, with thwick, thwack thirlery bouncing.

The bombastic style of Stanyhurst and Harvey is burlesqued in
Peele's *Old Wives' Tale* (1595); and in *2 Return from Parnassus*
(1602) Marlovian bombast is represented in the person of Furor
Poeticus. Marston has his fling at it in the induction to the first
part of *Antonio and Mellida* (1600):

> *Matzagente.* By the bright honor of a Milanoise and the re-
> splendent fulgor of this steel, I will defend the feminine to the
> death, and ding his spirit to the verge of hell, that dares divulge a
> lady's prejudice.
> *Feliche*...Rampum, scrampum, mount tufty Tamburlaine. What
> rattling thunderclap breaks from his lips?

Fletcher. *Chances* (1609) V iii:

> *John* This is an honest conjuror and a pretty poet;
> I like his words well; there's no bombast in 'em.

Massinger. *Parliament of Love* (1624) II ii:

> *Leonora.*   ... thy discourse,
> Though full of bombast phrases, never brought matter
> Worthy the laughing at, much less the hearing.

Ford. *Lover's Melancholy* (1628) I i:

> *Pelias.* To bestride
> The frothy foam of Neptune's surging waves,
> When blustering Boreas tosseth up the deep
> And thumps a thunder bounce.
> *Menaphon.* Where did'st thou learn this language?
> *Pelias.* I this language?
> Alas, sir, we that study words and forms
> Of compliment, must fashion all discourse
> According to the nature of the subject.

Massinger. Upon Shirley's *The Grateful Servant* (1630):

Here are no forc'd expressions, no rack'd phrase;
No Babel compositions to amaze
The tortured reader.

Shirley. On Massinger's *Renegado* (1630):

Others would fright the time
Into belief, with mighty words that tear
A passage through the ear.

Exaggerated alliteration is satirized by Chapman in *Gentleman Usher* (1602) II i 247:

Poggio. And so we come (gracing your gracious Graces)
To sweep care's cobwebs from your cleanly faces.

The Spanish Tragedy is burlesqued in *2 Return from Parnassus* (1602) I ii:

Ingenioso. I think we shall have you put finger in the eye and cry, "O friends, no friends."

And in Chapman's *M. D'Olive* (1605) IV ii 229, attention is called to "too many O's." Both of these devices had long before been ridiculed by Shakespeare.

In *Love in a Maze* (1632) II ii, Shirley indulges in a long tirade against the abuse of adjectives:

Goldsworth. Master Caperwit, before you read pray tell me, have your verses any adjectives?
Cap. Adjectives! Would you have a poem without adjectives? They are the flowers, the grace, of all language.
A well chose epithet doth give new soul
To fainting poesy, and makes every verse
A bride. With adjectives we bait our lines
When we do fish for gentlewomen's loves,
And with their sweetness catch the nibbling ear
Of amorous ladies. With the music of
These ravishing nouns we charm the silken tribe,
And make the gallant melt with apprehension
Of the rare word. I will maintain it against
A bundle of grammarians: in poetry

The substantive itself cannot subsist
Without an adjective.
   Goldsworth. But, for all that,
Those words would sound more full, methinks, that are not
So larded; and if I might counsel you,
You should compose a sonnet clean without them;
Carry their weight, show fair, like deeds enroll'd,
Not writs that are first made and after fil'd.
Then first came up the title of blank verse.
You know, sir, what blank signifies? When the sense,
First fram'd, is tied with adjectives like points,
And could not hold together without wedges,
Hang't, 'tis pedantic, vulgar poetry.
Let children, when they versify, stick here
And there these piddling words for want of matter.
Poets write masculine numbers.

That there is a difference between poetic diction and prose
diction was early recognized. Gascoigne explains the presence of
the marginal glossary in *Jocasta* (1572):

> . . . certain words which are not common in use are noted and
> expounded in the margent . . . at request of a gentlewoman who
> understood not poetical words or terms.

We noted above that Nash was willing to admit in verse some
of the words which he objected to in Harvey's prose. Other pertinent citations follow.

Chapman. *Sir Giles* (1601) III ii 25:

> *Clarence.* Prose is too harsh, and verse is poetry;
> Why should I write then?

Ibid. *Widow's Tears* (1605) IV i 47:

> *Lycus.* . . . Humanity broke loose from my heart and streamed
> from mine eyes.
> *Tharsalio.* In prose, thou weptst.

Puttenham, in 1589, classified style as high, medium and low.

Ten years earlier Lodge had recognized that there were different levels of style. In his *Defence of Poetry* he says:

> . . . weigh considerately but of the writing of poets, and you shall see that when the matter is most heavenly their style is most lofty, a strange token of the wonderful efficacy of the same.

Tomkis. Lingua (1603) III v:

> *Communis Sensus.* . . . Lingua, go on, but in a less formal manner. You know an ingenious oration must neither swell above the banks with insolent words, nor creep too shallow in the ford with vulgar terms; but run equally, smooth and cheerful, through the clear current of a pure style.

Chapman. *Revenge of Bussy* (1608) I ii 38:

> *Montsurry.*　　　　　　. . . worthiest poets
> Shun common and plebeian forms of speech,
> Every illiberal and affected phrase,
> To clothe their matter; and together tie
> Matter and form with art and decency.

The last line is particularly significant, possessing a wider applicability. Other utterances pertaining to the relation between matter and form follow.

Gascoigne. *Certain Notes* (1575)

> The first and most necessary point that ever I found meet to be considered in making of a delectable poem is this: to ground it upon some fine invention. For it is not enough to roll in pleasant words, nor yet to thunder in rhyme, *Ram, Ruff,* by letter (quoth my master Chaucer), nor yet to abound in apt vocables or epithets, unless the invention have in it also *aliquid salis.*

King James VI. *Ane schort Treatise* (1584):

> Ye man also take heid to frame your wordis and sentencis according to the mater.

Daniel. *Defence of Rhyme* (1603):

. . . it is matter that satisfies the judicial, appear it in what habit it will. . . . We admire them [the Greeks and Romans] not for their smooth-gliding words, nor their measures, but their inventions.

Chapman. *Revenge of Bussy* (1608) II i 184:

> *Clermont.*   And as the foolish poet that still writ
> All of his self-lov'd verse in paper royal,
> Or parchment rul'd with lead, smooth'd with pumice,
> Bound richly up, and strung with crimson strings; . . .
> Yet in his works behold him, and he show'd
> Like to a ditcher.

Homer's practice probably prompted the criticism of excessive description in Tomkis' *Lingua* (1603) II iv:

> *Phantastes.*   Chronologers, many of them, are so fantastic, as when they bring a captain to the combat, lifting up his revengeful arm to dispart the head of his enemy, they'll hold up his arms so long till they have bestowed three or four pages in describing the gold hilts of his threatening falchion; so that in my fancy the reader may well wonder his adversary stabs him not before he strikes.

The following quotations give utterance to a passionate yearning for the power of effective expression.
Marston. *Antonio's Revenge* (1599) Prol.:

> O that our power
> Could lackey or keep wing with our desires,
> That with unused peize of style and sense
> We might weigh massy in judicious scale.

Beaumont. *Salmacis and Hermaphroditus*:

> Command the god of love, that little king,
> To give each verse a slight touch with his wing,
> That, as I write, one line may draw the other,
> And every word skip nimbly o'er another.

Field. *On Faithful Shepherdess* (1629) :

> My ambition is
> (Even by my hopes and love to poetry)
> To live to perfect such a work as this,
> Clad in such elegant propriety
> Of words.

John Denham. *Cooper's Hill*:

> O could I flow like thee [the Thames], and make thy stream
> My great example, as it is my theme;
> Though deep, yet clear; though gentle, yet not dull;
> Strong without rage, without overflowing, full.

Chapman on the art of translating. Address to the Reader of the *Seven Books of the Iliads* (1598):

> The worth of a skillful and worthy translator is to observe the sentences, figures, and forms of speech proposed in his author, his true sense and height, and to adorn them with figures and forms of oration fitted to the original in the same tongue to which they are translated.
> . . . how pedantical and absurd an affectation it is in the interpretation of an author (much more of Homer) to turn him word for word, when (according to Horace and other best lawgivers to translators) it is the part of every knowing and judicial interpreter, not to follow the number and order of words, but the material things themselves, and sentences to weigh diligently, and to clothe and adorn them with words, and such style and form of oration as are most apt for the language into which they are converted.

According to Drayton (*Elegies of Poets and Poesy*) Chapman's translations did not read like translations:

> . . . reverend Chapman, who hath brought to us
> Musaeus, Homer, and Hesiodus
> Out of the Greek; and by his skill hath rear'd
> Them to that height, and to our tongue endear'd,
> That were those poets at this day alive, . . .
> They would think, having neglected them so long,
> They had been written in the English tongue.

Chapman's idea of a well organized oration (*Byron's Conspiracy*, IV i):

And as the cunning orator reserves
His fairest similies, best adorning figures,
Chief matter, and most moving arguments
For his conclusion; and doth then supply
His ground stream laid before, glides over them,
Makes his full depth seen through; and so takes up
His audience in applause past the clouds; . . .

PROSODY

Two topics under this head were the subject of heated dispute: the naturalization of classic meters, and the employment of rhyme. Nash, Daniel, and Chapman made direct contributions to the controversy. Other dramatists sprinkled allusions to matters of prosody in their dialogue; but these are usually in a jocular vein, and concerned merely with metrical details.

The scholars were emphatically for the adoption of the classic meters, and, curiously enough, they won over the young Spenser to their side. (Fortunately his conversion in theory did not affect his practice.) Their attitude is understandable in view of their education, the poor showing English poetry had made in comparison with the classics, and the absurdly complicated rhyme schemes of English medieval poetry and drama. Even Chaucer, who was universally admired, did not help, for his rhythms were not understood at the time. How strongly they felt on the subject is evident from the way Ascham states the case in his *Schoolmaster* (Smith, I. p. 30):

> But now, when men know the difference, and have the examples, both of the best and of the worst, surely to follow rather the Goths in rhyming than the Greeks in true versifying were even to eat acorns with swine, when we may freely eat wheat bread amongst men.

But the monosyllabic character of English forces him to make a concession:

> And although *carmen exametrum* doth rather trot and hobble than run smoothly in our English tongue, yet I am sure our English tongue will receive *carmen iambicum* as naturally as either Greek or Latin.

Nash's statement for the opposition in his reply to Harvey in *Strange News* (1592) is no less graphic:

> The hexameter verse I grant to be a gentleman of an ancient house (so is many an English beggar); yet this clime of ours he cannot thrive in. Our speech is too craggy for him to set his plough in; he goes twitching and hopping in our language like a man running upon quagmires, up the hill in one syllable, and down the dale in another, retaining no part of that stately smooth gait which he vaunts himself with amongst the Greeks and Latins.
>
> Homer and Virgil . . . wrote in hexameter verses: *ergo*, Chaucer and Spenser, the Homer and Virgil of England, were far overseen that they wrote not all their poems in hexameter also. In many countries velvet and satin is a commoner wear than cloth amongst us: *ergo*, we must leave wearing of cloth, and go every one in velvet and satin, because other countries use so.

Chapman, in *Shadow of Night* (1594), declares that English poetry

> Will not be clad in her supremacy
> With those strange garments (Rome's hexameters),
> As she is English; but in right prefers
> Our native robes (put on with skillful hands—
> English heroics) to those antic garlands.

Bacon's simple comment in *Advancement of Learning*:

> Though men in learned tongue do tie themselves to the ancient measures, yet in modern languages it seemeth to me as free to make new measures of verses as of dances.

Daniel's famous *Defence of Rhyme* (1603) was prompted by the appearance the year before of Campion's *Observations on the Art of English Poesy*; but Ascham's words, "you that praise this rhyming," prove that the controversy started far back of Campion and Daniel. Gascoigne informs the reader of his blank-verse satire, *Steel Glass* (1576), that the walls of fame

> are wondrous hard to climb,
> And much too high for ladders made of rhyme.

And of course we remember Marlowe's blast that he would rescue the English drama "from jigging veins of rhyming mother-wits;" but he was for the adoption of blank verse, not a return to classic meters. The same is true of the others quoted.

Nash. *Anatomy of Absurdity* (1589):

Now, whether rhyming be poetry I refer to the judgment of the learned. Yea, let the indifferent reader divine what deep mystery can be placed under plodding meter. Who is it that, reading *Bevis of Hampton,* can forbear laughing if he mark what scrambling shift he makes to end his verses alike.

Rhyme and meter seem to be identified in Brome's *Jovial Crew* (1641), IV ii:

Hilliard. That's no rime, poet.
Poet. There's as good poetry in blank verse as in meter.

Even Daniel was willing to concede that for tragedy blank verse is to be preferred to rhyme. Comedy, apparently, he excludes from the privilege:

I must confess my adversary hath wrought this much upon me, that I think a tragedy would indeed best comport with a blank verse and dispense with rhyme, saving in the chorus, or where a sentence shall require a couplet.

This concession is typical of the broad-minded attitude maintained in the whole of this admirable treatise.

Chapman, in the following allusion to Daniel's *Complaint of Rosamond* (148-150), must have felt a mean satisfaction in delivering a palpable hit.

Sir Giles (1601) IV iii 58:

Momford. But our most court-received poet says
That painting is pure chastity's abater.
Clarence. That was to make up a poor rhyme to 'nature.'

Most of the references to rhyme relegate it, by implication, to a lower sphere.

James IV (1590) III end:

> *Bohan.* The rest is ruthful; yet, to beguile the time,
> 'Tis interlaced with merriment and rhyme.

Dekker. *Seven Deadly Sins* (1606) (Percy Reprints p. 20):

> I would fain see a prize set up that the welted usurer and the
> politic bankrupt might rail one against another for it:
> O, it would beget a rhyming comedy.

Shirley. *Bird in a Cage* (1633) IV i:

> *Mardona.* . . . there be some call themselves poets, make their
> rhymes straddle so wide, a twelvemonth will hardly reconcile them;
> I hope a lady may straddle a little by poetical license.

Ibid.

> *Mar.* If aught else do clog thy thoughts with unkind
> Thoughts, unload the dark burden of thy mind,
> Pronounce thy grief aloud, my amorous darling,
> And I will—
> *Cassiana.* Let him choose his rhyme, I beseech you, madam.
> *Mar.* Uh, uh—cold phlegm obstructs my language—
> Barling, carling,—
> *Donella.* Ha, ha, 'tis time to make an end;
> He was almost choked with his own phrase.

Stephen Gosson, in his *Plays Confuted in Five Actions*, written
about 1582, before Marlowe issued his blast against rhyme, finds
rhyme to be one of the alluring attractions utilized by the devil
to draw people to the theater:

> Because the sweet numbers of poetry flowing in verse do wonder-
> fully tickle the hearer's ears, the devil hath tied this to most of
> our plays, that whatsoever he would have stick fast to our souls
> might slip down in sugar by this inticement; for that which de-
> lighteth never troubleth our swallow.

Lyly. *Endymion* (1585) IV ii:

Epiton.   The beggar, Love, that knows not where to lodge,
At last within my heart, when I slept,
He crept;
I walked, and so my fancies began to fodge.
Samias.   That's a very long verse.
Epiton.   Why, the other was short.

Robert Tailor. *The Hog Hath Lost His Pearl* (1613) I i:

Player.   Methinks the end of this stave is a foot too long.
Haddit.   O no; sing it but in tune, and I dare warrant you.
Player.   Why, hear ye:
   And you that delight in trulls and minions,
   Come buy my four ropes of hard St. Thomas's onions.
Look ye there; *St. Thomas* might very well have been left
out; besides, *hard* should have come next to *onions.*

In *All Fools* (1599) Chapman indulges in a humorous enumeration of metrical forms:

Haddit.   Fie! no; the dismembering of a rhyme to bring in reason shows the more efficacy in the writer.

Gostanzo.   I could have written as good prose and verse
As the most beggarly poet of them all;
Either acrostic, exordium,
Epithalamions, satires, epigrams,
Sonnets in dozens, or your quatorzains
In any rhyme, masculine, feminine,
Or sdrucciola, or couplets, blank verse;
Y'are but bench-whistlers nowadays to them
That were in our times.

In the dedication of *Caesar and Pompey* (1605), Chapman, in obscure prose, argues the superiority of verse over prose in a drama:

. . . the hasty prose the style avoids obtain to the more temperate and staid numerous elocution some assistance and grace of it.

Thomas Carew has praise for good metrical effects in his lines upon *The Heir*, by Thomas May (1622) :

You shall observe his words in order meet,
And softly stealing on with equal feet,
Slide into even numbers with such grace,
As each word had been molded for that place.
You shall perceive an amorous passion spun
Into so smooth a web as, had the sun,
When he pursued the swiftly flying maid,
Courted her in such language, she had staid.

Heywood's boast, in the *Apology*, of the capacity of English for metrical forms is amusing:

Neither Sapphic, Ionic, Iambic, Phaleutic, Adonic, Gliconic, Chori-ambic, nor any other measured verse used among the Greeks, Latins, Italians, French, Dutch, or Spanish writers, but may be exprest in English, be it in blank verse or meter, in distichon, or hexastichon, or in what form or feet, or what number you can desire.

THE THEATER ON THE DEFENSIVE

Thomas Heywood, in his *Apology for Actors* (1612), deplores the fact that poets and playwrights have themselves been remiss in the face of the onslaught on poetry and the theater:

And, amongst our modern poets who have been industrious in many an elaborate and ingenious poem, even they whose pens have had the greatest traffic with the stage, have been in the excuse of these muses most forgetful.

Where was *he* all the while? His own involvement must have flashed upon him, so he thought it better to stop right there: "But leaving these, lest I make too large a head to a small body, and so misshape my subject, I will begin with the antiquity of acting comedies, tragedies, and histories."

It is true that the published statements issued from the public theaters in reply to Gosson and his followers were not numerous. However, the playwrights were not apathetic to Gosson's invective. In fact, they showed commendable activity. First, as Gosson tells us, they tried to get the universities to take up the cudgels for them. Failing in that they met the attack in their own way. They placed Gosson in a ridiculous position by presenting two plays that he had written, and also produced, Gosson informs us, an allegorical play in defense of the theater, entitled *The Play of Plays*. Gosson also tells us of the appearance of a pamphlet on the subject, entitled *News out of Affrick,* but he does not mention the author.

Besides, Lodge immediately leaped to the defense, and Nash later came out vigorously both in his preface to Greene's *Menaphon* and in his *Pierce Penniless*, in the latter of which he devotes a section entitled *An Invective against the Enemies of Poetry*, and one entitled *The Defense of Plays.* In the former he blames the Puritans for the prevailing low state of literature.

In the first scene of the last act of *The Mayor of Quinborough* (1596), Middleton has an amusing situation in which a Puritan is tormented by being compelled to witness a play:

> *Oliver.* . . . I understand there are players in thy house; despatch me, I charge thee, in the name of all the brethren.
> *Simon.* Nay, now, proud rebel, I will make thee stay:
> And, to thy greater torment, see a play.
> *Oliv.* O devil! I conjure thee by Amsterdam!
> *Sim.* Our word is past;
> Justice may wink a while, but see at last.
> The play begins. Hold, stop him, stop him!
> *Oliv.* O that profane trumpet! O, O!
> *Sim.* Set him down there, I charge you, officers.
> *Oliv.* I'll hide my ears and stop my eyes.
> *Sim.* Down with his golls. I charge you.
> *Oliv.* O tyranny, tyranny! revenge it, tribulation!
> For rebels there are many deaths; but sure the only way
> To execute a puritan, is seeing of a play.
> O, I shall swound!
> *Sim.* Which if thou dost, to spite thee,
> A player's boy shall bring thee aqua-vitae.

We have a moving defence of poetry (and, by implication, of the drama) from a source itself not friendly to the public theater. It appears in the last act of the university play, *The Pilgrimage to Parnassus* (1598):

> *Philomusus.* No sour reforming enemy of art
> Could do delightful poetry more wrong
> Than thy unwary slippery tongue hath done.
> Are these the thanks thou givest for her mirth
> Wherewith she did make short thy pilgrim's way,
> Made months seem minutes spent in her fair soil?
> O do not wrong this music of the soul,
> The fairest child that e'er the soul brought forth,
> Which none contemn but some rude foggy squires
> That know not to esteem of wit or art!
> No epitaph adorn his baser hearse
> That in his lifetime cares not for a verse!

Nor think Catullus, Ovid, Martiall,
Do teach a chaste mind lewder luxuries.
Indeed if lechers read a wanton clause,
It tickles up each lustful impure vein;
But who reads poets with a chaster mind
Shall ne'er infected be by poesy.
An honest man that ne'er did stand in sheet
May chastely dwell in unchaste Shoreditch street.

This argument is echoed in the closing lines of Beaumont and Fletcher's *Triumph of Honor*:

Emanuel.   Sweet poetry's
A flower, where men, like bees and spiders, may
Bear poison, or else sweets and wax, away.

I am afraid Philomusus' reasoning is hardly calculated to convince a Gosson; especially as he and his cousin Studioso have just come through an experience with Catullus, Ovid, and Martiall, which forces Studioso to declare:

Here had we nigh made shipwreck of our youth,
And nipt the blossoms of our budding spring—

an experience which they had embarked upon with misgiving, Studioso feeling sure that

Chaste thoughts can lodge no longer in that soul
That lends an ear to wanton poesy.

Of course we must avoid the notion that the right in this cause was all on one side. We do not know the plays that brought Gosson to his conviction at that early date——they are not extant. But would it have been surprising if he had been prompted to issue a fresh invective after hearing (or reading) a prologue like the following to Fletcher's *Rule a Wife and Have a Wife* (1624), interpreting it as an admission of pornography and an invitation to wantonness?

Pleasure attend ye! and about ye sit
The spring of mirth, fancy, delight, and wit
To stir you up! ...

Nor, ladies, be not angry if you see
A young fresh beauty, wanton, and too free,
Seek to abuse her husband; still 'tis Spain;
No such gross errors in your kingdom reign;
You're vestals all; . . .
Take no example neither to begin,
For some by precedent delight to sin.

Or the alluringly suggestive promise (really unkept) which Middleton makes his reader of *The Roaring Girl* (1611), heading the address, "To the Comic Play-readers, Venery and Laughter":

. . . for venery, you shall have enough for sixpence, but well couched and you mark it; for Venus, being a woman, passes through the play in doublet and breeches; a brave disguise and a safe one, if the statute untie not her codpiece point.

There is a virtual admission of guilt in *The Actor's Remonstrance* (1643):

For ribaldry or any such paltry stuff as may scandal the pious and provoke the wicked to looseness, we will utterly expel it, with the bawdy and ungracious poets, the authors, to the Antipodes.

An impassioned defence of the drama is offered by Chapman
in *The Revenge of Bussy d'Ambois* (1608) I i 322:

   Guise.   I would have these things
Brought upon stages, to let mighty misers
See all their grave and serious miseries play'd,
As once they were in Athens and old Rome.
   Clermont. Nay, we must now have nothing brought on stages
But puppetry, and pied ridiculous antics.
Men thither come to laugh, and feed fool-fat,
Check at all goodness there, as being profan'd:
When, wheresoever goodness comes, she makes
The place still sacred, though with other feet
Never so much 'tis scandal'd and polluted.
Let me learn anything that fits a man,
In any stables show, as well as stages.
   Baligny. Why, is not all the world esteem'd a stage?

Cler.   Yes, and right worthily; and stages too
Have a respect due them, if but only
For what the good Greek moralist says of them:
'Is a man proud of greatness, or of riches?
Give me an expert actor, I'll show all
That can within his greatest glory fall.
Is a man fray'd with poverty and lowness?
Give me an actor, I'll show every eye
What he laments so, and so much doth fly,
The best and worst of both.' If but for this then,
To make the proudest outside, that most swells
With things without him and above his worth,
See how small cause he has to be so blown up,
And the most poor man to be griev'd with poorness,
Both being so easily borne by expert actors,
The stage and actors are not so contemptful
As any innovating puritan,
And ignorant sweater-out of zealous envy,
Would have the world imagine.

Presently Chapman cannily pronounces this effusion a "virtuous digression."

The most eloquent and extensive defense of the theater, afte[r] Heywood's *Apology*, offered by a playwright, is put into the mout[h] of the actor Paris in Massinger's *Roman Actor* (1626). To includ[e] it here would mean to quote practically the whole of the thir[d] scene of the first act.

A formidable effort at a rejoinder was made by Thomas Ran[]dolph in 1634, when he wrote *The Muses' Looking Glass*. It is [a] piece of propaganda, hardly a play, as he himself admits throug[h] the person of Roscius, the chorus:

            . . . he brings you
No plot at all, but a mere ollo-podrida,
A medley of ill-plac'd and worse-penn'd humors.
His desire was in single scenes to show
How comedy presents each single vice
Ridiculous.

Two puritans are persuaded to witness the performance to lear[n] how mistaken they have been in their opinion of the theater[.]

Bird.   Are you a player?
Roscius.   I am, sir; what of that?
Bird.   And is it lawful?
Good sister, let's convert him. [Aside] Will you use
So fond a calling?
Mis. Flowerdew.   And so impious?
Bird.   So irreligious?
Mis. Flo.   So unwarrantable?
Bird.   Only to gain by vice?
Mis. F.   To live by sin?
Ros.   My spleen is up. . . . O dull ignorance!
How ill 'tis understood what we do mean
For good and honest! They abuse our scene,
And say we live by vice. Indeed, 'tis true,
As the physicians by diseases do,
Only to cure them. They do live, we see,
Like cooks, by pamp'ring prodigality,
Which are our fond accusers. On the stage
We set an usurer to tell this age
How ugly looks his soul: a prodigal
Is taught by us how far from liberal
His folly bears him. Boldly I dare say,
There has been more by us in some one play
Laugh'd into wit and virtue, than hath been
By twenty tedious lectures drawn from sin
And foppish humors; hence the cause doth rise:
Men are not won by th'ears so well as eyes.

A weaker claim for the dignity of plays, made by Chapman and
others, is that they have received recognition from important
personages.

Chapman. *Widow's Tears* (1612) Ded.:

Other countrymen have thought the like worthy of dukes' and
princes' acceptations. *Ingiusti Sdegni, Il Petamento Amoroso, Calisto, Pastor Fido,* etc. (all being but plays) were all dedicate to
princes of Italy.

There is a similar plea in the *Revenge of Bussy* dedication; and
dedications following the same pattern will be found in Webster's
Duchess of Malfi (1623), Davenant's *Cruel Brother* (1630),

Massinger's *New Way* (1633), Heywood's *English Traveller* (1633) and his *Love's Mistress* (1636), Rowley and Dekker's *Noble Soldier* (1634), Ford's *Fancies Chaste* (1638).

Two men present themselves as incredible snobs—and traitors, each expressing contempt for the art of the theater, and bragging that he doesn't need to practice it for a living. One is Jasper Mayne, author of *The City Match* (1639), the other, Thomas Rawlins, author of *The Rebellion* (1639). Mayne's words in the prologue are:

> Nor would he write still, were't to succeed i' the bays;
> For he is not o' the trade, nor would excel
> In this kind, where 'tis lightness to do well.

Rawlins' scornful words to the reader are:

> Take no notice of my name, for a second work of this nature shall hardly bear it. I have no desire to be known by a threadbare cloak, having a calling that will maintain it wooly.

A third renegade is Thomas Lodge, who had been the first to leap to the defense of stage plays against the onslaught of Gosson. His *Glaucus and Scylla* ends with these lines:

> At last he [Cupid] left me, where at first he found me,
> Willing me let the world and ladies know
> Of Scylla's pride, and then by oath he bound me
> To write no more of that whence shame doth grow,
> Or tie my pen to penny-knaves' delight,
> But live with fame and so for fame to write.

Perhaps I ought to add the name of Samuel Daniel. But his was a case of rue with a difference. As an academic classicist, he could not be expected to have respect for the public theater of his day. In the Apology appended to *Philotas*, one of his two admirable dramas composed according to the French Senecan ideal, he expresses regret that sheer necessity compelled him to plan a public production:

> . . . driven by necessity to make use of my pen, and the stage to be the mouth of my lines, which before were never heard to

speak but in silence, I thought the representing so true a history, in the ancient form of a tragedy, could not but have had an unreprovable passage with the time, and the better sort of men; seeing with what idle fictions, and gross follies, the stage at this day abused men's recreations.

One of the serious objections that the Puritans had to the theater was the practice of dressing boys as women—a direct violation of a Scriptural prohibition. Heywood's defense is that no deception is intended (*Apology*. Shak. Soc., p. 28):

. . . to see our youths attired in the habit of women, who knows not what their intents be? who cannot distinguish them by their names, assuredly knowing they are but to represent such a lady, at such a time appointed.

For support Heywood could have fallen back on the authority of Doctor Gager, in his letter to Doctor Rainolds.

Finally, we must recall that Heywood, in the passage quoted above from the Apology (p. 57), stresses the theater's contribution to the improvement of English speech.

The same claim is advanced in *The Actors' Remonstrance* (1643):

. . . plays, comedies and tragedies, being the lively representations of men's actions, in which vice is always sharply glanced at and punished, and virtue rewarded and encouraged, the most exact and natural eloquence of our English language expressed and daily amplified, and yet, for all this, we suffer.

In *The Stage-Players' Complaint* (1641) the actor Reed tells why he does not believe that the theaters will be shut down, and at the same time affords us information on the composition of a London audience:

. . . we are very necessary and commodious to all the people: first, for strangers, who can desire no better recreation than to come and see a play; then for citizens to feast their wits; then for gallants, who otherwise perhaps would spend their money in drunkenness and lasciviousness, do find a great delight and delectation to see

a play; then for the learned it doth increase and add wit construc-
tively to wit; then for gentlewomen, it teacheth them how to deceive idleness; then for the ignorant, it does augment their knowledge. Pish, a thousand more arguments I could add, but that I
should weary your patience too much. Well, in a word, we are so
needful for the common good, that in some respect it were almost
a sin to put us down.

FUNCTION OF THE DRAMA

What Schelling would call "the earliest regular English play," namely, *Calisto and Meliboea,* written between 1520 and 1530, is modelled on *Celestina,* the earliest modern Spanish drama. But the English version, as Schelling puts it, "transformed the tragedy of the original into a moral interlude and added an 'exhortacyon to vertew.' No other ending could have been possible in these early years of the sixteenth century." Traditionally the function of the English drama had been didactic. It was brought into being because it seemed an effective method of teaching the people. We know, however, how soon it brought down upon itself the hostility of the very agents that had given it existence, because forces beyond their control, yet innate in its creation, developed for it additional functions which they considered anything but desirable. Nevertheless the ostensible purpose of dramatic production remained didactic to the end of the medieval drama. Now the end of the medieval drama almost coincided with the culmination of the Elizabethan drama, and the distinction between the two forms was, popularly, not great enough to prevent the application of the same theories to both, no matter what the practice was; particularly since such application is made unconsciously. Furthermore, the conscious critical views of English critics had their source largely on the continent; chiefly in the writings of the elder Scaliger, whose *Poetics* (1561), like the other similar continental works, was little more than a monumental perversion of Aristotle. Scaliger's prestige in England was unlimited. Here is what this god of criticism had to say of the function of the drama as one of the divisions of poetry, albeit in his scheme it held only fourth place in order of excellence:

The end is the giving of instruction in pleasurable form; fo
poetry teaches, and does not simply amuse, as some used to think
. . . because primitive poetry was sung its design seemed merely t
please; yet underlying the music was that for the sake of whicl
music was provided only as a sauce. In time this rude and pristin
invention was enriched by philosophy, which made poetry th
medium of its teaching. Now is there not one end, and only one
in philosophical exposition, in oratory, and in the drama? Assuredl
such is the case. All have one and the same end—persuasion.

Presently, however, authors had the courage to admit th
additional motive of pleasure, and would speak of "profit and
delight;" and eventually they might even ignore the profit motiv
entirely in their declarations. The three groups will be illustrated
consecutively and in chronological order.

John Rastell. *Calisto and Malibœa* (c. 1530) Introduction:

A new comedy in English in manner if an interlude, right elegan
and full of craft of rhetoric, wherein is showed and described a
well the beauty and good properties of women, as their vices and
evil conditions; with a moral conclusion and an exhortation to
virtue.

The Prologue to *The Conflict of Conscience* (1560), by Na
thaniel Woodes, announces the presentation of

A strange example done of late, which might, as he suppose,
Stir up their minds to godliness, which should it see or hear,
And therefore humbly doth you pray to give attentive ear.

Edwards, Richard. *Damon and Pythias* (1564) (Dodsley IV
p. 99) :

Dionysius. O noble gentlemen, the immortal gods above
Hath made you play this tragedy for my behalf.

The Tragical Comedy of Appius and Virginia (1568) Epil.:

And by this poet's feigning example do you take
Of Virginia's life of chastity, of duty to thy make;
Of love to wife, of love to spouse, of love to husband dear,
Of bringing up of tender youth: all these are noted here.

Gascoigne. *Glass of Government* (1575) Title page:

A tragical comedy so entitled because therein are handled as well the rewards for virtues as also the punishment for vices.

Ibid. Argument:

. . . the whole comedy a figure of the rewards and punishments of virtues and vices.

Ibid. Epil.:

For every man that lists his faults to mend,
This was my mind, and thus I make an end.

The prologue warns those to leave who have come to laugh.

Whetstone. *Promos and Cassandra* (1578) Title page:

In the second part is discoursed the perfect management of a noble king in checking vice and favoring virtue, wherein is shown the ruin and overthrow of dishonest practices, with the advancement of upright dealing.

Ibid. Dedication:

The effects of both [the two parts of the play] are good and bad: virtue intermixed with vice; unlawful desires (if it were possible) quenched with chaste denials—all needful actions (I think) for public view. For by the reward of the good, the good are encouraged in well-doing; and with the scourge of the lewd, the lewd are feared from evil attempts; maintaining this my opinion with Plato's authority: 'Naughtiness comes of the corruption of nature, and not by hearing or reading the lives of the good or lewd (for such publication is necessary), but goodness (saith he) is beautiful by either action.' And to these ends Menander, Plautus, and Terence, themselves many years since entombed, by their comedies in honor live this day. The ancient Romans held their shows of such prize that they not only allowed the public exercise of them, but the grave senators themselves countenanced the actors with their presence, who from these trifles won morality, as the bee sucks honey from weeds. . . . But this I am assured: what actions soever passeth in this history, either merry or mournful, grave or lascivious, the conclusion shows the confusion of vice, and the cherishing of virtue.

The gist of Lodge's *Defence of Poetry, Music, and Stage Plays* (1579) is that they are morally beneficial; and the Introduction to *The Misfortunes of Arthur* (a work composed in 1588 by a number of Gentlemen of Gray's Inn, Bacon being one of the number) tells us:

The matter which we purpose to present
In tragic notes the plague of vice recounts.

Lodge's contention that the theater is morally beneficial is challenged by Gosson in his *Plays Confuted* (1582):

Sometime you shall see nothing but the adventures of an amorous knight, passing from country to country for the love of his lady, encountering many a terrible monster made of brown paper, and at his return is so wonderfully changed, that he can not be known but by some posy in his tablet, or by a broken ring, or by a handkercher, or a piece of cockle shell—what learn you by that? When the soul of your plays is either mere trifles, or Italian bawdry, or wooing of a gentlewoman, what are we taught?

And farther on:

How are they [the players] able to pull us up that gravel as flat in the dust as we? What credit hath any good counsel in players' lips, when it works no amendment in themselves?

A Looking Glass for London and England (1589), by Lodge and Greene, as the name implies, is avowedly a didactic work. After each episode the prophet Oseas explains "what lessons the events do here unfold;" and at the end Jonah addresses London:

Repent, O London! lest for thy offence
Thy shepherd fail, whom mighty God preserve,
That she may bide the pillar of His church
Against the storms of Romish Anti-Christ.

In 1591 Robert Wilmot, in his dedication of *Tancred and Gismunda* (a revised version of *Gismond of Salerne*), says of the authors:

. . . herein they all agree: commending virtue, detesting vice, and lively deciphering their overthrow that suppress not their unruly affections. . . . my purpose in this tragedy tendeth only to the exaltation of virtue, and the suppression of vice.

Nash. *Pierce Penniless* (1592) :

In plays, all cozenages, all cunning drifts overgilded with outward holiness, all stratagems of war, all the cankerworms that breed on the rust of peace, are most lively anatomiz'd. They show the ill success of treason, the fall of hasty climbers, the wretched end of usurpers, the misery of civil dissension, and how just God is evermore in punishing of murder . . . what should I say more? They are the sour pills of reprehension, wrapt up in sweet words.

He thus proceeds at some length.

Day. *Parliament of Bees*. End:

Art has banished ignorance,
And chased all flies of rape and stealth
From forth our winged commonwealth.

Webster. *Malcontent* (1604) Induction:

Burbage. Shall we protest to the ladies that their paintings make them angels? or to my young gallant that his expense in the brothel gain him reputation? No, sir; such vices as stand not accountable to law should be cured as men heal tetters,—by casting ink upon them.

Beaumont, Fletcher. *Triumph of Honor* (1608) End:

Eman. What hurts now in a play, 'gainst which some rail
So vehemently? Thou and I, my love,
Make excellent use, methinks: I learn to be
A lawful lover void of jealousy,
And thou a constant wife.

Ibid. *Philaster* (1609) End:

> *King.*   Let princes learn
> By this to rule the passions in their blood;
> For what Heaven wills can never be withstood.

Ibid. *Maid's Tragedy* (1610) End:

> *Lysippus.*   May this a fair example be to me,
> To rule with temper; for in lustful kings
> Unlook'd-for sudden deaths from Heaven are sent.

Nathaniel Field, commending *The Faithful Shepherdess* (1610), describes it as

> Clad in such elegant propriety
> Of words, including a morality
> So sweet and profitable.

Thomas Heywood, in his *Apology* (1612), dwells mainly on the efficaciousness of the theater as an educational force. He contends that the lesson

> can no way be so exquisitely demonstrated, nor so lively portrayed, as by action.

Which is good pedagogics.

All of John Taylor's thirty-six lines prefixed to Heywood's *Apology* are pertinent. The theme they develop is:

> A play's a brief epitome of time,
> Wherein man may see his virtue or his crime
> Lay'd open.

Chapman, in his dedication (1613) of *The Revenge of Bussy,* states the purpose of playing:

> . . . material instruction, elegant and sententious excitation to virtue, and deflection from her contrary, being the soul, limbs, and limits of an autentical tragedy.

This practically repeats what he had said in 1605 in his lines on Jonson's *Sejanus*:

> Besides, thy poem hath this due respect,
> That it lets nothing pass without observing
> Worthy instruction; or that might correct
> Rude manners, and renown the well-deserving.

In II i of Massinger's *Roman Actor,* Philargus is forced to see a play in order to be cured of avarice.

The following quotation is not confined to the drama, but affirms the value of all literature. I think I shall be pardoned for including it here. (Fletcher. *Elder Brother* I ii 60):

> *Charles.*   Give me leave
> To enjoy myself. That place that doth contain
> My books, the best companions, is to me
> A glorious court, where hourly I converse
> With the old sages, and philosophers;
> And sometimes, for variety, I confer
> With kings and emperors, and weigh their counsels;
> Calling their victories, if unjustly got,
> Unto a strict account, and, in my fancy,
> Deface their ill-placed statues. Can I then
> Part with such constant pleasures, to embrace
> Uncertain vanities?

In 1619 was printed *Two Wise Men and All the Rest Fools,* a dull piece of work, which Winstanley and Langbaine incomprehensibly attributed to Chapman. The title-page describes it as "a comical moral, censuring the follies of this age, as it hath been divers times acted." The Prologue addresses the audience thus:

> Right noble and worthy assembly: it hath been a very ancient and laudable custom in the best governed commonwealths to admit and favorably to allow interludes and discourses upon the stage for divers reasons; but especially two: the one, to entertain the well-conditioned people with some delightful and fruitful conceits, thereby as it were to deceive idleness of that time which it hath allotted for worse purposes; the other, for the just reprehension of such as with serious and more grave advisings cannot or will not be so freely

admonished and corrected. The latter of these two respects hath begotten this dialogue ready to be acted, principally and specially pointing to that imp, which is unfortunately fostered up to this day, to ruin itself with infamy. Only this comfort is afforded, that if he be presented and withal silent, he may suppose that of all others it concerns not him. If he be absent (as most likely he is) then every other that finds himself parcel-guilt may see the deformity and forebear the excess. Other touches and passages are which our author and we present, not with mind to offend any, but to please the well-disposed.

The echo of Quince with which he closes forms a fitting introduction to the play that follows.

Anon. *Noble Soldier* (1631) III:

> *Poet.*   A poet's ink can better cure some sores
> Than surgeon's balsam.

Randolph. *Muses' Looking Glass* (1634) I iii:

> *Roscius.*   So comedies, as poets do intend them,
> Serve first to show our faults, and then to mend them.

Wm. Habington. *On Master John Fletcher's Dramatic Poems* (1647):

> Instruct the envious with how chaste a flame
> Thou warm'st the lover; how severely just
> Thou wert to punish, if he burn'd to lust;
> How epidemic errors by thy play
> Were laugh'd out of esteem, so purg'd away;
> How to each sense thou so didst virtue fit
> That all grew virtuous to be thought t'have wit.
> But this was much too narrow for thy art:
> Thou didst frame governments, give kings their part,
> Teach them how near to God, while just, they be,
> But how dissolv'd, stretch'd forth to tyranny;
> How kingdoms in their channels safely run,
> But rudely overflowing, are undone.

Jasper Mayne. *On the Works of Beaumont and Fletcher* (1647):

              . . . vices, which were
Manners abroad, did grow corrected there;
They who possess'd a box, and half-crown spent
To learn obsceneness, return'd innocent,
And thank'd you for this cozenage.

Shirley. Preface to Beaumont and Fletcher Folio (1647):

> . . . the three hours' spectacle, while Beaumont and Fletcher were presented, was usually of more advantage to the hopeful young heir than a costly, dangerous foreign travel, with the assistance of a governing monsieur or signor to boot; and it cannot be denied but that the young spirits of the time, whose birth and quality made them impatient of the sourer ways of education, have, from the attentive hearing these pieces, got ground in point of wit and carriage of the most severely-employed students, while these recreations were digested into rules, and the very pleasure did edify.

According to Milton the function of literature was to be an attractive teacher, especially to those unable to face the naked truth. (*Reason of Church Government*, Bohn ed., p. 479) :

> . . . teaching over the whole book of sanctity and virtue through all the instances of example, with such delight to those especially of soft and delicious temper, who will not so much as look upon truth herself, unless they see her elegantly dressed, that whereas the paths of honesty and good life appear now rugged and difficult, though they be indeed easy and pleasant, they will then appear to all men both easy and pleasant, though they were rugged and difficult indeed. And what a benefit this would be to our youth and gentry may be soon guessed by what we know of the corruption and bane which they suck in daily from the writings and interludes of libidinous and ignorant poetasters, who having scarce ever heard of that which is the main consistence of a true poem, the choice of such persons as they ought to introduce, and what is moral and decent to each one, do for the most part lay up vicious principles in sweet pills to be swallowed down, and make the taste of virtuous documents harsh and sour.

That his view was not as narrow and puritanic as this statement might lead one to believe is proved by his appreciation of Shakespeare.

Richard Flecknoe. *Discourse of the English Stage* (1660):

The stage being a harmless and innocent recreation, where the mind is recreated and delighted, and that *Ludus Literarum,* or School of good Language and Behavior, that makes youth into man, and man soonest good and virtuous, by joining example to precept, and the pleasure of seeing to that of hearing. Its chiefest end is, to render folly ridiculous, vice odious, and virtue and nobleness so amiable and lovely, as every one shu'd be delighted and enamored with it; from which when it deflects as *corruptio optimi pessima,* of the best it becomes the worst of recreation.

Cicero's doctrine that the drama is *imitatio vitae, speculum consuetudinis,* made familiar to us by Shakespeare, came down to the Renaissance through Donatus, and was paraphrased by a number of playwrights in such association as to imply that it was tantamount to the assignment of a didactic function.

In Spenser's *Tears of the Muses* (1591), Thalia complains about the condition of the theater:

All places they with folly have possessed,
And with vain toys the vulgar entertain,

having banished

Fine counterfesance and unhurtful sport,
Delight and laughter deckt in seemly sort.
All these, and all that else the comic stage
With seasoned wit and goodly pleasance graced,
By which man's life in his likest image
Was limned forth, are wholly now defaced;
And those sweet wits which wont the like to frame,
Are now despised, and made a laughing game. . . .
Instead thereof, scoffing scurrility
And scornful folly with contempt is crept,
Rolling in rhymes of shameless ribaudry,
Without regard, or due decorum kept.
Each idle wit at will presumes to make,
And doth the learned's task upon him take.

Tomkis. *Lingua* (1603) IV ii:

Anamnestes.   Both [comedy and tragedy] vice detect and virtue
          beautify,
By being death's mirror, and life's looking glass.

Marston. *Fawn* (1604) Prol.:

But if the nimble form of comedy,
Mere spectacle of life and public manners,
May gratefully arrive at your pleased ears,
We boldly dare the utmost death of fears.

Field. *Woman is a Weathercock* (1612) To the Reader:

. . . nor slight my presentation because it is a play; for I tell thee,
reader, if thou be'st ignorant, a play is not so idle a thing as thou
art, but a mirror of men's lives and actions.

Randolph. *Muses' Looking Glass* (1634) I iii:

Roscius.   . . . the soul sees her face
In comedy, and has no other glass.

During the Middle Ages the reading of the pagan classics was
justified on the ground that poetry is allegorical, conveying a
hidden message beneath the surface—hidden so as to keep the
message from reaching the untutored, who were unworthy to
receive it, as Sidney explains. Dante admonishes us:

O voi che avete gl'intelletti sani,
Mirate la dottrina che s'asconde
Sotto il velame degli versi strani.

And Rabelais characteristically teases us, first telling us in the
address to the reader that he has no other *argument* than to produce laughter, and then stating in the prologue that we shall have
to use our wits to penetrate the significance of the Pythagorean
symbols. The principle prevailed through the Renaissance, and
was accepted by the English dramatists, if we take the following
citations as representative.

Udall. *Ralph Royster Doyster* (1553) Prol.:

The wise poets long time heretofore,
Under merry comedies secrets did declare,
Wherein was contained very virtuous lore,
With mysteries and forewarnings very rare.
Such to write neither Plautus nor Terence did spare,
Which among the learned at this day bears the bell.

Jack Juggler (c. 1553) Epil.:

This trifling interlude that before you hath been rehearsed,
May signify some further meaning if it be well searched.

Lodge. *Defence of Poetry* (1579):

. . . if, saith he [Lactantius], we examine the Scriptures literally, nothing will seem more false, and if we weigh poets' words and not their meaning, our learning in them will be very mean.

Nash, in *The Anatomy of Absurdity* (1589), describes poetry as

. . . a more hidden and divine kind of philosophy, enwrapped in blind fables and dark stories, wherein the principles of more excellent arts and moral precepts, . . . are contained. . . . But grant the matter to be fabulous, is it therefore frivolous? Is there not under fables, even as under the shadow of green and flourishing leaves, most pleasant fruit hidden in secret, and a further meaning closely comprised?

Heywood. *Love's Mistress* (1636) To the Reader:

. . . The argument is taken from Apuleius, an excellent moral, if truly understood, and may be called a golden truth contained in a leaden fable, which, though it be not altogether conspicuous to the vulgar, yet to those of learning and judgment no less apprehended in the paraphrase than approved in the original.

While the didactic function of the drama retained its recognition to the end of the period, it was early coupled with another; namely, entertainment. The union of the two, commonly worded "profit and delight," deriving its authority from Horace's *Aut prodesse solent, aut delectare,* probably represented the most popularly accepted principle, undoubtedly harbored, unexpressed, even by those who proclaimed a didactic motive only. The great number of commendatory verses prefixed to the Beaumont and Fletcher Folio harp on this theme, ascribing the greatness of the two authors to the fact that they successfully met this double aim.

The very expression, "profit and delight," became a catchphrase, as illustrated in Brome's *English Moor,* IV ii:

> *Vincent.*   We left him with his foster-father, Arnold,
> Busy at rehearsal, practicing their parts.
> *Edmond.*   They shall be perfect by tomorrow night.
> *Nathaniel.*   If not unto our profit, our delight.

The double function had the encouragement of the academic critics.

Sidney. *Apology* (c. 1582) :

> [Poets] imitate both to delight and teach: and delight to move men to take that goodness in hand, which without delight they would fly as from a stranger.

Webbe. *Discourse* (1586) :

> The perfect perfection of poetry is this: to mingle delight with profit in such wise that a reader might by his reading be a partaker of both.

The earliest extant modern English play, Medwell's *Fulgens and Lucrece,*[1] performed about 1497, announces the double purpose. Part II. 888:

> . . . all the substance of this play
> Was done specially therfor
> Not onely to make folke myrth and game,
> But that suche as be gentilmen of name
> May be somewhat mouyd

---

[1] Schelling attached this distinction to *Calisto and Meliboea* before this play was discovered.

By this example for to eschew
The way of vyce and fauour vertue. . . .
This was the cause principall,
And also for to do withall
This company some myrth.

Udall. *Ralph Royster Doyster* (1553) Prol.:

What creature is in health, either young or old,
But some mirth with modesty will be glad to use,
As we in this enterlude shall now unfold; . . .
For mirth prolongeth life, and causeth health. . . .
Mirth is to be used both of more and less,
Being mixed with virtue in decent comeliness.
Our comedy . . . against the vainglorious doth inveigh.

The prologue to *Jack Juggler* (1553), like that to *Royster Doyster*, dilates on the need for recreation, appealing to the authority of Cicero, who

. . . above all other things commendeth the old comedy,
The hearing of which may do the mind comfort,
For they be replenished with precepts of philosophy.
They contain much wisdom, and teach prudent policy.

Ulpian Fulwell. *Like Will to Like* (1561) Prol.:

Our author thought good such a one for to choose
As may show good example, and mirth may eke be found. . . .
Some do matters of mirth and pastime require;
Other some are delighted with matters of gravity;
To please all men is our author's chief desire,
Wherefore mirth in measure to sadness is annexed:
And sith mirth for sadness is a sauce most sweet,
Take mirth then with measure, that best sauceth it.

Lodge. *Defence* (1579):

You see then how comedians . . . are requisite both for their antiquity and for their commodity, for the dignity of the writers, and the pleasure of the hearers.

Lyly. *Alexander and Campaspe* (1580) Prol.:

We have mixed mirth with counsel, and discipline with delight.

Ibid. *Sappho and Phao* (1581) Prol.:

Our intent was at this time to move inward delight, not outward lightness, and to breed soft smiling, not loud laughing: knowing it to the wise to be as great pleasure to hear counsel mixed with wit, as to the foolish to have sport mingled with rudeness.

Sir Clyomon (1570-1584) Prol.:

Wherein, as well as famous facts, ignominies placed are,
Wherein the just reward of both is manifestly shown,
That virtue from the root of vice might openly be known. . . .
What he hath done for your delight, he gave not me in charge.

Greene. *Never Too Late* (1589) :

Thus did Menander win honor in Greece with his works, and reclaim both old and young from their vanities by the pleasant effect of his comedies. After him this faculty grew to be famous in Rome, practiced by Plautus, Terence, and others that excelled in this quality, all aiming, as Menander did, in all their works to suppress vice and advance virtue.

Nash. *Anatomy of Absurdity* (1589):

I am a professed peripatician, mixing profit with pleasure, and precepts of doctrine with delightful invention.

Locrine. Title page (1595):

No less pleasant than profitable.

Marston. *Sophonisba*. To the General Reader (1606) :

. . . if aught shall please thee thank not me, for I confess in this it was not my only end.

Massinger. *Roman Actor* (1626) . I. i:

> *Paris.*   ... grudge us,
> That with delight join profit, and endeavor
> To build their minds up fair, and on the stage
> Decipher to the life what honors wait
> On good and glorious actions, and the shame
> That treads upon the heels of vice, the salary
> Of six sestertii.

Heywood's motto, printed on the title-page of all the plays that he edited, was the dictum of Horace quoted above: *aut prodesse aut delectare*; and in the address to the reader of *The English Traveller* (1633) he signs his name after the leave-taking: "Studious of thy pleasure and profit."

Henry Shirley, in his address to the reader of *The Martyred Soldier* (1638), affirms:

> ... it hath drawn even the rigid stoics of the time; who, though not for pleasure yet for profit have gathered something.

The title-page of James Mabbe's *Spanish Bawd* (1631), a translation of Rojas's *Celestina*, reads:

> Wherein is contained, besides the pleasantness and sweetness of the style, many philosophical sentences, and profitable instructions necessary for the younger sort.

It is important to note that pursuing a didactic purpose was not looked upon as identical with sermonizing. This we learn from Whetstone's dedication of *Promos and Cassandra* (1578):

> For at this day the Italian is so lascivious in his comedies that honest hearers are grieved at his actions; the Frenchman and Spaniard follow the Italian's humor. The German is too holy, for he presents on every common stage what preachers should pronounce in pulpits.

A considerable number of plays lay claim to no other purpose than amusement; but it will be observed that nearly all such plays are comedies. The drama as a whole did not yet feel sufficiently emancipated from religion and morality to take up its dwelling frankly in the realm of art.

The interludes included in the old John Heywood canon, printed in the first third of the century, are advertised as "merry interludes."

William Stevenson's *Gammer Gurton's Needle*, performed in the winter of 1552-3, announces on the title-page: A Right Pithy, Pleasant, and Merry Comedy.

The prologue to Lyly's *Endymion* (1585) facetiously lets us know that the play is a product of pure imagination, therefore not subject to rational explanation:

> . . . we must tell you a tale of the Man in the Moon, which, if it seem ridiculous for the method, or superfluous for the matter, or for the means incredible, for three faults we can make but one excuse: it is a tale of the Man in the Moon . . . there liveth none under the sun that knows what to make of the Man in the Moon.

Mucedorus (c. 1588) Induction:

> *Comedy.*   Comedy is mild, gentle, willing to please,
> And seeks to gain the love of all estates;
> Delighting in mirth, mixt all with lovely tales,
> And bringeth things with treble joy to pass. . . .
> And mix not death amongst pleasing comedies,
> That treat nought else but pleasure and delight.

Nash. *Summer's Last Will* (1592) Prol.:

> *Placeat sibi quisque licebit.*
> What's a fool but his bauble? Deep-reaching wits, here is no stream for you to angle in. . . . As the Parthians fight flying away, so will we prate and talk, but stand to nothing that we say.

Ibid. (Dodsley, VIII. p. 30):

> *Will Sum.*   . . . we come hither to laugh and be merry, and we hear a filthy, beggarly oration in praise of beggary. It is a beggarly poet that writ it.

Marston. *Jack Drum's Entertainment* (1600) Intr.:

> He vows if he could draw the music from the spheres
> To entertain this presence with delight,

Or could distil the quintessence of heaven
In rare composed scenes, and sprinkle them
Among your ears, his industry should sweat
To sweeten your delights.

Contention between Liberality and Prodigality (1601) Prol.:

But this we bring is but to serve the time,
A poor device to pass the day withal.

Dekker and Webster. *Westward Ho* (1603) Last lines:

   Justiniano.   Gold that buys health can never be ill spent,
Nor hours laid out in harmless merriment.

Marston. *Dutch Courtizan* (1604) Prol.:

And if our pen in this seem over slight,
We strive not to instruct, but to delight.

Ibid. *Fawn* (1604) Prol.:

Your modest pleasure is our author's scope.

Dekker. *Shoemaker's Holiday* Dedication (1600) :

. . . nothing is purposed but mirth; mirth lengtheneth long life.

Fletcher. *Woman's Prize* (1606) Prol. (not by Fletcher):

The end we aim at is to make you sport;
Yet neither gall the city nor the court.
Hear, and observe his comic strain, and when
Ye are sick of melancholy, see't again.
'Tis no dear physic, since 'twill quit the cost,
Or his intentions, with our pains, are lost.

Ibid. *Woman Hater* (1607) Prol.:

I dare not call it comedy or tragedy; 'tis perfectly neither: a play it
is, which was meant to make you laugh.

Fletcher, Massinger. *Little French Lawyer* (1619) Prol.:

And such a play as shall (as should plays do)
Imp time's dull wings, and make you merry too.
'Twas to that purpose writ.

Fletcher. *Two Noble Kinsmen* (1612) Prol.:

     If this play do not keep
A little dull time from us, we perceive
Our losses fall so thick, we must needs leave.

Fletcher, Jonson, Middleton. *Widow* (c. 1620) Prol.:

A sport only for Christmas is the play
This hour presents to you. To make you gay
Is all th' ambition 't has, and fullest aim
Bent on your smiles, to win itself a name;
And if your edge be not quite taken off,
Wearied with sports, I hope 'twill make you laugh.

Fletcher. *Spanish Curate* (1622) Prol.:

     . . . to tell ye too 'tis merry,
And meant to make ye pleasant, and not weary.

Middleton. *Family of Love* (1607) Epil.:

Gentles, whose favors have o'erspread this place,
And shed the real influence of grace
On harmless mirth, we thank you.

Dekker. *The Devil Is in It* (1612) Epil.:

If for so many moons and midnights spent
To reap three hours' mirth. . . .

Thomas May. *The Heir* (1620) Prol.:

     . . . he does not mean
To rub your galls with a satiric scene;

Nor toil your brains to find the fustian sense
Of those poor lines that cannot recompense
The pains of study. Comedy's soft strain
Should not perplex, but recreate the brain.

Webster, Middleton. *Anything for a Quiet Life* (1612) Prol.:

> ... if to you
> It yield content, and usual delight,
> For our parts, we shall sleep secure tonight.

Brome. *Antipodes* (1638) I v:

> *Letoy.*　　　　　　Sir, I have
> For exercises, fencing, dancing, vaulting;
> And for delight, music of all kinds;
> Stage-plays and masques are nightly my pastimes.

Brome. *Jovial Crew* (1641) Epil.:

> ... the course we took today,
> Which was intended for your mirth, a play;
> Not without action, and a little wit.

SATIRE IN THE DRAMA

Lodge defended the drama against the attacks of Gosson on the ground that it was didactic; more specifically, that it was satirical, and stung hard the abuses of the time. Subsequently playwrights were more cautious about pushing the claims of satire as a legitimate function of the drama. The reason was that satire had largely degenerated into personal abuse. Most of the references to satire, therefore, took the form of a disclaimer of personal allusion. Important people were touchy on the subject, and probably saw allusions that did not exist. Nash complains of this in his letter to the printer of *Pierce Penniless* (1592):

> In one place of my book, Pierce Penniless saith but to the knight of the post, 'I pray you, how might I call you?' and they say I meant one Howe, a knave of the trade, that I never heard of before.

And Fulke Greville burned his play, *Antony and Cleopatra,* because it was "apt to be construed or strained to a personating of vices in the present governors, and government." Essex complained to the queen: "Shortly they will play me in what forms they list upon the stage." Lyly found it politic, in the prologue to *Endymion,* to express the hope that "none will apply pastimes, because they are fancies," even though his play was not a satire; for it *was* an allegory.

Daniel's *Philotas* was suspected of having a bearing on the Essex rebellion; hence a disclaimer was issued in an appended Apology:

> ... taking a subject that lay (as I thought) so far from the time, and so remote a stranger from the climate of our present courses, I could not imagine that envy or ignorance could possibly have made it to

take any particular acquaintance with us, but as it hath a general alliance to the frailty of greatness, and the usual workings of ambition, the perpetual subjects of books and tragedies.

A note in the Shakespeare Society edition of Heywood's *Apology* quotes a passage from the epistle before H. Parrot's *More the Merrier* (1608) :

As for satiric inveighing at any man's private person (a kind of writing which, of late, seems to have been very familiar among our poets and players, to their cost) my reader is to seek it elsewhere.

Undoubtedly, notwithstanding disclaimers, the abuse was a common one. We have Hamlet's word for it. It must have got started early, for Udall declares in the prologue to *Ralph Royster Doyster* (1553) that

... all scurrility we utterly refuse,
Avoiding such mirth wherein is abuse.

The pertinent passages need not all be included here. Only those that have a measure of individuality will be quoted.

Not many, outside of Jonson, had the courage to come out squarely with an affirmation of the legitimacy of satire. John Day was one.

Parliament of Bees V.:

   Stuprata. A scholar speak with me? Admit him; do it;
I have business for him.
   Servant.   Business? He's a poet,
A common beadle, one that lashes crimes,
Whips one abuse, and fetches blood o' the times. ...
   Iltriste.   Assume thy brightest flames
And dip thy pen in wormwood juice for me.
Canst write a satire? Tart authority
Do call 'em libels: canst write such a one?
   Poet. I can mix ink with copperas.
   Ilt. So; go on. ...
Thou hast the theory?
   Poet. Yes: each line must be
A cord to draw blood. ...

A lie to dare
The stab from him it touches. . . .
Such satires, as you call 'em, must lance wide
The wounds of men's corruptions; ope the side
Of vice; search deep flesh and rank cores.
A poet's ink can better cure some sores
Than surgeon's balsam.

Day even boasts of his skill in personal attack. This is the
"Author's Commission to His Bees:"

If then they mew, reply not you, but bring
Their names to me; I'll send out wasps shall sting
Their malice to the quick; if they cap words,
Tell 'em your master is atwisting cords
Shall make pride skip. If I must needs take pains,
'T shall be to draw blood from detraction's veins:
Though shriveled like parchment, Art can make 'em bleed;
And what I vow Apollo has decreed.
Your whole commission in one line's enrolled:
Be valiantly free, but not too bold.

Nash. *Summer's Last Will* (1592) Prol.:

Moralizers, you that wrest a never meant meaning out of everything, applying all things to the present time, keep your attention
for the common stage; for here are no quips in character for you to
read. Vain glosers, gather what you will; spite, spell backward what
thou canst.

Chapman. *All Fools* (1599) Prol.:

Who can show cause why th' ancient comic vein
Of Eupolis and Cratinus (now reviv'd
Subject to personal application)
Should be exploded by some bitter spleens,
Yet merely comical and harmless jests
(Though ne'er so witty) be esteem'd but toys,
If void of th' other satirism's sauce?

Ibid. II i 375:

113

Claudio.   Faith, that same vein of railing
Became now most applausive; your best poet is
He that rails grossest.

Marston. *Malcontent* (1600) Prol.:

To wrest each hurtless thought to private sense
Is the foul use of ill-bred impudence.

Ibid. *What You Will* (1601) II i 184:

What's out of railing's out of fashion.

Ibid. V i. Quadratus curses Pippo:

... Through every comic scene be drawn.

Ibid. *Fawn* (1603) Prol.:

Spectators, know you may with freest faces
Behold this scene; for here no rude disgraces
Shall taint a public or a private name.
This pen at viler rate doth value fame
Than at the price of others' infamy
To purchase it.

Tomkis. *Lingua* (1603) II iv:

Phantastes.   Meanwhile he's somewhat acquainted with you, for
he's bold to bring your person upon the stage.
Communis Sensus.   What, me? I can't remember that I was ever
brought upon the stage before.
Phan.   Yes, you and you, and myself with all my fantastical
tricks and humors. ...
Com. Sen.   O times! O manners! when boys dare to traduce men
in authority; was ever such an attempt heard?
Memory.   I remember there was; for, to say the truth, at my last
being at Athens, it is now, let me see, about one thousand eight
hundred years ago, I was at a comedy of Aristophanes' making. I
shall never forget it. The arch-governor of Athens took me by the
hand, and placed me; and there, I say, I saw Socrates abused most

grossly, himself being then a present spectator. I remember he sat full against me, and did not so much as show the least countenance of discontent.

    Com. Sen. In those days it was lawful, but now the abuse of such liberty is insufferable.

    Phan. Think what you will of it, I think 'tis done.

Ibid. IV ii:

    Phan. That fellow in the bays, methinks I should have known him; O, 'tis Comedus; 'tis so; but he is become nowadays something humorous, and too too satirical, up and down, like his great-grand-father Aristophanes.

Puritan Widow (1606) I iv 207:

    Pyeboard. . . . thou must be employed as an actor.

    Nicholas. An actor? O no, that's a player; and our parson rails against players mightily, I can tell you, because they brought him drunk upo' th' stage once,—as he will be horribly drunk.

Ibid. III iii 10:

    Ravenshaw. . . . why, sergeant, 'tis natural in us, you know, to hate scholars, natural; besides, they will publish our imperfections, knaveries and conveyances upon scaffolds and stages. . . .

    Puttock. They say you're a scholar: nay, sir, . . . you'll rail again sergeants, and stage 'em! you'll tickle their vices!

Beaumont. *Knight of the Burning Pestle* (1607) Ind.:

    Citizen. . . . you have no good meaning. These seven years there hath been plays at this house: I have observed it, you have still girds at citizens.

Beaumont. *Woman Hater* (1606) Prol.:

But you shall not find in it the ordinary and overworn trade of jesting at lords, and courtiers, and citizens, without taxation of any particular or new vice by them found out, but at the persons of them. Such, he that made this thinks vile.

Dekker, Webster. *Northward Ho* (1605) III i:

Philip. No, sir, I'll kill no poet, lest his ghost write satires against me.

Dekker. *Gull's Hornbook* (1609) :

. . . the stage, like time, will bring you to most perfect light, and lay you open.

Ibid.:

Now, sir, if the writer be a fellow that hath either epigrammed you, or hath had a flirt at your mistress, or hath either your feather, or your red beard, or your little legs, etc., on the stage, you shall disgrace him worse than by tossing him in a blanket, . . . if, in the middle of the play, you rise with a screwed, and discontented face from your stool to be gone.

Barry. *Ram-Alley* (1609) Prol.:

The satire's tooth, and waspish sting,
Which most do hurt when least suspected,
By this play are not affected. . . .
Free from the loathsome stage disease,
(So overworn, so tired, and stale,
Not satirising but to rail). . . .
He vows by paper, pen, and ink,
And by the learned Sisters' drink,
To spend his time, his lamps, his oil,
And never cease his brains to toil,
Till from the silent hours of night
He doth produce, for your delight,
Conceits so new, so harmless, free,
That Puritans themselves may see
A play, yet not in public preach
That players such lewd doctrine teach,
That their pure joint do quake and tremble
When they do see a man resemble
The picture of a villain.

In his address To the Comic Play-Readers (1611) in the *Roaring Girl*, Middleton adds an original touch to the conventional disclaimer:

. . . we rather wish in such discoveries, where reputation lies bleeding, a slackness of truth than fulness of slander.

In the revised epilogue to *Mucedorus* the author creates a graphic portrait of the satiric poet, who jeopardizes the very existence of the theater:

> *Comedy.*   Envy, spit thy gall,
> Plot, work, contrive; create new fallacies,
> Teem from thy womb each minute a black traitor,
> Whose blood and thoughts have twins' conception;
> Study to act deeds yet unchronicled,
> Cast native monsters in the molds of men,
> Case vicious divels under sancted rochets,
> Unhasp the wicket where all perjureds roost,
> And swarm this ball with treasons: do thy worst;
> Thou canst not cross my star tonight,
> Nor blind that glory where I wish delight.
> *Envy.*   I can, I will.
> *Comedy.*   Nefarious hag, begin,
> And let us tug, till one the mast'ry win.
> *Envy.*   Comedy, thou art a shallow goose;
> I'll overthrow thee in thine own intent,
> And make thy fall my comic merriment.
> *Com.*   Thy policy wants gravity; thou art
> Too weak. Speak, fiend, as how?
> *Envy.*   Why, thus:
> From my foul study will I hoist a wretch,
> A lean and hungry meager cannibal,
> Whose jaws swell to his eyes with chawing malice:
> And him I'll make a poet.
> *Com.*   What's that to the purpose?
> *Envy.*   This scrambling raven, with his needy beard,
> Will I whet on to write a comedy,
> Wherein shall be compos'd dark sentences,
> Pleasing to factious brains:
> And every otherwhere place me a jest,
> Whose high abuse shall more torment than blows;
> Then I myself (quicker than lightning)
> Will fly me to a puissant magistrate,
> And waiting with a trencher at his back,
> In midst of jollity, rehearse those galls
> (With some additions)

So lately vented in your theater.
He, upon this, cannot but make complaint,
To your great danger, or at least restraint.
   Com.   Ha, ha, ha! I laugh to hear thy folly;
This is a trap for boys, not men, nor such
Especially desertful in their doings,
Whose stay'd discretion rules their purposes.
I and my faction do eschew those vices.

The reference to the "boys" would indicate that the children's companies were the chief culprits in what was apparently a recent intensification of the practice of ragging prominent personalities. This surmise is confirmed by Heywood, in his *Apology*, published shortly after (1612):

Now, to speak of some abuse lately crept into the quality, as an inveighing against the state, the court, the law, the city, and their governments, with the particularizing of private men's humors (yet alive), noblemen, and other: I know it distastes many; neither do I any way approve it, nor dare I by any means excuse it. The liberty which some arrogate to themselves, committing their bitterness, and liberal invectives against all estates, to the mouths of children, supposing their juniority to be a privilege for any railing, be it never so violent, I could advise all such to curb and limit this presumed liberty within the bands of discretion and government.

Beaumont, in his sonnet on *The Silent Woman*, points out the difference between the good writer's and the bad writer's handling of satirical material:

Hear, you bad writers, and, though you not see,
I will inform you where you happy be:
Provide the most malicious thoughts you can,
And bend them all against some private man,
To bring him, not his vices, on the stage;
Your envy shall be clad in some poor rage,
And your expressing of him shall be such,
That he himself shall think he hath no touch.
Where he that strongly writes, although he mean
To scourge but vices in a labor'd scene,
Yet private faults shall be so well express'd
As men do act 'em, that each private breast

That finds these errors in itself, shall say,
"He meant me, not my vices, in the play."

Fletcher, Massinger. *Custom of the Country* (1619) Prol.:

> We dare look
> On any man that brings his table-book
> To write down what again he may repeat
> At some great table, to deserve his meat:
> Let such come swell'd with malice, to apply
> What is mirth here, there for an injury.
> Nor lord, nor lady, we have tax'd; nor state,
> Nor any private person; their poor hate
> Will be starv'd here; for Envy shall not find
> One touch that may be wrested to her mind.

Ibid. *Spanish Curate* (1622) Prol.:

> To tell ye 'tis familiar, void of glory,
> Of state of bitterness,—of *wit*, you'll say,
> For that is now held wit that tends that way
> Which we avoid.

Randolph. *Aristippus* (1629) Praeludium:

> But first with tears wash off thy guilty sin;
> Purge out those ill-digested dregs of wit,
> That use their ink to blot a spotless fame.
> Let's have no one particular man traduc'd;
> But, like a noble eagle, seize on vice,
> As she flies, bold and open—spare the persons.

Heywood. *Iron Age*, Part Two. To the Reader (1632):

> I know not how they may be received in this age, where nothing but *satirica dictaeria*, and *comica scommata* are now in request. For mine own part, I never affected either, when they stretched to the abuse of any person, public or private.

Marmion treats the subject with pleasant sarcasm in the prologue to *A Fine Companion* (1633), imitating a passage in onson's *Poetaster* (cf. p. 343a):

Critic.   'Tis this licentious generation
Of poets trouble the peace of the whole town.
A constable can't get his maid with child,
A baker nor a scrivener lose his ears,
Nor a justice of peace share with his clerk;
A gallant can't be suffer'd to pawn's breeches,
Or leave his cloak behind him at a tavern,
But you must jerk him for it.
   Author.   In all ages
It hath been ever free for comic writers,
If there were any that were infamous,
For lust, ambition, or avarice,
To brand them with great liberty.

Cartwright. *The Ordinary* (1638) Prol.:

No guilty line traduceth any; all
We now present is but conjectural.

Brome. *Antipodes* (1638) II v:

   Quailpipe.   For nothing can
Almost be spoke, but some or other man
Takes it unto himself; and says the stuff,
If it be vicious or absurd enough,
Was woven upon his back. Far, far be all
That bring such prejudice mixed with their gall.
This play shall no satiric timist be
To tax or touch at either him or thee,
That art notorious. 'Tis so far below
Things in our orb, that do among us flow,
That no degree, from keyser to the clown,
Shall say this vice or folly was mine own.

The list of quotations will close with two from Shirley, in which
he stands up for the business of the dramatist to expose prevailing
vices. The first is from the opening scene of *The Lady of Pleasure*
(1635). The allusion is to Middleton's play, *The Family of Love*.
The speaker is discussing an immoral ball:

   Bornwell.   'Tis but the *Family of Love* translated
Into more costly sin'. There was a play on 't,

And had the poet not been bribed to a modest
Expression of your antic gambols in't,
Some darks had been discovered, and the deeds too:
In time he may repent, and make some blush,
To see the second part danced on the stage.

Shirley. *Duke's Mistress* (1636) Prol.:

For satire, they do know best what it means
That dare apply; and if a poet's pen,
Aiming at general errors, note the men,
'Tis not his fault. The safest cure is, they
That purge their bosoms may see any play.

DRAMA AS LITERATURE

Only Marston came out against the notion insisted on by Jonson that a play should appeal equally well to the reader as to the spectator.

Marston. *Malcontent*. To the Reader (1604):

... one thing afflicts me, to think that scenes invented merely to be spoken should be inforcively published to be read.

But even he confined the strict application of his theory to comedy: a tragedy could conceivably be effective reading.

Ibid. *The Fawn*. To my equal Reader (1606):

If any wonder why I print a comedy, whose life rests much in the actor's voice, let such know that it cannot avoid publishing. . . . Comedies are writ to be spoken, not read. Remember the life of these things consists in action; and for your such courteous survey of my pen, I shall present a tragedy to you which shall boldly abide to most curious perusal.

The tragedy which he here promises to publish is *Sophonisba*. The way he puts it, it would seem that the radical difference he sees between comedy and tragedy was a generally recognized one. If so, the attitude ought to be a key to Elizabethan technique. However, the opinions implied by the remaining quotations do not coincide with Marston's.

Webster. *Devil's Law Case*. To the Judicious Reader (1623):

A great part of the grace of this, I confess, lay in action; yet can no action ever be gracious where the decency of the language and the ingenious structure of the scene arrive not to make a perfect harmony.

Davenant. *The Wits*. Dedication (1636) merely concedes that stage presentation is an advantage.

Shirley. *The Brothers*. Dedication (1652):

. . . though it appear not in that natural dress of the scene, nor so powerful, as when it had the soul of action.

Dekker, on the other hand, tries to persuade the reader of *The Whore of Babylon* (printed 1607) that the author can be judged fairly only in the reading, since most actors spoil the lines. He argues that the relation between author and actor is analogous to that between musical composer and player. One must suspect, however, that he spoke thus to improve the sale of the book.

The remaining citations support the claim of both eye and ear. *Common Conditions* (1570) Prol.:

You skillful heads that sit in place to see, likewise to hear.

Heywood. *Brazen Age* (1596) Epil.:

        . . . for more than sight
We seek to please.

Chapman (of course) on Jonson's *Sejanus* (1605):

Performing such a lively evidence
In thy narrations, that thy hearers still
Thou turn'st to thy spectators; and the sense
That thy spectators have of good and ill,
Thou subject'st jointly to thy readers' souls.

Henry Shirley (who must not be confused with his more famous namesake). *Martyred Soldier* (1627) Epil.:

Two senses must be pleased; . . .
And he that only seeks to please but either,
While both he doth not please, he pleaseth neither.

PLAYMAKING

The Elizabethan drama early revealed the presence of an advanced critical consciousness. For example, the prologue to *Common Conditions*, written shortly after the middle of the century, tries to impress upon the audience the fact that a play is a unit, and cannot be judged properly except as a whole:

> ... we pray you bide
> The last as well as first to see, then uprightly judge and weigh
> Our author's mind and doing his, in that which we display.
> Let judgment then from you proceed discreetly to be shown,
> And let not rashness oversoon too much abroad be blown.

And Whetstone tells us that he had to divide his *Promos and Cassandra* (1578)

> ... into two comical discourses, for that, decorum used, it would not be carried into one.

which anticipated by nearly half a century what Fletcher says in the prologue to *Lovers' Progress*:

> ... his powers
> Could not, as he desired, in three short hours
> Contract the subject, and much less express
> The changes and the various passages
> That will be look'd for.

By the end of the century the theater could look upon itself as an old established institution, with traditions, and a long history of evolution, as charmingly illustrated by Chapman in the second scene of *A Humorous Day's Mirth* (1597):

Lemot. . . . I will sit like an old king in an old-fashioned play, having his wife, his council, his children, and his fool about him, to whom he will sit and point very learnedly, as followeth:

'My council grave, and you, my noble peers,
My tender wife, and you, my children dear,
And thou, my fool—'

By this time the dramatists knew what they wanted, and how to go about getting it. What they wanted was expressed by Dekker in his portrait of the ideal playwright in the prologue to *If It Be Not Good* (1610):

Give me that man
Who, when the plague of an imposthumed brains,
Breaking out, infects a theater and hotly reigns,
Killing the hearers' hearts, that the vast rooms
Stand empty, like so many dead men's tombs,
Can call the banish'd auditor home, and tie
His ear with golden chains to his melody:
Can draw with adamantine pen even creatures
Forg'd out of th' hammer on tiptoe to reach up,
And, from rare silence, clap their hands,
T' applaud what their charm'd soul scarce understands.
That man give me, whose breast, fill'd by the Muses
With raptures, into a second them infuses:
Can give an actor sorrow, rage, joy, passion,
Whilst he again, by self-same agitation,
Commands the hearers; sometimes drawing out tears,
Then smiles, and fills them both with hopes and fears.
That man give me. And to be such a one
Our poet this day strives, or to be none.

The following quotations illustrate awareness of dramatic development. The first is particularly significant, because of its date, 1589, pointing as it does to a past which was evidently crowded with dramatic activity, but which to us is sunk in oblivion, very little having survived.

Lyly. *Midas* Prol.:

Gentlemen, so nice is the world that for apparel there is no fashion, for music no instrument, for diet no delicate, for plays no invention, but breedeth satiety before noon, and contempt before night.

Middleton. *Roaring Girl.* To the Comic Play-Readers (1611):

The fashion of play-making I can properly compare to nothing so naturally as the alteration in apparel; for in the time of the great crop-doublet, your huge bombastic plays, quilted with mighty words to lean purpose, was only then in fashion: and as the doublet fell, neater inventions began to set up. Now, in the time of spruceness, our plays follow the niceness of our garments, single plots, quaint conceits, lecherous jests, dressed up in hanging sleeves: and those are fit for the times and termers.

In the prologue he informs us that "tragic passion, and such grave stuff, is this day out of fashion;" which is historically correct. Shakespeare had done his *Coriolanus* three years back, and he had for some time been struggling against the tide.

Heywood. *Four Prentices of London.* Dedication (1615):

... knowing withal that it comes short of that accurateness both in plot and style, that these more censorious days with greater curiosity acquire, I must excuse: that as plays were then—some fifteeen years ago—it was in the fashion.

Ibid. *Royal King.* To the Reader (1637):

That this play's old, 'tis true; but now if any
Should for that cause despise it, we have many
Reasons, both just and pregnant, to maintain
Antiquity, and those, too, not all vain.
We know (and not long since) there was a time
Strong lines were not looked after, but if rhyme,
O then 'twas excellent. Who but believes
That doublets with stuffed bellies and big sleeves
And those trunk-hose which now our life doth scorn,
Were all in fashion, and with custom worn? ...
With rigor therefore judge not, but with reason,
Since what you read was fitted to that season.

Shirley. *Imposture* (1640) Prol.:

126

He has been stranger long to the English scene,
Knows not the mode.

Shirley had been some years in Ireland, writing plays there in the meantime, yet he feared that the fashion might have already changed at home.

The practical playwright must take into consideration all the conditions involved.

Chapman. Preface to *Masque of the Middle Temple* (1613):

... all the courtly and honoring inventions (having poesy and oration in them, and a fountain to be expressed from whence their rivers flow) should expressively arise out of the places and persons for and by whom they are presented, without which limits they are luxurious and vain.

Tailor. *The Hog Hath Lost His Pearl* I i (1613):

Player. I hope you have made no dark sentence in't; for, I assure you, our audience commonly are very simple idle-headed people; and if they should hear what they understand not, they would quite forsake our house.
Haddit. O, ne'er fear it; for what I have writ is both witty to the wise, and pleasing to the ignorant: for you shall have those laugh at it far more heartily that understand it not, than those that do.

Heywood frankly acknowledges the necessity of making concessions. In *Love's Mistress* (1634), Apuleius has to admit that "art sometimes must give way to ignorance." Throughout the play dances are introduced as concessions to Midas with the long ears.

The following citations give evidence of the concern of the dramatist with the innumerable details that demand the attention of those occupied with the writing and producing of plays.

In the prologue to *Endymion,* already quoted, Lyly lists three elements that enter into the making of a play: matter, which should be worthwhile, means, which should be credible, method which should be rational.

127

Cartwright in his lines, *In the memory of the most worthy Benjamin Jonson*, indicates that the drama must be objective:

Nor dost thou pour out, but dispense thy vein,
Skill'd when to spare, and when to entertain.
Not like our wits, who into one piece do
Throw all that they can say, and their friends too;
Pumping themselves for one term's noise so dry,
As if they made their wills in poetry.
And such spruce compositions press the stage
When men transcribe themselves, and not the age.
Both sorts of plays are thus like pictures shown:
Thine of the common life, theirs of their own.

In the following tribute to Fletcher, contributed to the Beaumont and Fletcher Folio, Cartwright seems to try to think of all the items which, taken together, would constitute the perfect play.

No vast uncivil bulk swells any scene,
The strength's ingenious, and the vigor clean;
None can prevent the fancy, and see through
At the first opening; all stand wondering how
The thing will be, until it is; which thence
With fresh delight still cheats, still takes the sense;
The whole design, the shadows, the lights, such
That none can say he shows or hides too much;
Business grows up, ripen'd by just increase,
And by as just degrees again doth cease;
The heats and minutes of affairs are watch'd,
And the nice points of time are met, and snatch'd;
Nought later than it should, nought comes before,—
Chemists and calculators do err more;
Sex, age, degree, affections, country, place,
The inward substance, and the outward face,
All kept precisely, all exactly fit.

He wrote another poem on the same theme, portions of which are quoted in other connections.

Claptrap disdained in the prologue to Heywood's *English Traveler* (1632):

A strange play you are like to have, for know,
We use no drum, nor trumpet, nor dumb show;
No combat, marriage, not so much today
As song, dance, masque, to bombast out a play;
Yet these all good, and still in frequent use
With our best poets.

Fletcher. *The Captain* (1613). V. v.:

> *Angelo.* I thought you, Julio, would not thus have stolen a
> marriage
> Without acquainting your friends.
> *Julio.* Why, I did give you inklings.
> *Angelo.* If a marriage should be thus stubber'd up in a play,
> ere almost
> Anybody had taken notice you were in love, the spectators
> Would take it to be but ridiculous.

This trick to disarm the audience Fletcher borrowed from
Shakespeare, who employed it more than a dozen years earlier in
Twelfth Night.

Fletcher, Massinger. *Lover's Progress* (1623). V. i.:

> *Lisander.* I will not, like a careless poet, spoil
> The last act of my play, till now applauded.

In the same scene, near the end, there is a hint of the desirability of adequate motivation:

> *Alcidon.*   ... it may
> Find passage to the mercy of the king,
> The motives urg'd in his defence, that forc'd him
> To act that bloody scene.

A play must not be too long.

Kyd. *Spanish Tragedy* (1583). IV. i. 184:

> *Hieronimo.* And all shall be concluded in one scene,
> For there's no pleasure ta'en in tediousness.

Webster. *Devil's Law Case* (1619). III. iii.:

> *Romelio.* Is not the shortest fever the best? and are not bad plays
> The worse for their length?

The well known importance of a substantial and responsive audience to the success of a performance is stressed by Webster in his address to the reader of *The White Devil* (1612):

> . . . it was acted in so dull a time of winter, presented in so open and black a theater, that it wanted (that which is the only grace and setting-out of a tragedy) a full and understanding auditory; and since that time I have noted most of the people that come to that playhouse resemble those ignorant asses who, visiting stationers' shops, their use is not to inquire for good books, but new books.

Even the wide practice of making additions to plays had to bear its comment. Middleton. *Mayor of Quinborough* (1596) V i:

> *Simon.* A pox on your new additions! they spoil all the plays that ever they come in: the old way had no such roguery in it.

Simon is a fool, and the speech is probably intended as a sly reflection on this very play.

Villiers' dramatic satire on Dryden, *The Rehearsal,* belongs to the Restoration. However, I quote one passage, because of its direct allusion to a favorite practice of the Elizabethans. Shakespeare gave it a name: "the swelling act." V i:

> *Bayes.* Now, gentlemen, I will be bold to say, I'll show you the greatest scene that England ever saw: I mean not for words, for those I do not value; but for state, show, and magnificence. In fine, I'll justify it to be as grand to the eye every whit, egad, as that great scene in *Harry the Eight,* and grander too, egad; for, instead of two bishops, I have brought in two other cardinals.

Shirley. *The Imposture* (1640). Prol.:

> In all his poems you [the ladies] have been his care,
> Nor shall you need to wrinkle now that fair

Smooth alabaster of your brow; no fright
Shall strike chaste ears, or dye the harmless white
Of any cheek with blushes: by this pen
No innocence shall bleed in any scene.

This passage illustrates what an anemic product the decadent Elizabethan drama found it necessary to boast of as an ideal.

In *An Apology for Actors* Heywood states the proper composition of a comedy as determined by the sixteenth century critics and commentators on Terence:

> . . . the *Prologue*, that is, the preface; the *Protasis*, that is, the proposition, which includes the first act, and presents the actors; the *Epitasis*, which is the business and body of the comedy; the last, the *Catastrophe*, and conclusion.[1]

---

[1] For a full treatment of the subject, including the connotation and history of these terms, the reader is referred to T. W. Baldwin's comprehensive *Shakespeare's Five-Act Structure*.

MATERIAL

With the passing of the Middle Ages sacred history ceased to be a noteworthy source of drama material. Indeed, resorting to it was not looked upon with favor. In *Wit's Misery* IV. (1596) Lodge declares:

> ... in stage plays to make use of historical Scripture I hold with the Legists odious, and, as the Council of Trent did, I condemn it.

The drama became, in the words of Ascham, "a fair, lively, painted picture of the life of every degree of man." This virtually removed all restrictions on the material that the dramatist might use. The great variety of themes employed even during the early stages of the modern drama, of whose evidently extensive products so little is extant, is indicated in the prologue, composed in a typical jigging vein, to Robert Wilson's *Three Ladies of London* (1583):

> We list not ride the rolling racks that dim the crystal skies,
> We mean to set no glimmering glance before your courteous eyes;
> We search not Pluto's pensive pit, nor taste of Limbo's lake;
> We do not show of warlike fight, as sword and shield to shake;
> We speak not of the powers divine, ne yet of furious sprites;
> We do not seek high hills to climb, nor talk of love's delights;
> We do not here present to you the thresher with his flail;
> We do not here present to you the milkmaid with her pail;
> We show not you of country toil, as hedger with his bill;
> We do not bring the husbandman to lop and top with skill;
> We play not here the gardener's part to plant and set and sow;
> You marvel then what stuff we have to furnish out our show.

More than three decades later, after the zenith has been passed, Heywood supplies a similar enumeration, impressing on us the fact that no possible source has been left untapped.

Royal King (1618) . Prol.:

To give content to this most curious age,
The gods themselves we've brought down to the stage,
And figured them in planets; made even hell
Deliver up the furies, by no spell
  (Saving the Muses' rapture). Further, we
Have traffickt by their help: no history
We have left unrifled; our pens have been dipt
As well in opening each hid manuscript
As tracts more vulgar, whether read or sung,
In our domestic, or more foreign, tongue,
Of fairy elves, nymphs of the sea and land,
The lawns and groves. No number can be scann'd
Which we have not given feet to. Nay, 'tis known
That when our chronicles have barren grown
Of story, we have all invention stretcht,
Div'd low as the center, and then reacht
Unto the *primum mobile* above,
  (Nor 'scapt things intermediate) for your love.
These have been acted often; all have past
Censure, of which some live, and some are cast.

Two conventional themes are listed in the prologue to *2 Return from Parnassus* (1603), one modern, one ancient:

Frame as well we might with easy strain,
With far more praise, and with as little pain,
Stories of love, where 'fore the wondering bench
The lisping gallant might injoy his wench;
Or make some sire acknowledge his lost son,
Found when the weary act is almost done.
Nor unto this nor unto that our scene is bent:
We only show a scholar's discontent.

For a time Seneca was a fruitful source. In his preface to Greene's *Menaphon* Nash derides its exploitation to the point of exhaustion:

English Seneca read by candle light yields many good sentences, as *Blood is a beggar,* and so forth; and if you intreat him fair in a frosty morning, will afford you whole *Hamlets*—I should say, handfuls of tragical speeches. But O grief! *tempus edax rerum*; what's that will last always? The sea exhaled by drops will in continuance be dry, and Seneca let blood line by line and page by page, at length must needs die to our stage.

By admitting what he did *not* do, Massinger, in the prologue to *Believe as You List*, informs us what others did do:

> He dares not boast
> His pains and care, or what books he hath tost
> And turned to make it up.

As Ascham pointed out, man was now the material out of which plays were to be fashioned. The challenging complexity of this material was vividly comprehended by Chapman, who adopted the principle later enunciated by Browning (with whom he possessed an artistic kinship) that dramatic writing was concerned with incidents in the development of a soul. *Byron's Tragedy* (1608) V. iii:

> *Epernon.* Oh of what contraries consists a man!
> Of what impossible mixtures! Vice and virtue,
> Corruption, and eternness, at one time,
> And in one subject, let together loose!
> We have not any strength but weakens us,
> No greatness but doth crush us into air.
> Our knowledges do but light us but to err,
> Our ornaments are burthens, our delights
> Are our tormenters, fiends that, rais'd in fears,
> At parting shake our roofs about our ears.

The young Cartwright realized that sufficient understanding of the complexity of life to qualify a playwright, must come with years and experience. *The Ordinary* (1634). Prol.:

> His conversation will not yet supply
> Follies enough to make a comedy . . .
> That web of manners which the stage requires,
> That mass of humors which poetic fires
> Take in, and boil, and purge, and try, and then,
> With sublimated follies cheat those men

That first did vent them, are not yet his art . . .
He hath not yet seen vice enough to write.[1]

Shirley puts the idea succinctly in his commendatory verses on
Brome's *Jovial Crew*:

Learning, the file of poesie, may be
Fetch'd from the Arts and University;
But he that writes, and good, must know,
Beyond his books, men, and their actions too.

Richard Flecknoe expatiates along the same line on the prov-
ince and qualifications of the playwright in his *Discourse of the
English Stage*:

Of all arts that of the dramatic poet is the most difficult and most
subject to censure; for in all others, they write only of some particular subject, as the mathematician of mathematics, or philosopher
of philosophy; but in that, the poet must write of every thing, and
every one undertakes to judge of it.
   A dramatic poet is to the stage as a pilot to the ship; and to the
actors, as an architect to the builders, or master to his scholars: he
is to be a good moral philosopher, but yet more learned in men
then books. He is to be a wise, as well as a witty man, and a good
man, as well as a good poet; and I'd allow him to be so far a good
fellow too, to take a cheerful cup to whet his wits, so he take not so
much as to dull 'um, and whet 'um quite away.

When Ascham said that tragedy and comedy treated of the life
of every degree of man, he did not mean to imply that every
degree was treated in both tragedy and comedy. Tragedy was
reserved for the higher degrees, in accordance with the dictum of
Aristotle that "the nobility of the agents is what distinguishes
tragedy from comedy." Richard Puttenham (*Art of English Poesy*,
ed. Arber, p. 41) expressed the principle thus:

There were also poets that wrote only for the stage, I mean plays
and interludes, to recreate the people with matters of disport, and to

---

[1] Cartwright, one of the "sons of Ben," must have learned from his
master that what was required of the playwright was "the exact knowledge of all virtues and their contraries," as expressed in the *Discoveries*.

that intent did set forth in shows and pageants, accompanied with speech, the common behaviors and manner of life of private persons, and such as were the meaner sort of men, and they were called comical poets . . . Besides these poets comic there were other who served also the stage, but meddled not with so base matters, for they set forth the doleful falls of unfortunate and afflicted princes, but were called poets tragical.

The requirement that the serious drama be maintained on a lofty plane found ready recognition from the public, not because of Aristotle's authority, of which it was innocent, but because of inherited tradition; as the themes of the medieval drama had been the loftiest imaginable. Those who ventured to depart from this principle felt apologetic as indicated by the epilogue to *A Warning for Fair Women* (1598):

> Bear with this true and home-born tragedy,
> Yielding so slender argument and scope
> To build a matter of importance.

This plea follows an explanation why the author had not followed the expected conventional lines in the development of his plot:

> Perhaps it may seem strange unto you all
> That one hath not revenged another's death,
> After the observation of such course:
> The reason is that now of truth I sing;
> And should I add, or else diminish aught,
> Many of these spectators then could say
> I have committed error in my play.

This epilogue draws our attention to two points: that material gathered from local and contemporary life could not possess the quality of loftiness, and that the use of such material restricted the author's artistic freedom. The play deals with a recent murder, of which the audience knew the details, so the author felt that in such a case he was denied the liberty of the imaginative artist. (Think of *The Ring and the Book!*)

We find at the end of the period that the attitude has not changed. The prologue to *The Late Lancashire Witches* (1633), likewise a play based on a recent local occurrence, advances the same kind of apologetic explanation:

> No accidents abroad worthy relation
> Arriving here, we are forced from our own nation
> To ground the scene that's now in agitation.
> The project unto many here well-known:
> Those witches the fat jailer brought to town.
> An argument so thin, persons so low
> Can neither yield much matter, nor great show.
> Expect no more than can from such be raised,
> So may the scene pass pardoned though not praised.

The apprehensiveness expressed in these passages concerning the reaction of the audience is justified by a statement in Brome's *Jovial Crew* (1641), V. i.:

> *Oldrents.* True stories and true jests do seldom thrive on stages.

Even the themes of comedy were expected to possess a certain degree of importance.

Marston. *What You Will* (1601). Prol.:

> A silly subject too, too simply clad,
> Is all his present.

Dekker and Middleton. *Roaring Girl* (1611). Epil.:

> Some perhaps do flout
> The plot, saying, 'tis too thin, too weak, too mean;
> Some for the person will revile the scene,
> And wonder that a creature of her being
> Should be the subject of a poet, seeing
> In the world's eye none weighs so light.

Heywood, indeed, in the prologue to *A Challenge for Beauty* (1635), asserts the superiority of the English drama over the foreign partly on the ground that its themes are more dignified:

> They do not build their projects on that ground,
> Nor have their phrases half the weight and sound
> Our labored scenes have had.

The apprehensiveness expressed in the prologue to *The Late Lancashire Witches* is supported by Richard Brome in the prologue to *The Antipodes* (1638). With characteristic candor he concedes the superior claims of the lofty theme, but, at the same time, maintains that plays dealing with homely local material might achieve merit entitling them to go down to posterity; that, indeed, such plays *have* been written, referring, of course to the works of his master Ben Jonson:

Opinion, which our author cannot court,
(For the dear daintiness of it) has, of late,
From the old way of plays, possest a sort
Only to run to those that carry state
In scene magnificent and language high,
And clothes worth all the rest, except the action.
And such only are good, those leaders cry;
And into that belief draw on a faction
That must despise all sportive, merry wit,
Because some such great play had none of it.

But it is known (peace to their memories)
The poets late sublimed from our age,
Who best could understand, and best devise
Works that must ever live upon the stage,
Did well approve, and lead this humble way,
Which we are bound to travel in tonight.
And though it be not trac'd so well as they
Discover'd it by true Phoebean light,
Pardon our just ambition, yet, that strive
To keep the weakest branch o' th' stage alive.

I mean the weakest in their great esteem
That count all slight that's under us, or nigh;
And only those for worthy subjects deem,
Fetch'd or reach'd at (at least) from far, or high;
When low and home-bred subjects have their use,
As well as those fetch'd from on high, or far;
And 'tis as hard a labour for the Muse
To move the earth, as to dislodge a star.
    See, yet, those glorious plays; and let their sight
Your admiration move; these your delight.

His appeal was apparently without effect; for three years later, in the last act of *The Jovial Crew*, Oldrents remarks:

"True stories and true jests do seldom thrive on stages."

Miscellaneous comments on the availability of material follow. In *Gammer Gurton's Needle* (1552-3), a play written in academic circles, the possibility of a play being based on simple actuality is affirmed. In II. i., Diccon, commenting on the situation that has developed, remarks:

A man, I think, might make a play,
And need no words to this they say,
Being but half a clark.

Dekker, Webster. *Northward Ho* (1605). I i:

Bellamont.   . . . I could make an excellent description of it [Sturbridge Fair] in a comedy.

Beaumont. *Knight of the Burning Pestle* (1604). Induction:

From all that's near the court, from all that's great
Within the compass of the city walls,
We now have brought our scene.

Massinger. *The Picture* (1629) . V. ii.:

Ubaldo.   Some poet will,
From this relation, or in verse or prose,
Or both together blended, render us
Ridiculous to all ages.

Marston. *Jack Drum's Entertainment* (1600). Introduction:

And vows not to torment your list'ning ears
With moldy fopperies of stale poetry,
Impossible dry musty fictions.

Middleton. *Mayor of Quinborough* (1597) . I. Chorus:

> *Raynulph.*   What Raynulph, monk of Chester, can
> Raise from his Polychronicon, ...
> That best may please this round fair ring,
> With sparkling diamonds circled in,
> I shall produce. . . .
> Ancient stories have been best;
> Fashions, that are now called new,
> Have been worn by more than you;
> Elder times have used the same,
> Though these new ones get the name:
> So in story what now told
> That takes not part with days of old?
> Then to approve time's mutual glory,
> Join new time's love to old time's story.

Dekker, Webster. *Westward Ho* (1604). I. i.:

> *Justiniano.*   . . . Have amongst you, city dames! You that are
> indeed the fittest and most proper persons for a comedy.

Kyd. *Spanish Tragedy* (1583). IV. i.:

> *Hieronimo.*   . . . what's a play without a woman in it?

As the prologue declares, Shirley did not expect the crowd to enjoy his *Doubtful Heir* (1640), because of the absence of so many things that they like:

> No shows, no dance, and, what you most delight in,
> Grave understanders, here's no target-fighting
> Upon the stage, all work for cutlers barr'd;
> No bawdry, nor no ballads; this goes hard;
> But language clean; and, what affects you not,
> Without impossibilities the plot;
> No clown, no squibs, no devil in't.

Tomkis. *Lingua* (1603). Prol.:

> Our muse describes no lover's passion,
> No wretched father, no unthrifty son,
> No craven subtle whore, or shameless bawd,
> No stubborn clown, or daring parasite,
> No lying servant, or bold sycophant.

Middleton. *Mayor of Quinborough* (1597). V i:

> *Simon.*   Give me a play without a beast, I charge ye.
> *2nd. Player.*   That's hard; without a cuckold or a drunkard?
> *Simon.*   O, those beasts are often the best men in a parish, and must not be kept out.

Beaumont. *Woman Hater* (1606). Prol.:

> Some things in it you may meet with which are out of the common road. A duke there is, and the scene lies in Italy, as those things lightly we never miss.

Heywood, toward the close of the period, laments the fall of the prevailing practice, under foreign influence, from the lofty heights of the imperial theme.

Challenge for Beauty (1635). Prol.:

> For where before great patriots, dukes, and kings
> Presented for some high facinorous things,
> Were the stage subject, now we strive to fly
> In their [continental plays'] low pitch who never could soar high.
> For now the common argument intreats
> Of puling lovers, crafty bawds, or cheats.

The romantic notion satirized above by Beaumont that the scene must lie in Italy, or some other remote region, anywhere but at home, did not apply to history. Plays drawn from the English past were pursued with patriotic fervor.

Ford. *Perkin Warbeck* (1633). Prol.:

> He shows a History, couched in a play:
> A history of noble mention, known,
> Famous, and true; most noble, 'cause our own:
> Not forged from Italy, from France, from Spain,
> But chronicled at home; as rich in strain
> Of brave attempts as ever fertile rage,
> In action, could beget to grace the stage.

Nash. *Pierce Penniless* (1592) :

. . . what if I prove plays to be . . . a rare exercise of virtue? First, for the subject of them (for the most part) it is borrowed out of our English chronicles, [interesting information concerning stage activity following the destruction of the Armada] wherein our forefathers' valiant acts (that have lyne longe buried in rusty brass and worm-eaten books) are revived, and they themselves raised from the grave of oblivion, and brought to plead their aged honors in open presence. . . .

How would it have joy'd brave Talbot (the terror of the French) to think that after he had lyne two hundred years in his tomb, he should triumph again on the stage, and have his bones new embalmed with the tears of ten thousand spectators at least, (at several times) who, in the tragedian that represents his person, imagine they behold him fresh bleeding?

I will defend it against any collian, or club-fisted usurer of them all, there is no immortality can be given a man on earth like unto plays.

The principle of the superiority of poetry to history as enunciated by Sidney and Bacon (supra. p. 32), applies of course to the drama. The first citation is obviously a rap at Jonson's *Sejanus*.

Marston. *Sophonisba*. To the general Reader (1606) :

Know that I have not labored in this poem to tie myself to relate anything as an historian, but to enlarge everything as a poet. To transcribe authors, quote authorities, and translate Latin prose orations into English blank verse, hath, in this subject, been the least aim of my studies.

Dekker. *The Whore of Babylon*. Lectori (1607) :

And whereas I may (by some more curious in censure than sound in judgment) be critically taxed that I falsify the account of time, and set not down occurrents according to their true succession, let such (that are so nice of stomach) know that I write as a poet, not as an historian, and that these two do not live under one law.

Chapman. *Revenge of Bussy*. Dedication (1613):

And for the autentical truth of either person or action, who (worthy the respecting) will expect it in a poem, whose subject is not truth, but things like truth?

Heywood. *Apology* (1612) :

Why should not the lives of these worthies, presented in these our days, effect the like wonders in the princes of our times, which can in no way be so exquisitely demonstrated, nor so lively portrayed, as by action. . . . A description is only a shadow, received by the ear, but not perceived by the eye, but can neither show action, passion, motion, or any other gesture to move the spirits of the beholder to admiration: but to see a soldier shap'd like a soldier, walk, speak, act like a soldier; to see a Hector all besmeared in blood, trampling upon the bulks of kings . . . oh, these were sights to make an Alexander!

Chapman. *Caesar and Pompey*. Dedication (1631):

. . . scenical representation is so far from giving just cause of any least diminution, that the personal and exact life it gives any history, or other such delineation of human actions, adds to them luster, spirit, and apprehension.

In the prologue to *Believe as You List*, Massinger, with posed humility characteristic of him, disclaims credit for whatever interest his play may possess, that being due entirely to the material supplied by history. The following year, however, in the prologue to another historical play, *The Emperor of the East*, he suggests that perhaps the author is entitled to some credit for the skill with which he handles the material supplied by history.

Believe as You List (1630) . Prol.:

> The rarity
> Of the events in this strange history
> Now offered to you, by his own confession,
> Must make it good, and not his weak expression.

The Emperor of the East (1631). Prol.:

> He hath done his best: and, though he cannot glory
> In his invention (this work being a story

Of reverend antiquity) he doth hope
In the proportion of it, and the scope,
You may observe some pieces drawn like one
Of a steadfast hand.

The fact that several dramatists, as we see, thought it necessary
to urge their point of view concerning history plays, would indicate that they were responding to considerable criticism. It is not
difficult to understand that the way the stage taught history
would not meet with the approval of the historian. A particularly
vituperative utterance is afforded by Sir George Buc, who, in his
History of King Richard the Third, classes historical plays with
the ignoble ballad to be fed to the ignorant masses:

> For the ignorant and never understanding vulgar, whose faith
> (in history) is drawn from pamphlet and ballad, and their reverend
> and learned authors, the stage, or those that play the bands to it
> for a living, let fly their own pitch; for they are but kites and daws,
> and can digest naught (so well) as stench and filth; to which I leave
> them.[1]

On the other hand, Sir William Alexander, who wrote a number of curious historical plays in rhyme, argues in his *Anacrisis*
(1634) that a theme drawn from history is best for tragedy:

> Many would bound the boundless liberty of a poet, binding him
> only to the birth of his own brains, affirming that there can be no
> perfection but in a fiction. . . . I would allow that an epic poem
> should consist altogether of a fiction; that the poet, soaring above
> the course of nature, . . . may liberally furnish his imaginary man
> with all the qualities requisite for the accomplishing of a perfect
> creature, having power to dispose of all things at his own pleasure.
> But it is more agreeable with the gravity of a tragedy, that it be
> grounded upon a true history, where the greatness of a known
> person, urging regard, doth work the more powerfully upon the
> affections.

Milton. *Reason of Church Government* (1641). Bohn ed., Vol.
II, p. 479:

---

[1] Quoted in advertisement at end of Frank Marcham: *William
Shakespeare and his Daughter Susannah.*

... to celebrate in glorious and lofty hymns the throne and equipage of God's almightiness, and what he works, and what he suffers to be wrought with high providence in his church; to sing victorious agonies of martyrs and saints, the deeds and triumphs of just and pious nations, doing valiantly through faith against the enemies of Christ, to deplore the general relapses of kingdoms and states from justice and God's true worship. Lastly, whatever in religion is holy and sublime, in virtue amiable or grave, whatever hath passion or admiration in all the changes of that which is called fortune from without, or the wily subtleties and refluxes of a man's thoughts from within; all these things with a solid and treatable smoothness to paint out and describe.

As evidenced by his practice, Milton would have this enumeration apply to both dramatic and non-dramatic poetry. The latter part, particularly, pertains most appropriately to the drama. As we should expect from the quotation, he finds great poetry and drama in the Bible (ibid., p. 479) :

The Scripture also affords us a divine pastoral drama in the Song of Solomon, consisting of two persons, and a double chorus, as Origen rightly judges. And the Apocalypse of St. John is the majestic image of a high and stately tragedy, shutting up and intermingling her solemn scenes and acts as a sevenfold chorus of hallelujahs and harping symphonies; and this my opinion the grave authority of Pareus, commenting that book is sufficient to confirm. . . . But those frequent songs throughout the law and prophets beyond all these [i. e. Pindar, Callimachus, etc.), not in their divine argument alone, but in the very critical art of composition, may be easily made appear over all the kinds of lyric poesy to be incomparable.

Interestingly, the Book of Job, which is commonly compared to a Greek tragedy, Milton classified as an epic poem (ibid., p. 478):

... that epic form whereof the two poems of Homer, and those other two of Virgil and Tasso, are a diffuse, and the Book of Job a brief, model.

THE PLOT

Meres calls Munday "our best plotter," indicating the presentation of a moot topic. The construction of the perfect plot is briefly and effectively described by Tourneur in *The Atheist's Tragedy* (1603). II. iv:

> *Borachio.* 'T has crowned the most judicious murder that
> The brain of man was e'er delivered of.
> *D'Anville.* Ay, mark the plot. Not any circumstance
> That stood within the reach of the design,
> Of persons, dispositions, matter, time, or place,
> But by this brain of mine was made
> An instrumental help; yet nothing from
> The induction to the accomplishment seemed forced,
> Or done o' purpose, but by accident.

A fuller account is given by Richard Flecknoe in his *A Discourse of the English Stage*:

> There are few of our English plays (excepting only some few of Jonson's) without some faults or other; and if the French have fewer than our English, 'tis because they confine themselves to narrower limits, and consequently have less liberty to err.
>
> The chief faults of ours are our huddling too much matter together, and making them too long and intricate; we imagining we never have intrigue enough, till we lose ourselves and auditors, who shu'd be led in a maze, but not a mist; and through turning and winding ways, but so still as they may find their way at last.
>
> A good play shu'd be like a good stuff, closely and evenly wrought, without any breaks, thrums, or loose ends in 'um, or like a good picture well painted and designed; the plot or contrivement, the design, the writing, the coloris, and counterplot, the shadowings, with other embellishments; or, finally, it shu'd be like a well con-

triv'd garden, cast into its walks and counterwalks, betwixt an alley
and a wilderness, neither too plain, nor too confus'd.

Thomas Carew. Upon *The Heir*, by Thomas May (1622) :

The whole plot doth alike itself disclose
Through the five acts, as doth a lock that goes
With letters; for, till every one is known,
The lock's as fast as if you had found none.

Shirley. *Cardinal* (1641). Prol.:

A poet's art is to lead on your thought
Through subtle paths and working of a plot.

Cartwright, on Fletcher (1647) :

No vast uncivil bulk swells any scene,
The strength's ingenious and the vigor clean:
None can prevent the fancy, and see through
At the first opening; all stand wondering how
The thing will be until it is; which thence
With fresh delights still cheats, still takes the sense;
The whole design, the shadows, the lights, such
That none can say he shows or hides too much:
Business grows up, ripened by just encrease,
And by as just degrees again doth cease;
The heats and minutes of affairs are watched,
And the nice points of time are met and snatched;
Nought later than it should, nought comes before,—
Chemists and calculators do err more;
Sex, age, degree, affections, country, place,
The inward substance, and the outward face,
All kept precisely, all exactly fit;
What he would write, he was before he writ.

Jay. On Massinger's *New Way to Pay Old Debts* (1633):

The crafty mazes of the cunning plot,
The polished phrase, the sweet expression, the conceit
Fresh and unsullied.

Fletcher, Massinger. *Custom of the Country* (1619) . Prol.:

147

                            The play
Is quick and witty; so the poets say,
And we believe them; the plot neat and new;
Fashion'd like those that are approv'd by you.
Only, 'twill crave attention in the most,
Because, one point unmark'd, the whole is lost.

Lyly. *Sapho and Phao* (1581). Epil.:

We fear we have led you all this while in a labyrinth of conceits,
divers times hearing one device, and have now brought you to the
end where we first began. Which wearisome travail you must impute
to the necessity of the history.

Even though the plot be intricate it should be within the con-
trol of the author, who must not resort to the *deus ex machina*.
Cartwright. In the memory of the most worthy Benjamin
Jonson:

No strange perplexed maze doth pass for plot;
Thou always dost untie, not cut the knot.
Thy labyrinth's doors are open'd by one thread
That ties, and runs through all that's done or said:
No power comes down with learned hat and rod;
Wit only, and contrivance, is thy god.

Tomkis. *Lingua* (1603) . V. i.:

  Mendacio. My lady Lingua is just like one of these lean-witted
comedians who disturbing all to the fifth act, bring down some
Mercury or Jupiter in an engine to make all friends.

The simple plot too had its champions, among them Fletcher,
whose skill in developing an intricate plot was commended by
Cartwright.
Fletcher. *Woman's Prize* (1606). Prol.:

We do entreat the angry men would not
Expect the mazes of a subtle plot.

Ibid. *Chances* (1609) . Prol.:

... we do entreat that you would not
Expect strange turns and windings in the plot.

Heywood. *Fair Maid of the West*. To the Reader (1631):

I hold it no necessity to trouble thee with the argument of the story,
the matter itself lying so plainly before thee in acts and scenes, without any deviations, or winding incidents.

The last act should be the best.

Cromwell (1592). IV. Chorus:

Pardon the errors is already past,
And live in hope the best doth come at last.

Webster. *Devil's Law Case* (1619). II. iii.:

   Romelio.   O look the last act be the best in the play.

Fletcher. *Prophetess* (1622). IV. Chorus:

We ... are bold,
In that which follows, that the most shall say,
'Twas well begun, but the end crown'd the play.

2 Return from Parnassus (1603). Prol.:

   Momus.   For catastrophe there's ne'er a tale in Sir John Mande-
ville or Bevis of Southampton but hath a better turning.

Middleton. *Roaring Girl* (1610). Epil.:

       ... some perhaps do flout
The plot, saying 'tis too thin, too weak, too mean.

Heywood. *Wise Woman* (1604). III. i.:

   Wise W.   Here were even a plot to make a play on.

Dekker, Webster. *Northward Ho* (1605). IV. i.:

   Mayberry.   A comedy! a Canterbury tale smells not half so sweet as the comedy I have for thee, old poet: thou shalt write upon't, poet.

Bellamont. Nay, I will write upon't, if 't be a comedy, for I have been at a most villainous female tragedy: come, the plot, the plot. [Then follows an account of a clever intrigue.]

Brome. *Antipodes* (1638). V. viii.:

Letoy.   The music, songs,
And dance I gave command for, are they ready?
Quailpipe. All, my good lord; and (in good sooth) I cannot enough applaud your honor's quaint conceit in the design; so apt, and so (withal) *poetice legitimate,* as I may justly say with Plautus—
Letoy. Prithee say no more; but see upon my signal given, they act as well as I designed.

That stealing plots was not an unknown practice in those free-and-easy days is indicated by a passage in Middleton and Rowley's *Spanish Gypsy* (1623), III i:

Roderigo.   ... if my pen
From my invention can strike music-tunes,
My head and brains are yours. ...
Sancho. A magpie of Parnassus! welcome again! I am a firebrand of Phoebus myself; we'll invoke together, so you will not steal my plot.
Rod. 'Tis not my fashion.
San. But nowadays 'tis all the fashion.

Conventional claptrap is ridiculed in Brome's *English Moor* (1636) V i. Two fathers give the reason for disappearing and pretending to be dead:

Rashly. Nor was it to make trial of
What husbands they would be; how spend, or save;
How manage, or destroy; how one or both
Might play the tyrants over their poor tenants,
Yet fall by prodigality into the compters;
And then the dead, by pulling off a beard,
After a little chiding and some whining,
To set the living on their legs again,
And take 'em into favor; pish! old play plots.

CHARACTER

Regarding the characters in a play Aristotle said: "They must be true to type." But he added: "They must be true to life, which is something different from making them true to type." The latter admonition the Renaissance critics did not digest. They seized upon the former, and based upon it the rigid principle of *Decorum*, according to which human beings were rigidly classified into types, the speech and behavior of each type uniformly regulated. Among the Elizabethan dramatists there are two early statements of adherence to the principle.

Edwards. *Damon and Pythias* (1564). Prol.:

In comedies the greatest skill is this: rightly to touch
All things to the quick; and eke to frame each person so,
That by his common talk you may his nature know:
A royster ought not preach, that were too strange to hear;
But as from virtue he doth swerve, so ought his word appear;
The old man is sober, the young man rash, the lover triumphing
    in joys;
The matron grave, the harlot wild and full of wanton toys,
Which all in one course they nowise do agree;
So, correspondent to their kind their speeches ought to be.

Whetstone. *Promos and Cassandra* (1578). Dedication:

And their ground is not so unperfect as their working indiscreet; not weighing, so the people laugh, though they laugh them, for their follies, to scorn. Many times (to make mirth) they make a clown companion with a king; in their grave counsels they allow the advice of fools; yea, they use one order of speech for all persons— a gross indecorum—for a crow will counterfeit ill the nightingale's sweet voice: even so, affected speech doth misbecome a clown. For to work a comedy kindly grave old men should instruct; young men should show the imperfections of youth; strumpets should be lascivious; boys unhappy; and clowns should be disorderly.

A later reference in the prologue to Fletcher's *Chances*, but composed after Fletcher's death:

Familiar language, fashion'd to the weight
Of such as speak it.

The phrase, "fashion'd to the weight of such as speak it," would indicate that the writer, whoever he was, still had in mind the doctrine of *Decorum*; for in that doctrine the principle of division was social rank.

In the induction to the first part of *Antonio and Mellida* (1600) we are told that for a certain character Marlovian bombast is deliberately chosen for its appropriateness.

Feliche. . . . What rattling thunderclap breaks from his lips?
Alberto. O, 'tis native to his part. For, acting a modern bradoch under the person of Matzagente, the Duke of Milan's son, it may seem to suit with good fashion of coherence.

QUALITIES AIMED AT

Lyly's practice coincided with his theory. Quotation by George P. Baker in *Camb. Hist. of Eng. Lit.* V. 143:

It is wit that allureth, when every word shall have his weight, when nothing shall proceed but it shall either savor of a sharp conceit or a secret conclusion.

Chapman (?) *Alphonsus Emperor of Germany* (1590). To Reader:

The design is high, the contrivance subtle.

In *2 Antonio and Mellida* Marston makes his own play the subject of the last speech in the play:

Andrugio.   And oh, if ever time create a muse
That to th' immortal fame of virgin faith
Dares once engage his pen to write her death,
Presenting it in some black tragedy,
May it prove gracious; may his style be deckt
With freshest blooms of purest elegance;
May it have gentle presence, and the scenes suckt up
By calm attention of choice audience.

Chapman. *Gent. Usher* (1602). III. 2:

Vincentio.   Besides, good sir, Your show did show so well.
Bassioli.   Did it, indeed, my lord?
Vin.   Oh, sir, believe it!
'Twas the best fashion'd and well-ordered thing
That ever eye beheld; . . .
                          . . . every part
Concurring to one commendable end—

Marston. *Sophonisba* (1603). Epil.:

If words well-sens'd, best suiting subject grave,
Noble true story, may once boldly crave
Acceptance gracious, . . .
If scenes exempt from ribaldry, or rage
Of taxing indiscreet, may please the stage,
If such may hope applause, he not commands,
Yet craves as due, the justice of your hands.

Ibid. *Fawn* (1604). Epil.:

            . . . if you shall judge this flame
Distemperately, weak, as faulty much
In style, in plot, in spirit. . . .

Dekker. *Whore of Babylon* (1604). Prol.:

            . . . we present
Matter above the vulgar argument,
Yet drawn so lively that the weakest eye
Through those thin veils we hang between your sight
And this our piece, may reach the mystery.

Tourneur. *Revenger's Tragedy* (1606). III. iv.:

  Vendice.   When the bad bleeds, then is the tragedy good.

Greene. *Selimus* (1588). Conclusion:

If this first part, gentles, do like you well,
The second part shall greater murthers tell.

Fletcher. *Woman's Prize* (1606). Prol.:

We do entreat the angry men would not
Expect the mazes of a subtle plot,
Set speeches, high expressions, and, what's worse
In a true comedy, politic discourse.

The prologue to Barry's *Ram-Alley* (1609) promises "conceit
with quick-turn'd scenes."

Fletcher. *Love's Cure* (1626) . Epil.:

Such will be apt to say there wanted wit,
The language low, very few scenes are writ
With spirit and life.

Ford. *Broken Heart* (1629). Epil.:

Let some say, "This was flat!" some, "Here the scene
Fell from its height;" another that the "mean
Was ill observed in such a growing passion
As it transcended either state or fashion."

Massinger. On Shirley's *Grateful Servant* (1630):

Here are no forc'd expressions, no rack'd phrase,
No Babel compositions, to amaze
The tortur'd reader.

Jay. On Massinger's *New Way* (1633) :

The crafty mazes of the cunning plot,
The polished phrase, the sweet expression, the conceit
Fresh and unsullied.

Ford. *The Fancies* (1635) . Epil.:

Fancy and judgment are a play's full matter.

Ibid. *Lady's Trial* (1638). Prol.:

Language and matter, with a fit of mirth
That sharply savors more of air than earth,
Like midwives, bring a play to timely birth.

Suckling. *Goblins* (1638) . Epil.:

   . . . who goes about
To take asunder, oft destroys (we know)
What all together made a pretty show.

Fletcher, Massinger. *Fair Maid of the Inn* (1626). Prol.:

A worthy story, howsoever writ,
For language, modest mirth, conceit, or wit.

W. B. Verses on Massinger's *Bondman* (1624):

Here are no gypsy jigs, no drumming stuff,
Dances, or other trumpery to delight,
Or take, by common way, the common sight.

Heywood. *English Traveller* (1632). Prol.:

A strange play you are like to have, for know,
We use no drum nor trumpet nor dumb show;
No combat, marriage, not so much today
As song, dance, masque, to bombast out a play.

Shirley. *Doubtful Heir* (1640). 2 Prol.:

No shows, no dance, and, what you most delight in,
Grave understanders, here's no target-fighting
Upon the stage, all work for cutlers barr'd;
No bawdry, nor no ballads; this goes hard;
But language clean, and, what affects you not,
Without impossibilities the plot:
No clown, no squibs, no devil in't.

J. Cumber. *Two Merry Milkmaids* (1619). Prol.:

'Tis a fine play;
For we have in't a conqueror, a divel,
And a clown too; but I fear the evil,
In which, perhaps, unwisely we may fail,
Of wanting squibs and crackers at their tail.

The reason why I have placed the two preceding extracts consecutively is plain. A number of the quotations in this section give indication of the popular demands which the good playwright felt himself called upon to defy.

PROPRIETY

Disclaimers of indecency are numerous. Practically all the dramatists issued them. There is little variation in them, and most of them are not worth quoting. I shall confine myself to a few, and list some others.

Udall. *Ralph Royster Doyster* (1553). Prol.:

. . . all scurrility we utterly refuse,
Avoiding such mirth wherein is abuse.

Lyly. *Sapho and Phao* (1583). Prol.:

We have endeavored to be as far from unseemly speeches to make your ears glow. . . .

Nash. *Pierce Penniless* (1592):

Our players are not as the players beyond sea, a sort of squirting, bawdy comedians, that have whores and common curtizans to play women's parts, and forbear no immodest speech or unchaste action that may procure laughter.

Lodge. *Wit's Misery* (1596) . IV.:

For all of that sect [players] I say thus much: if they use no other mirth but Eutrapelian urbanity, and pleasure mixed with honesty, it is to be borne withal; but filthy speaking, scurrility, unfit for chaste ears, that I wish with the Apostle that it should not be named amongst Christians. . . . The conclusion shall be Tully's, and, good fellows, mark it: *nihil est tam tetrum, nihil tam aspernandum, nihil homine indignius, quam turpitudo.* There is nothing more vild, nothing more to be despised, nothing more unworthy a man, than villainy and filthiness; and if you will follow my counsel therefor, write this over your theaters:

Nihil dictu foedom visuque haec limina tangat.
Let nought unfit to see or to be said
Be toucht, or in these houses be bewraid.

Beaumont. On Jonson's *Fox*:

But since our subtle gallants . . . have, at best,
Stomachs so raw that nothing can digest
But what's obscene, or barks. . . .

Barry. *Ram-Alley* (1609). Prol.:

He doth produce for your delight
Conceits so new, so harmless, free,
That Puritans themselves may see
A play, yet not in public preach
That players such lewd doctrines teach
That their pure joints do quake and tremble
When they do see a man resemble
The picture of a villain.

Middleton. *Fair Quarrel* (1616). IV. iv.:

Meg. Bawd and whore? Out, you unprofitable rascal! Hast not thou been at the new play yet, to teach thee better manners? Truly, they say they are the finest players, and good speakers of gentle-women of our quality; bawd and whore are not mentioned among 'em, but the handsomest narrow-mouthed names they have for us, that some of them may serve as well for a lady, as for one of our occupation.

Cartwright. In the memory of the most worthy Benjamin Jonson:

No rotten talk broken for a laugh; no page
Commenc'd man by th' instructions of the stage;
No bargaining line there, provocative verse;
No need to make good countenance ill, and use
The plea of strict life for a looser muse.

The plea in the last line is familiar to us in modern criticism. Not so many years ago Eugene O'Neill used it when he appeared before a New York City Magistrate because of the language employed in *The Hairy Ape*. The magistrate's reply was that the language was not true to life anyway. "Come into the next room and I'll give you a sample of what would be true to life." (Which was correct criticism too.)

Departure from conventional morality, if not excessive, is justified by Fletcher in the prologue to *Rule a Wife* (1624):

> Nor blame the poet if he slips aside
> Sometimes lasciviously, if not too wide.

And prudery is ridiculed in the person of Gullio in *1 Return from Parnassus* (1601), IV i:

> *Gullio.* . . . there's a word in the last canto which my chaste lady will never endure the reading of. Thou shouldest have insinuated so much, and not told it plainly. What is become of art?

Appropriate to this section is Cartwright's evaluation of Shakespeare's humor, in his lines on Fletcher quoted on page 8f. That judgment is rendered all the more remarkable by two noteworthy facts: first, that Shakespeare never protested to the public that he shunned indecency; second, that Shakespeare is to a modern audience about the least indecent of Elizabethan playwrights.

Other references under this head: Dekker, *Shoemaker's Holiday*, Ded.; Dekker, Middleton, *Roaring Girl*, Epil.; Beaumont, *Woman Hater*, Prol.; *Knight of the Burning Pestle*, Prol.; Fletcher, *Henry VIII*, Prol.; Fletcher, Massinger, *Custom of the Country*, Prol.; Massinger, *Emperor of the East*, Prol.; Carew, on May's *Heir*; Heywood, *A Maidenhead*, To the Reader; Shirley, *Politician*, Ded.; *Coronation*, Prol.; *Doubtful Heir*, Prol. 1 and 2; *Duke's Mistress*, Prol.; *Imposture*, Prol.; Marmion, *Fine Companion*, Prol.; Glapthorne, *Whitehall*, (p. 247) ; Ford, *Broken Heart*, Prol.; Middleton, *Roaring Girl*, Address to the Reader.

ORIGINALITY

Probably the earliest utterance under this head by a playwright is Greene's famous attack on Shakespeare. To the same period belongs Nash's vigorous assertion of the originality of his style, in *Strange News,* already quoted on page 59. R. B., in *Greene's Funerals,* paraphrases Greene's own statement:

Greene made the ground to all that wrote upon him.
Nay, more, the men who so eclipst his fame
Purloined his plumes; can they deny the same?

In *2 Return from Parnassus,* I. ii., Daniel is thus admonished:

Only let him more sparingly make use
Of others' wit, and use his own the more,
That well may scorn base imitation.

Fletcher, Massinger. *False One* (1620). Prol.:

New titles warrant not a play for new,
The subject being old; and 'tis as true,
Fresh and neat matter may with ease be fram'd
Out of their stories that have oft been nam'd
With glory on the stage. What borrows he
From him that wrote old Priam's tragedy,
That writes his love to Hecuba? Sure, to tell
Of Caesar's amorous heats, and how he fell
In the Capitol, can never be the same
To the judicious: nor will such blame
Those that penn'd this for barrenness, when they find
Young Cleopatra here, and her great mind
Express'd to the height, with us a maid, and free,

And how he rated her virginity.
We treat not of what boldness she did die,
Nor of her fatal love to Antony.
What we present and offer to your view,
Upon their faiths, the stage yet never knew.
Let reason, then, first to your wills give laws,
And after judge them and of their cause.

Ford. *Lover's Melancholy* (1628). Prol.:

Our writer for himself would have you know
That in the following scenes he doth not owe
To others' fancies, nor hath lain in wait
For any stol'n invention, from whose height
He might command his own, more than the right
A scholar claims may warrant for delight.

Ibid. *The Fancies, Chaste and Noble* (1635). Prol.:

The Fancies! that's our play. In it is shown
Nothing but what our author knows his own
Without a learned theft. . . .
His free invention runs but in conceit
Of mere imaginations.

Heywood. *English Traveller* (1632). Prol.:

   . . . no help, no strain,
Or flash that's borrowed from another's brain.

With less courage than is displayed in the prologue to *The False One*, quoted above, Massinger, in the prologue to *The Emperor of the East* (1631), justifies the treating of an old subject. The passage has already been quoted under the heading of Material.

Cartwright. On Fletcher (1647):

Thou wert not like some, our small poets. . . .
Whose wit is pilfering, and whose vein and wealth
In poetry lies merely in their stealth.

THE QUESTION OF AUTHORITY

The question of authority as affecting the drama is touched upon by Richard Edwards in the prologue to *Damon and Pythias* (1564) :

> If this offend the lookers-on, let Horace then be blamed,
> Which hath our author taught at school, from whom he doth not
>   swerve.

Note that classical authority with Edwards meant Latin authority. How completely this view was taken for granted is illustrated by a letter written by Ascham to Sturm in 1568 (Wks. ed. Giles, II. 189), in which the English scholar says:

> Scripsit idem Baptista Pigna . . . alterum librum, *Questiones Sophocleas*: ubi de tota doctrina tragica, de *Senecae vitiis* de *Graecorum Tragicorum virtutibus* fuse tractavit. Nec minori hujus libri videndi desiderio teneor, mi Sturmi: quoniam Sophocles et Euripides, mea certe opinione, cum Platone et Xenephonte in omni civilis cognitionis explicatione conferri possunt.

We see from this that the view expressed by Pigna was heretical, and we observe that Ascham does not attempt to defend the startling doctrine that the Greek dramatists were superior to Seneca by comparing their relative merits as playwrights, but merely endeavors to make the view less repellent by advancing the eminence of the former as political thinkers.

Two years later Ascham writes again, in his *Schoolmaster* (ed. Arber, 139):

> Some in England, more in France, Germany, and Italy, also have written tragedies in our time: of which, not one I am sure is able

to abide the touch of Aristotle's precepts, and Euripides' examples, save only two that ever I saw: M. Watson's *Absalon,* and Georgius Buckananus' *Jephte.*

Seneca and Horace are quietly disregarded. But how far such ideas were ahead of the time is evidenced by the fact that Webbe, in his *Discourse of English Poetry,* published in 1586, appends, as a matter of course, a synopsis of Horace's rules. Elizabethan taste could not escape its Latin training, which left its mark on the entire Elizabethan drama. Ascham's preference could not have been a very positive thing; for, as Boas points out, "there is no trace in [*Jephte*] of the distinctive influences of Greek dramatic art. It is even more strictly Senecan in form and spirit than *Baptistes.*"[1] Similarly, Edwards evidently did not realize to what extent he was controlled by native influences in the composition of *Damon and Pythias.* One can about imagine what Horace would have thought of the play that claimed him as a foster father.

The force of the native influences is strikingly illustrated in the case of the earliest extant university play in England: Nicholas Grimald's *Christus Redivivus,* printed in 1543. In it the unities are disregarded, and there is a mixture of the high and the low, the grave and the gay; all of which met with the approval of his tutor, John Airy. "It is astonishing," observes Boas, "to find this Oxford scholar, in his observations to Grimald upon his play, setting forth the distinctive principles of Romantic dramatic art."[2] Interesting, but not astonishing. There was a tradition of dramatic practice woven into the literary consciousness of Airy, and Grimald, and Edwards, scholars or no scholars. And the theorizers had not yet formulated rigid rules presumed to be based upon "Aristotle's precepts."

When the Elizabethan dramatists were confronted with those rules, the majority probably were willing to recognize their theoretical validity, but as practical playwrights they felt that they had to forget them, and very likely with a troubled conscience. To the point is Webster's statement to the reader of *The White Devil:*

If it be objected this is no true dramatic poem, I shall easily confess it; *non potes in nugas dicere plura meas ipse ego quam dixi.*Will-

---

[1] *University Drama in the Tudor Age.* p. 60.

[2] Ibid., p. 28.

ingly, and not ignorantly, in this kind have I faulted; for, should a man present to such an auditory the most sententious tragedy that ever was written, observing all the critical laws, as height of style, and gravity of person, enrich it with the sententious Chorus, and, as it were, liven death in the passionate and weighty Nuntius; yet, after all this divine rapture, *O dura messorum ilia*, the breath that comes from the uncapable multitude is able to poison it.

This as late as 1612, from a man who had witnessed a succession of the greatest plays the world had ever seen, and who himself was about to add to that succession a play that Gosse ranks second only to Shakespeare's *King Lear*! It seems incredible, yet he was only echoing opinions that had been voiced only a few years earlier by such great men as Cervantes and Lope de Vega. We are assisted in grasping the paradox if we recall that all he could see in Shakespeare was a "right happy and copious industry." The Elizabethan drama was simply not conscious of its own greatness.

Perhaps the typical attitude is expressed by Dekker in the prologue to *Old Fortunatus* (1599) :

[Our Muse] begs your pardon, for she'll send [a Chorus] forth,
Not when the laws of poesy do call,
But as the story needs.

In other words, the laws are all right, but the show must go on. Some took a definite stand against the domination of the rules. Marston. *What You Will* (1601) . Induction:

  . . . hold this firm:
Music and poetry were first approv'd
By common sense; and that which pleased most
Held most allow'd to pass. Your rules of art
Were shap'd to pleasure, not pleasure to your rules.
Think you if that his scenes took stamp in mint
Of three or four deem'd most judicious,
It must inforce the world to current them?

Daniel. *Defence of Rhyme* (1603):

Methinks we should not so soon yield our consents captive to the authority of antiquity, unless we saw more reason. All our understandings are not to be built by the square of Greece and Italy. We are the children of nature as well as they; we are not so placed out of the way of judgment but that the same sun of discretion shineth upon us.

In the same work he speaks of "custom, that is before all law; nature that is above all art."

Ford asserts the impossibility of formulating fixed and final laws of dramatic composition.

Lover's Melancholy (1628). Prol.:

To tell you, gentlemen, in what true sense
The writer, actors, or the audience
Should mold their judgments for a play, might draw
Truth into rules; but we have no such law.

Back in 1599 Chapman, in the prologue to *All Fools*, had pointed out that there are always incalculable factors involved in the determination of the success or failure of a play.

The fortune of a stage (like Fortune's self)
Amazeth great judgments; and none knows
The hidden causes of those strange effects
That rise from this hell, or fall from this heaven.

Hardly consistent with the foregoing extract, and hardly consistent with itself, is a statement by Chapman in his preface to *The Masque of the Middle Temple and Lincoln's Inn* (1613), in which the ancient laws of poetry are defended:

But what rules soever are set down to any art or act (though without their observation no art, nor act, is true and worthy) yet they are nothing the more followed; or those few that follow them credited. Every vulgarly-esteemed upstart dares break the dreadful dignity of ancient and autentical poesy; and presume luciferously to proclaim in place thereof repugnant precepts of their own spawn.

There is confusion here, the second sentence contradicting the first. Chapman was in a bitter frame of mind, the whole preface being a personal invective against Campion.

Beaumont. Upon Jonson's *Fox* (1607):

> ... the art which thou alone
> Hast taught our tongue, the rules of time, of place,
> And other rites, ..

Barry. *Ram-Alley* (1609) . Prol.:

> Observing all those ancient streams
> Which from the horse-foot fount do flow,
> As time, place, person. . .

Middleton. *World Tost at Tennis* (1620):

> This our device we do not call a play,
> Because we break the stage's laws today
> Of acts and scenes.

Cartwright. On Fletcher (1647) :

> ... thou couldst thine own free fancy bind
> In stricter numbers, and run so confined
> As to observe the rules of art which sway
> In the contrivance of a true-born play.

Yet, perhaps Fletcher himself was not so sure that his own free fancy could create as effectively under restrictions, judging by a passage in the first scene of *The Maid's Tragedy* (1609):

> *Lysippus.*   Strato, thou hast some skill in poetry:
> What think'st thou of the masque? will it be well?
> *Strato.*   As well as masques can be.
> *Lys.*   As masques can be!
> *Stra.*   Yes; they must commend their king, and speak in praise
> Of the assembly, bless the bride and bridegroom
> In person of some god: they're tied to rules of flattery.

Adherence in theory to the principle of the unities was probably due to the influence of Sidney, who declared that

> the stage should always represent but one place; and the uttermost time presupposed in it should be, by Aristotle's precept, and common reason, but one day.

He emphasized the idea with his famous illustration, holding up to ridicule the consequences of violation:

> . . . you shall have Asia of the one side, and Affrick of the other, and so many under-kingdoms that the player, when he cometh in, must ever begin with telling where he is, or else the tale will not be conceived. Now ye shall have three ladies walk to gather flowers, and then we must believe the stage to be a garden. . . . Now, of time they are much more liberal; for ordinary it is that two young princes fall in love. After many traverses, she is got with child, delivered of a fair boy, he is lost, groweth a man, falls in love, and is ready to get another child, and all this in two hours space. . . .

Sidney was anticipated by Whetstone, who, about five years earlier, in the dedication of *Promos and Cassandra*, gives a similar illustration:

> The Englishman in this quality is most vain, indiscreet, and out of order. He first grounds his work on impossibilities; then in three hours runs through the world, marries, gets children, makes children men, men to conquer kingdoms, murder monsters, and bringeth gods from heaven, and fetches devils from hell.

Jasper Mayne. On Jonson. (Bradley and Adams. *Jonson Allusion Book*, p. 227):

> Thy scene was free from monsters; no hard plot
> Call'd down a god t' untie th' unlikely knot;
> The stage was still a stage; two entrances
> Were not two ports o' the world, disjoin'd by seas.
> Thine were land tragedies. No prince was found
> To swim a whole scene out, then o' the stage drown'd;
> Pitch'd fields, as Red Bull wars, still felt thy doom;
> Thou laid'st no sieges to the music room.

It is interesting to observe that Sidney, who came so close to proclaiming a basic romantic principle when he said that the poet "goeth hand in hand with Nature, not inclosed within the narrow warrants of her gifts, but freely ranging only within the zodiac of his own wit," could not sufficiently overcome the effects of his classical training to take another step forward, and realize that art is primarily subject to the jurisdiction, not of "common reason," but of imagination. The Elizabethan dramatists might then, perhaps, have suffered fewer pangs of conscience.

Samuel Butler's sarcastic jingle, *Upon critics who judge of modern plays by the rules of the Antients,* is too delightful not to be quoted. Here are the opening lines:

Reduce all tragedy by rules of art
Back to its antique theater, a cart,
And make 'em henceforth keep the beaten roads
Of reverend choruses and episodes;
Reform and regulate a puppet play
According to the true and ancient way,
That not an actor shall presume to squeak
Unless he have a licence for 't in Greek.

APPEAL TO THE IMAGINATION

What Sidney exaggerated and held up to ridicule is justified by the playwrights on the ground that the appeal is to the imagination, not to the "common reason."

Cromwell (1592). Chorus after II.:

Now let your thoughts, as swift as the wind,
Skip some few years that Cromwell spent in travel,
And now imagine him in England.

This, of course, is an echo of the Chorus in Shakespeare's *Henry V*, first produced in 1590.

Drayton. *Merry Devil of Edmonton* (1600). Prol.:

Imagine now that whilst he is retired
From Cambridge back unto his native home,
Suppose the silent, sable-visaged night
Casts her black curtain over all the world;
And whilst he sleeps within his silent bed,
Toiled with the studies of the passed day,
The very time and hour wherein that spirit
That many years attended his command, ...
Comes now to claim the scholar for his due.

Beaumont. *Knight of the Burning Pestle* (1607). IV. i:

Boy. Sir, if you will imagine all this to be done already, you shall hear them talk together; but we cannot present a house covered with black velvet, and a lady in beaten gold.

Dekker. *Whore of Babylon* (1604). Prol.:

... as in landscape towns and woods appear
Small afar off, yet to the optic sense
The mind shows them as great as those more near;
So, winged Time that long ago flew hence,
You must fetch back with all those golden years
He stole, and here imagine still he stands,
Thrusting his silver lock into your hands.
There hold it but two hours, it shall from graves
Raise up the dead; upon this narrow floor
Swell up an ocean, with an armed fleet,
And lay the dragon at a dove's soft feet.
These wonders sit and see, sending as guides
Your judgment, not your passions. Passion slides,
When judgment goes upright. For though the Muse
That's thus inspir'd a novel path doth tread,
She's free from foolish boldness.

Ibid. *Old Fortunatus* (1596). Prol.:

And for this small circumference must stand
For the imagined surface of much land,
Of many kingdoms, and since many a mile
Should here be measured out, our Muse entreats
Your thoughts to help poor art.

Heywood. *Fair Maid of the West* (1603). Chorus after IV.:

Our stage so lamely can express a sea,
That we are forced by Chorus to discourse
What should have been in action. Now, imagine....

Fletcher. *The Prophetess* (1622). IV. Chorus, beginning and end:

So full of matter is our history
... that there wants
Room in this narrow stage, and time, to express
In action to the life, our Dioclesian
In his full luster. Yet (as the statuary,
That by the large size of Alcides' foot,
Guess'd at his whole proportion) so we hope
Your apprehensive judgments will conceive

Out of the shadow we can only show,
How fair the body was; and will be pleas'd,
Out of your wonted goodness, to behold
As in a silent mirror, what we cannot
With fit conveniency of time allow'd
For such presentments, clothe in vocal sounds. . . .
                              Now be pleas'd
That your imaginations may help you
To think them safe in Persia, and Dioclesian
For this disaster circled round with sorrow,
Yet mindful of the wrong.

Heywood. *Love's Mistress* (1634) . I., end:

   Midas.   And for thy scene: thou bringest here on the stage
A young green sickness baggage to run after
A little ape-faced boy thou term'st a god;
Is not this absurd?
   Apuleius.   Misunderstanding fool, thus much conceive:
Psyche is Anima, Psyche is the soul;
The soul's a virgin, longs to be a bride;
The soul's immortal—whom can she woo
But heaven? whom wed but immortality?

STANDARD OF JUDGMENT

A. VARIETY OF DEMAND

The Elizabethan dramatists complain of the difficulty of pleasing their audience, giving as one reason the fact that the audience was not homogeneous in its taste.

Contention between Liberality and Prodigality (1565. rev. 1601):

> The proverb is: How many men so many minds. . . .
> No play, no part, can all alike content.
> The grave divine calls for divinity,
> The civil servant for philosophy;
> The courtier craves some rare sound history,
> The baser sort for knacks of pleasantry.

Daniel. *Defence of Rhyme* (1603) :

> . . . the slippery foundation of opinion, and the world's inconstancy, which knows not well what it would have.

Heywood, in the epilogue to *A Woman Killed with Kindness* (1603), expresses himself in a parable, which concludes thus:

> Unto this wine we do allude our play;
> Which some will judge too trivial, some too grave. . . .
> Excuse us, then; good wine may be disgraced,
> When every several mouth hath sundry taste.

Middleton, Dekker, in *Roaring Girl*, Epilogue, similarly employ a parable, concluding thus:

If we to every brain that's humorous
Should fashion scenes, we, with the painter, shall,
In striving to please all, please none at all.

Middleton. *No Wit, No Help, Like a Woman's* (1613). Prol.:

How is't possible to suffice
So many ears, so many eyes?
Some in wit, some in shows,
Take delight, and some in clothes;
Some for mirth they chiefly come,
Some for passion,—for both some;
Some for lascivious meetings, that's their arrant;
Some to detract, and ignorance their warrant.
How is't possible to please
Opinion tossed on such wild seas?

Fletcher. *Henry VIII* (1613). Epilogue:

'Tis ten to one this play can never please
All that are here. Some come to take their ease
And sleep an act or two; but those, we fear,
We've frighted with our trumpets; so, 'tis clear,
They'll say 'tis naught; others, to hear the city
Abused extremely, and to cry, "That's witty!"
Which we have not done neither.

Glapthorne. *Revenge for Honor* (1624). Prol.:

Our author thinks 'tis not i' th' power of wit,
Invention, art, nor industry, to fit
The several fantasies which in this age,
With a predominant humor, rule the stage.
Some men cry out for satire, other choose
Merely to story to confine each muse;
Most like no play but such as gives large birth
To that which they judiciously term mirth,
Nor will the best works with their liking crown,
Except 't be grac'd with part of fool or clown.
Hard and severe the task is then to write
So as may please each various appetite.

Shirley, H. *Martyred Soldier* (bef. 1627). Epil.:

Who once made all, all rules, all never pleas'd.
Fain would we please the best, if not the many.

Fletcher. *Wife for a Month* (1624). Prol.:

> Who writ this bid me say,
> He had rather dress, upon a triumph day,
> My lord-mayor's feast, and make him sauces too,
> Sauce for each several mouth; nay, further go,
> He had rather build up those invincible pies,
> And castle-custards, that affright the eyes,
> Nay, eat 'em all and their artillery,
> Than dress for such a curious company
> One single dish.

Massinger. *Bashful Lover* (1635). Prol.:

> 'Tis no crime,
> He hopes as we do, in this curious time,
> To be a little diffident, when we are
> To please so many with one bill of fare.

Shirley. *Duke's Mistress* (1636). Prol.:

> So various are the palates of our age,
> That nothing is presented on the stage,
> Though ne'er so square and apted to the laws
> Of poesy, that can win full applause.
> This likes a story, that a cunning plot;
> This wit, that lines; here one he knows not what.

Suckling. *Goblins* (1638). Epil.:

> O what a monster wit must that man have
> That could please all which now their twelve-pence gave!
> High characters (cries one) and he would see
> Things that ne'er were, nor are, nor ne'er will be.
> Romances, cries easy souls; and then they swear
> The play's well writ, though scarce a good line there.
> The women—Oh, if Stephen should be kill'd,
> Or miss the lady, how the plot is spill'd! . .
> One will like all the ill things in a play,
> Another some o' the good, but the wrong way; . . .

Day. *Parliament of Bees* (1641). To the Impartial Reader (1641):

... to content the judicious I hold it no great miracle. . . . But to please all: *Hic labor, hoc opus est*; and I utterly despair on't.

Shirley. *St. Patrick* (1639). Prol.:

We know not what will take; your palates are
Various, and many of them sick, I fear: ...
We should be very happy if, at least,
We could find out the humor of your taste,
That we might fit, and feast it, so that you
Were constant to yourselves, and kept that true.

Thomas Carew's address to the reader of Davenant's play, *The Wits* (printed 1641), besides being an appropriate citation, is a considered piece of esthetic criticism:

It hath been said of old that plays are feasts,
Poets the cooks, and the spectators guests,
The actors waiters. From this simile
Some have derived an unsafe liberty
To use their judgments as their tastes; which choose,
Without control, this dish, and that refuse;
But wit allows not this large privilege:
Either you must confess, or feel its edge.
Nor shall you make a current inference,
If you transfer your reason to your sense:
Things are distinct, and must the same appear
To every piercing eye, or well-tuned ear.
Though sweets with yours, sharps with my taste meet,
Both must agree this meat's or sharp or sweet:
But if I scent a stench or a perfume,
Whilst you smell nought at all, I may presume
You have that sense imperfect: so you may
Affect a sad, merry, or humorous play,
If, though the kind distaste or please, the good
And bad be by your judgment understood;
But if, as in this play, where with delight
I feast my Epicurean appetite
With relishes so curious, as dispense

The utmost pleasure to the ravished sense,
You should profess that you can nothing meet
That hits your taste, either with sharp or sweet,
But cry out, " 'Tis insipid," your bold tongue
May do its master, not the author, wrong;
For men of better palate will, by it,
Take the just elevation of your wit.

B. INSTABILITY OF PUBLIC DEMAND

Besides the diversity of demand, the rapidity with which play fashions changed contributed to the bedevilment of the playwright; at least so some of them would have us believe.

Lyly. *Midas* (1589). Prol.:

Gentlemen, so nice is the world that for apparel there is no fashion, for music no instrument, for diet no delicate, for plays no invention, but breedeth satiety before noon, and contempt before night.

In a passage already quoted (p. 126), from Middleton's address to the readers of *The Roaring Girl*, a parallel is drawn between fashion changes in clothes and in plays. The parallel is a tempting one, and is resorted to by Heywood in his address to the reader of *Royal King*, printed in 1637, about a score of years after its production (Supra 126).

The same author had been impelled to make the same apology once before, in 1615, to the readers of *The Four Prentices of London* (Supra 126).

The charges brought in these two sections are vague and exaggerated. Fortunately, however, we have a concrete example of the changes wrought between two specific dates. In the winter of 1567-8 the Gentlemen of the Inner Temple presented before the Queen a tragedy entitled *Gismond of Salerne*, written by five members of their body. In 1591 Robert Wilmot, one of the five took the trouble to rewrite the play in order to bring it up to date or, as he puts it, "according to the decorum of these daies." A comparison between the two versions is a most instructive lesson in the development of the English drama between the respective dates.[1] In the later version the diction is altered, the rhymes, except in what might be considered lyrical portions, are dropped for blank verse, the dialogue is more spirited, long speeches are broken up, set devices are introduced,—innovations all making for increased theatrical effectiveness. Prefaced to the revised version is a letter by William Webbe, author of the famous *Discourse*. This epistle being for the purpose of advertisement, the views expressed in it may be regarded as those of Wilmot, even as suggested by him. Here is a relevant extract:

> . . . I cannot sufficiently commend your charitable zeal and scholarly compassion toward him [i. e., the play], that have not only rescued and defended him from the devouring jaws of oblivion, but vouchsafed also to apparel him in a new suit at your own charges, wherein he may again more boldly come abroad, and by permission return to his old parents, clothed, perhaps not in richer or more costly furniture than it went from them, but *in handsomeness and fashion more answerable to these times, wherein fashions are so often altered*. Let one word suffice for your encouragement herein: namely, that your commendable pains in disrobing him of his *antique curiosity*, and adorning him with the approved guise of our stateliest English terms (not diminishing, but more augmenting, his artificial colors of absolute poesy derived from his first parents) cannot but be grateful to most men's appetites, who upon our experience we know highly to esteem such lofty measures of sententiously composed tragedies.

Such phrases as "stateliest English terms," and "lofty measures," make one think of Marlowe, who, in 1587, created an epoch by springing upon the world his *Tamburlaine*, with the much famed vaunt that

> From jigging veins of rhyming mother wits,
> And such conceits as clownage keeps in pay,
> We'll lead you to the stately tent of war,

---

[1] Cf. David Klein, *"According to the Decorum of these Daies."* MLA, XXXIII, 2. 1918.

Where you shall hear the Scythian Tamburlaine
Threat'ning the world with high astounding terms,
And scourging kingdoms with his conquering sword.

The play itself is a Kydian tragedy of blood, though not a typical revenge play.

C. CONTEMPT FOR JUDGMENT OF MASSES

Of course, the playwright aimed to please the public; but his ego found satisfaction in expressing contempt for the judgment of that public, especially the poorer portions of it. Support for his attitude was supplied by Horace. Rule 45 in the list of rules appended to Webbe's *Discourse* reads:

> The common people's judgments of poets is seldom true, and therefore not to be sought after.

Expressions of contempt are numerous; only the more significant ones will be quoted.

Common Conditions (1570). Prol.:

> Yet stays him on this steadfast hope: the wise his simple pain
> Will well accept, and that is all that he doth seek to gain.

Preston. *Sir Clyomon* (1570). Prol.:

> ... our author he is pressed to bide the brunt
> Of babblers' tongues, to whom he thinks is frustrate all his toil,
> As pearls cast filthy swine which in the mire do moil.

Nash. *Will Summer's Last Will and Testament* (1592). Prol.:

> ... as it is the nature of the serpent to hiss, so childhood and igno-
> rance would play the gosling, contemning and condemning wha
> they understood not. Their censures we weigh not whose senses ar
> not yet unswaddled. ... No man pleaseth all: we seek to please one

That Nash's attitude was not one of blind prejudice is indicated by a sober statement made three years earlier in his preface to Greene's *Menaphon*:

> Oft have I observed what I now set down: a secular wit, that hath lived all days of his life by what do you lack, to be more judicial in matters of conceit than our quadrant crepundios that spit *ergo* in the mouth of everyone they meet.

Heywood. *Brazen Age* (1595). End:

> *Homer.*   All we have done we aim at your content,
> Striving to illustrate things not known to all,
> In which the learn'd can censure right;
> The rest we crave, whom we unletter'd call,
> Rather to attend than judge; for more than sight
> We seek to please.

Marston is optimistic about the future of the masses, that now seem hopeless, in *Histriomastix* (bef. 1599). III.:

> *Chrisoganus.*   Write on, cry on, yawl to the common sort
> Of thick-skin'd auditors: such rotten stuffs
> More fit to fill the paunch of Esquiline,
> Than feed the hearings of judicial ears.
> Ye shades, triumph while foggy Ignorance
> Clouds bright Apollo's beauty. Time will clear
> The misty dulness of spectators' eyes.
> Then woeful hisses to your fopperies.

In one instance Marston sought to gain the favor of his audience by defending its judgment against the scorn heaped upon it by onson. *What You Will* (1601). Induction:

> *Doricus.*   What leprous humor
> Breaks from rank swelling of these bubbling wits?
> Now out upon 't. I wonder what tight brain
> Wrung in this custom to maintain contempt
> 'Gainst common censure; to give stiff counterbuffs,
> To crack rude scorn even on the very face
> Of better audience. 'Slight, is't not odious? . .
> Music and poetry were first approved
> By common sense; and that which pleased most

Held most allowed to pass: not rules of art
Were shaped to pleasure, nor pleasure to your rules.
Think you that if his scenes took stamp in mint
Of three or four deemed most judicious,
It would inforce the world to current them,
That you must spit defiance on dislike?
Now, as I love the light, were I to pass
Through public verdict, I should fear my form,
Lest aught I offered were unsquared or warped.

But he did not repeat this flattery. In the prologue and epilogue to *Sophonisba* (1603) he returned to the conventional tune. In the prologue to *The Fawn* (1604) he ironically extols the critical judgment of the audience, and ends up with calling his words "base soothings."

A similar sarcastic vein is employed by Chapman in the prologue and epilogue to *All Fools* (1599). The last lines of the latter read:

We can but bring you meat, and set you stools,
And to our best cheer say, you all are—welcome.

Beaumont, in his verses on *The Fox* (1607), stamps his approval on Jonson's attitude toward public opinion. What is noteworthy is that he directs his abuse, not against the groundlings, nor against the audience as a whole, but against the opinionated gallants who liked to display themselves on the stage:

But since our subtle gallants think it good
To like of nought that may be understood,
Lest they should be disproved, or have, at best
Stomachs so raw that nothing can digest
But what's obscene, or barks, let us desire
They may continue simply to admire
Fine clothes, and strange words; and may live, in age,
To see themselves ill brought upon the stage,
And like it. Whilst thy bold and knowing Muse
Contemns all praise, but such as thou would'st choose.

In his verses on Fletcher's *Faithful Shepherdess* Beaumont gives an amusing description of how the crowd makes up its mind

Why should the man whose wit ne'er had a stain,
Upon the public stage present his vein,
And make a thousand men in judgment sit,
To call in question his undoubted wit,
Scarce two of which can understand the laws
Which they should judge by, nor the party's cause?
Among the rout there is not one that hath
In his own censure an explicit faith:
One company, knowing they judgment lack,
Ground their belief on the next man in black;
Others, on him that makes signs and is mute;
Some like as he does in the fairest suit:
He, as his mistress doth; and she, by chance:
Nor want there those who, as the boy doth dance
Between the acts, will censure the whole play;
Some like, if the wax-lights be new that day;
But multitudes there are whose judgment goes
Headlong according to the actors' clothes.
For this, these public things and I agree
So ill, that, but to do a right to thee,
I had not been persuaded to have hurl'd
These few ill-spoken lines into the world,
Both to be read and censur'd of by those
Whose very reading makes verse senseless prose;
Such as must spend above an hour to spell
A challenge on a post, to know it well.
But since it was thy hap to throw away
Much wit, for which the people did not pay,
Because they saw it not, I not dislike
This second publication, which may strike
Their consciences, to see the thing they scorn'd,
To be with so much wit and art adorn'd.
Besides, one 'vantage more in this I see:
Your censurers must have the quality
Of reading, which I am afraid is more
Than half your shrewdest judges had before.

We know from this why Beaumont stopped writing for the theater. Writing on the same unsuccessful play, Nathaniel Field expresses his indebtedness to Jonson, who taught him to be indifferent to public opinion:

Opinion, that great fool, makes fools of all,
And once I fear'd her, till I met a mind
Whose grave instructions philosophical
Toss'd it like dust upon a March strong wind.
He shall ever my example be, . . .
His soul . . . it should me better satisfy
Than if the monster clapt his thousand hands,
And drown'd the scene with his confused cry.

Thomas Carew. On Davenant's *Just Italian.* (1630) :

Now noise prevails, and he is tax'd for drouth
Of wit, that with the cry spends not his mouth.
Yet, ask reason why he did not like;
Him, why he did: their ignorance will strike
Thy soul with scorn and pity . . .
. . . they'll still slight
All that exceeds Red Bull, or Cock-pit flight. . . .

Middleton. *No Wit, no Help, like a Woman's* (1613). Prol.:

> . . . if attention
Seize you above, and apprehension
You below. . . .

Fletcher. *Hen. VIII* (1613) . V. iv. 64:

> *Porter.* . . These are the youths that thunder at a playhouse and
> fight for bitten apples; that no audience but the Tribulation of
> Tower Hill, or the Limbs of Limehouse, their dear brothers, are
> able to endure.

Next to Jonson, Dekker was the bitterest vilifier of the common
sort. In the proemium to *The Gull's Hornbook* (1609) the poorer
portion of the audience are called "the garlick-mouthed stinkards;" and in the sixth chapter he says that in the theater the poets

> barter away that light commodity of words for a lighter ware than
> words: *plaudites*, and the breath of the great beast; which, like the
> threatenings of two cowards, vanish all into air.

In the prologue to *If This Be not a Good Play* (1610) he speaks
of them with similar contempt:

A play whose rudeness Indians would abhor,
If 't fill a house with fishwives, "Rare," they all roar.
It is not praise is sought for now but pence,
Though dropped from greasy-apron audience.

Daniel. *Musiphilus*:

And for any part if only one allow
The care my laboring spirits take in this,
He is to me a theater large enow,
And his applause only sufficient is.

Fletcher. *Chances*. Epil.:

> Our pains were eas'd
Could we be confident that all rise pleas'd;
But such ambition soars too high. If we
Have satisfied the best, and they agree
In a fair censure, we have our reward.

Marmion. *Fine Companion* (1633). Prol.:

> ... nor need we fear
Any their foul aspersions whilst the wise
Sit to control and judge; in whose clear eyes,
As we deserve, we look to stand or fall,
Passing profaner people.

Ford. *Broken Heart* (1629) . Epil.:

Our writer's aim, in the whole, addrest
Well to deserve of all, but please the best.

Shirley, in the prologue to *The Doubtful Heir* (1640), indulges
in a direct insult to the audience that patronized the Globe:

Our author did not calculate this play
For this meridian. The Bankside, he knows,
Is far more skillful at ebbs and flows
Of water, than of wit.

And in his lines on Massinger's *Renegado* (1630) he declares that
a poor poet is incapable of judging good poetry.

An interesting passage in *2 Return from Parnassus* (1602), IV. iii, satirizes the ignorant actor's opinion of university playwrights:

> *Kemp.* Few of the university pen plays well. They smell too much of that writer Ovid, and that writer Metamorphosis, and talk too much of Proserpina and Jupiter. Why here's our fellow Shakespeare puts them all down; ay, and Ben Jonson too.

The reference to Jonson is ambiguous. What follows would indicate that *Ben Jonson* is in the accusative.

One playwright who almost consistently capitulates to public opinion is Richard Brome. The Epilogue to *Lovesick Court* (1627) begins:

> 'Tis not the poet's art, nor all that we
> By life of action can present unt'ye
> Can justly make us to presume a play
> Is good till you approv't.

It is difficult to believe that a "Son of Ben" really meant what he says here. His real feeling is betrayed in the Prologue to *The Novella* (1632):

> He'll 'bide his trial, and submits his cause
> To you, the jury, so you'll judge by laws.
> If pride or ignorance should rule, he fears
> An unfair trial, 'cause not try'd by's peers.

Other references are the following:

Heywood, *Four Prentices* (1594), Epil.; Tomkis, *Lingua* (1603), Prol.; Chapman, *Rev. of Bussy* (1613), Ded.; Webster, *Devil's Law-Case* (1623), To the Judicious Reader; Fletcher and Massinger, *Fair Maid of the Inn* (1626), Prol.: Robert Tailor, *Hog Hath Lost His Pearl* (1613), Epil.: Ford, *Lover's Melancholy* (1629), Ded.; Ford, *Perkin Warbeck* (1633), Prol.; Ford, on Massinger's *Roman Actor* (1629); Shirley, *Hyde Park* (1637), Ded.; Mayne, *City Match* (1639), Epil.; Shirley, *Coronation* (1635), Prol.; Massinger, *New Way* (1625), Epil.; Randolph, *Eclogue to Master Jonson* (1632).

TYPES OF DRAMA

The longest list of dramatic types is provided by Polonius. Less varied lists are offered by Dekker and Marston.

Dekker. *Gull's Hornbook*:

. . . in the middle of the play, be it pastoral, comedy, moral, or tragedy. . . .

Marston. *What You Will*. Ind.:

Doricus. Is't comedy, tragedy, pastoral, moral, nocturnal, or history?
Phylomuse. Faith, perfectly neither; but even *What You Will*.

There were plays that did not fit into any classification.

Lyly. *Endymion* (1585) . Prol.:

We present neither comedy, nor tragedy, nor story, nor anything.

Nash. *Will Summer's Last Will and Testament* (1592) . Prol.:

Why, he has made a prologue longer than his play: nay, 'tis no play neither, but a show. I'll be sworn. The jig of Rowland's godson is a giant in comparison.

Randolph. *Muses' Looking-Glass* (1634). I iv:

Roscius.   . . . he brings you
No plot at all, but a mere *olla podrida*,
A medley of ill-placed, and worse-penn'd humors.

Shirley. *Cardinal* (1641). Prol.:

> We call it but a play.
> Whether the comic Muse, or ladies' love,
> Romance, or direful tragedy it prove,
> The bill determines not. And would you be
> Persuaded, I would have 't a comedy,
> For all the purple in the name, and state
> Of him that owns it.

Fletcher. *Woman Hater* (1607). Prol.:

> I dare not call it comedy or tragedy; 'tis perfectly neither.
> A play it is, which was meant to make you laugh.

Ibid. *Captain* (1613). Prol.:

> This is nor comedy, nor tragedy,
> Nor history, nor anything that may
> (Yet in a week) be made a perfect play.

Brome. *Jovial Crew* (1641). V i (Prologue to play within play):

> We promise you no dainty wit of court,
> Nor city pageantry, nor country sport;
> But a plain piece of action, short and sweet,
> In a story true.

The medieval view of the difference between tragedy and comedy is thus expressed by Webbe in his *Discourse of English Poetry* (ed. Arber, p. 39) :

There grew at last to be a greater diversity between tragedy writers and comedy writers, the one expressing only sorrowful and lamentable histories, bringing in only the persons of gods and goddesses, and great states, whose parts were chiefly to express most miserable calamities and dreadful chances, which increased worse and worse till they came to the most woeful plight that might be devised. The comedies, on the other side, were directed to a contrary end, which, beginning doubtfully, drew to some trouble or turmoil, and by some lucky chance always ended to the joy and appeasement of all parties.

The distinction is elaborated by John Tomkis in the university play, *Lingua* (1603), IV. ii:

Anamnestes.   These two, my lord, Comedus and Tragedus,
My fellows both, both twins, but so unlike,
As birth to death, wedding to funeral:
For this that rears himself in buskins quaint,
Is pleasant at the first, proud in the midst,
Stately in all, and bitter death at end.
That in the pumps doth frown at first acquaintance,
Trouble in the midst, but in the end concludes,
Closing up all with a sweet catastrophe.
This grave and sad, distained with brinish tears;
That light and quick, with wrinkled laughter painted;
This deals with nobles, kings and emperors,
Full of great fears, great hopes, great enterprises:
This other trades with men of mean condition,
His projects small, small hopes, and dangers little;

This gorgeous, broidered with rich sentences;
That fair and purfled round with merriments.
Both vice detect, and virtue beautify,
By being death's mirror, and life's looking-glass.

Randolph. *Muses' Looking-Glass* (1634). I. iii:

Upon our stage two glasses oft there be:
The comic mirror and the tragedy.
The comic glass is full of merry strife,
The low reflection of a country life.
Grave tragedy, void of such homely sports,
Is the sad glass of cities and of courts.

The next scene in this play is taken up with contentions between two pairs of contestants; one, Tragedy and Comedy; the
other, their respective attendants, Satire and Mime. The whole
scene is worth quoting. I shall confine myself to leading passages.

   Tragedy. I stalk in princes' courts: great kings and emperors,
From their close cabinets and council tables,
Yield me the fatal matters of my scene.
   Comedy. Inferior persons and the lighter vanities
(Of which this age, I fear, has grown too fruitful)
Yield subjects various enough to move
Plentiful laughter.
   Tra.   Laughter! a fit object
For poetry to aim at!
   Com. Yes, laughter is my object: 'tis a property
In man essential to his reason.
   Tra.   So;
But I move horror, and that frights the guilty
From his dear sins. . . .
   Com. You move with fear; I work as much with shame—
A thing more powerful in a generous breast. . . .
   Tra. The subject of my scene is in the persons
Greater, as in the vices: atheists, tyrants,
O'erdaring favorites, traitors, parasites,
The wolves and cats of state, which in a language
High as the men, and loud as are their crimes,
I thunder forth with terror and amazement
Unto the ghastly wondering audience. . . .

    Satire.   And, as my lady takes deserved place
Of thy light mistress, so yield thou to me,
Fantastic Mime.
    Mime.   Fond Satire, why to thee?
    Sat.   As the attendant of the nobler dame,
And of myself more worthy.
    Mime.   How more worthy?
    Sat.   As one, whose whip of steel can with a lash
Imprint the characters of shame so deep,
Even in the brazen forehead of proud sin,
That not eternity shall wear it out.
When I but frown'd in my Lucilius' brow,
Each conscious cheek grew red, and a cold trembling
Freez'd the chill soul; while every guilty breast
Stood fearful of dissection. . . .

It is interesting to note that satire is attendant upon tragedy,
not comedy.

The medieval conception of tragedy as a fall, is consciously ap-
proximated in Fletcher's *Henry VIII*, and Ford's *Perkin Warbeck*.

Henry VIII (1612). Prol.:

                Think you see them great
And follow'd with the general throng and sweat
Of thousand friends; then, in a moment, see
How soon this mightiness meets misery.

Perkin Warbeck (1633). Epil.:

Here has appear'd though in several fashion,
The threats of majesty, the strength of passion,
Hopes of an empire, change of fortunes; all
What can to theaters of greatness fall,
Proving their weak foundations.

In Tourneur's *Atheist's Tragedy* (1603), II. iv., (Mermaid ed.
p. 277) a rule from the Latin grammar is utilized to give a comic
twist to the medieval conception of comedy:

    D'Amville.   Here's a sweet comedy. 'T begins with *O Dolentis*
and concludes with ha, ha, he!

Tomkis. *Lingua* (1603). IV. viii.:

> *Lingua.* Why, this is good. By Common Sense's means,
> Lingua, thou has framed a perfect comedy.
> They are all good friends, whom thou mad'st enemies.

May. *Heir* (1620). V., near end:

> *1st. Judge.* How suddenly this tragic scene is chang'd,
> And turn'd to comedy.

We have an uncritical feeling that sorrow is something nobler, something profounder, than joy; hence we instinctively place tragedy at the top of the list of dramatic forms. So did the Elizabethans.

Kyd. *Spanish Tragedy* (1583). IV. i.:

> *Balthazar.* Hieronimo, methinks a comedy were better.
> *Hier...* A comedy?
> Fie! comedies are fit for common wits;
> But to present a kingly troop withal,
> Give me a stately-written tragedy;
> *Tragoedia cothurnata,* fitting kings,
> Containing matter, and not common things.

Marston. *What You Will* (1601). V. i.:

> *Quadratus.*   A comedy?
> No! and thy sense would banquet in delights
> Appropriate to the blood of emperors,
> Peculiar to the state of majesty,
> That none can relish but dilated greatness,
> Vouchsafe to view the structure of a scene
> That stands on tragic solid passion;
> Oh, that's fit traffic to commerce with births,
> Strained from the mud of base unable brains.
> Give them a scene may force their struggling blood
> Rise up on tiptoe in attention,
> And fill their intellect with pure elixed wit.
> Oh, that's for greatness apt, for princes fit.

Marston has used more words than Kyd—has he said any more?

Heywood. *Apology for Actors* (1612). Melpomene's speech:

Who lodge them in the bosom of great kings,
Save he that had a grave cothurnate muse?
A stately verse in an iambic style
Became a kesar's mouth.

Tragedy could not compete in popularity with comedy and history. In Spenser's *Tears of the Muses*, written before 1591, Melpomene complains:

My part it is and my professed skill
The stage with tragic buskin to adorn,
And fill the scene with plaint, and outcries shrill
Of wretched persons to misfortune born; . . .
So all with rueful spectacles is fild,
Fit for Megaera or Persephone;
But I, that in true tragedies am skild,
The flower of wit, find nought to busy me.

In the Induction to Lodge's *Warning for Fair Women* (1598), Tragedy exclaims to Comedy and History:

'Tis you have kept the theater so long
Painted in playbills upon every post,
While I am scorned of the multitude.

Ibid.:

　History.　And, Comedy, except thou canst prevail,
I think she means to banish us the stage.
　Comedy.　Tut, tut, she cannot; she may for a day
Or two, perhaps, be at some request;
But once a week if we do not appear,
She shall find few will attend her here.

Middleton, Dekker. *Roaring Girl* (1610). Prol.:

A Roaring Girl. . . .
Shall fill with laughter our vast theater.
That's all which I dare promise: tragic passion,
And such grave stuff, is this day out of fashion.

The presence of death was the characteristic of a tragedy. The nature of the following extracts would indicate that the writer had in mind the so-called Tragedy of Blood. In the Chorus preceding Kyd's *Soliman and Perseda* (1588), Death asks:

And what are tragedies but acts of Death?

and after the last act he turns to his two companions:

Pack, Love and Fortune! play in comedies;
For powerful Death best fitteth tragedies.

Tourneur. *Revenger's Tragedy* (1605). III. iv.:

Vendice. When the bad bleeds, then is the tragedy good.

Nath. Richards, on Rawlins' *The Rebellion* (1640):

Plots meet with counterplots, revenge, and blood,
Rebels' ruin, makes thy tragedy good.

Lodge. *Warning for Fair Women* (1598). Ind.:

... some damn'd tyrant, to obtain a crown,
Stabs, hangs, imprisons, smothers, cutteth throats.
And then a Chorus, too, comes howling in
And tells us of the worrying of a cat.
Then, too, a filthy whining ghost,
Lapt in some foul sheet or a leather pilch,
Comes screaming in, like a pig half-stick'd,
And cries "Vindicta! Revenge! Revenge!"

Massinger. *Maid of Honor* (1622). II. iv.:

Soldier. And if you please to be spectators of
The horrid scene, I will bring you where,
As in a theater, you may see their fates
In purple gore presented.

Dekker, Day, Haughton. *Lust's Dominion*. V. ii, 119:

Eleazar... I will have Philip's head, Hortenzo's head,
Mendoza's head, thy mother's head, and this,
This head that is so cross, I'll have't:

The scene wants actors; I'll fetch more, and clothe it
In rich cothurnal pomp. A tragedy
Ought to be grave, graves this shall beautify.

And now for the most charming quotation of all.

Greene. *Selimus* (1588). Epilogue:

If this first part, gentles, do like you well,
The second part shall greater murthers tell.

The inferior position of comedy was taken for granted. Marston
repeatedly speaks of his comedies as slight trifles.

Nash. *Will Summer's Last Will and Testament* (1592). Prol.:

Dydimus wrote four thousand books, or (as some say) six thousand,
on the art of grammar. Our author hopes it may be as lawful for
him to write a thousand lines of as light a subject.

Massinger. *Roman Actor* (1626). I i:

  Paris. The Greeks, to whom we owe the first invention
Both of the buskin'd scene and humble sock.

Marston. *Fawn* (1606). To the Reader:

If any desire to understand the scope of my comedy, know it hath
the same limits which Juvenal gives his satires:
    Quicquid agunt homines, votum, timor, ira, voluptas,
    Gaudia, discursus, nostri farrago libelli est.

Fletcher. *Woman's Prize* (1606). Prol.:

We do entreat the angry men would not
Expect the mazes of a subtle plot,
Set speeches, high expressions, and, what's worse
In a true comedy, politic discourse.

Comedy must have a happy ending.

2 Return from Parnassus (1602). Near end:

Ingenioso.   Nay, stay a while, and help me to content
So many gentle wits' attention,
Who ken the laws of every comic stage,
And wonder that our scene ends discontent.

Beaumont. *Knight of the Burning Pestle* (1607). V iii:

Wife.   Now, good husband, let him come out and die.
Cit.   He shall, Nell.—Ralph, come away quickly, and die, boy!
Boy.   'Twill be very unfit he should die, sir, upon no occasion—
and in a comedy too.

Middleton. *Mayor of Quinborough* (1596). V i:

Simon.   . . . Call you this a merry comedy, when a man's eyes are
put out in it?

Middleton here is poking fun at the practice of early title-pages
to describe a play as merry, when it was a confusion of horse-play
and tragedy.

Field. *Woman is a Weathercock* (1611). II i:

Katherine.   Nay, I'll think
As abjectly of thee as any mongrel
Bred in the city: such a citizen
As the plays flout still, and is made the subject
Of all the stages.

Ibid. III ii:

Saudmore.   What an internal joy my heart has felt,
Sitting at one of these same idle plays,
When I have seen a maid's inconstancy
Presented to the life!

Grazzini. *Bugbears.* V iv:

Donatus.   . . . if it fall
As we have devised, the case is such
That easily thereof a man might make a comedy.

194

Middleton, Rowley. *Spanish Gypsy* (1623). II i:

> *Cardochia.*   People already throng into the inn,
> And call for you into their private rooms.
> *Alvarez.*   No chamber-comedies.

Day, in *Humor out of Breath* (1608), I ii, presents an argument that would appeal to management:

> *Aspero.*   Your low comedy
> Craves but few actors.

Tomkis. *Albumazar* (1614). IV ii:

> *Antonio.*   Laughter proceeds
> From absurd actions that are harmless.

What was said on the subject of the chronicle play, or history, has been included in the section on material, including Nash's eloquent advocacy. Here may be added a passage from Peele's *David and Bethsabe* (1589), beginning with line 1577, which indicates the elastic nature of this type:

> *Chorus.*   Now, since this story lends us other store,
> To make a third discourse of David's life,
> Adding thereto his most renowned death,
> And all their deaths that at his death he judg'd,
> Here end we this.

Of the remaining types the tragicomedy is the most important. Though the name identifies the kind of play usually associated with Beaumont and Fletcher, they did not invent it. It was used by the earlier playwrights to describe the confused mixture of tragic and comic that then prevailed. What Fletcher meant by it is explained in a noteworthy statement (borrowed, according to Thorndike, from Guarini) in his preface to *The Faithful Shepherdess* (1610). As the play is at the same time a pastoral, that term too is explained:

> If you be not reasonably assured of your knowledge in this kind of poem, lay down the book, or read this, which I wish had been the

prologue. It is a pastoral tragicomedy, which the people seeing when it was first played, having ever a singular gift in defining, concluded to be a play of country-hired shepherds, in grey cloaks, with curtailed dogs in strings, sometimes laughing together and sometimes killing one another; and, missing whitsun-ales, cream, wassail, and morris-dances, began to be angry. In their error I would not have you fall, lest you incur their censure. Understand, therefore, a pastoral to be a representation of shepherds and shepherdesses, with their actions and passions, which must be such as may agree with their nature, at least not exceeding former fictions and vulgar traditions. They are not to be adorned with any art, but such improper ones as nature is said to bestow, as singing and poetry; or such experience may teach them, as the virtues of herbs and fountains, the ordinary course of the sun, moon, and stars, and such like. But you are ever to remember shepherds to be such as all the ancient poets, and modern, of understanding, have received them; that is, the owners of flocks, and not hirelings. A tragicomedy is not so called in respect of mirth and killing, but in respect it wants deaths, which is enough to make it no tragedy, yet brings some near it, which is enough to make it no comedy, which must be a representation of familiar people, with such kind of troubles as no life be questioned; so that a god is as lawful in this as in a tragedy, and mean people as in a comedy.

Dekker. *Satiromastix* (1602). Hawkins ed., p. 186:

> *Crispinus.*   My liege, to wed a comical event
> To presupposed tragic argument,
> Vouchsafe to exercise your eyes.

In *The Royal Master* (1638), II i, Shirley describes in uncomplimentary terms the contemporary method of constructing a masque. This was after the passing of Ben Jonson.

> *Bombo.*   ... though I appear not in't,
> I may have a humor to make a masque, if they stay supper.
> *Iacomo.*   Thou make a masque!
> *Bom.*   I do not say I'll write one, for I have not
> My writing tongue, though I could once have read:
> But can give, if need be, the design,
> Make work among the deal boards, and perhaps
> Can teach them as good language as another

Of competent ignorance. Things go not now
By learning. I have read, 'tis but to bring
Some pretty impossibilities for anti-masques,
A little sense and wit disposed with thrift,
With here and there monsters to make them laugh:
For the grand business, to have Mercury,
Or Venus' dandiprat, to usher in
Some of the gods, that are good fellows, dancing,
Or goddesses; and now and then a song,
To fill a gap:—a thousand crowns, perhaps,
For him that made it, and there's all the wit!
    Iac.   In what?
    Bom.   In getting of the money.

MIXTURE OF TYPES

The practice of mingling the comic with the serious in the English drama went back to the Middle Ages, when the Expositor in the Scriptural play informed the spectators that, "only to make sport," some things would be included that were "not warranted by any writ." The examples afforded by the extant early modern plays represent something far removed from an artistic fusion, and justified academic strictures on the vogue. The crude manner in which the clown (whose antics caused even Shakespeare to protest) is lugged into the action of a play, is delightfully satirized in the university play, *A Pilgrimage to Parnassus* (1598), V 671:

Enter Dromo, drawing a clown in with a rope.

Clown.   What now? thrust a man into the commonwealth whether he will or no? What the devil should I do here?

Dromo.   Why, what an ass art thou! Dost thou not know a play cannot be without a clown? Clowns have been thrust into plays by head and shoulders ever since Kemp could make a scurvy face; and therefore reason thou shouldst be drawn in with a cart-rope.

Clown.   But what must I do now?

Dromo.   Why, if thou canst but draw thy mouth awry, lay thy leg over thy staff, saw a piece of cheese asunder with thy dagger, lap up drink on the earth, I'll warrant thee they'll laugh mightily. Well, I'll turn thee loose to them; either say somewhat for thyself, or hang and be *non plus.*

Clown.   This is fine, i' faith! Now, when they have nobody to leave on the stage, they bring me up, and, which is worse, tell me not what I should say! Gentles, I dare say you look for a fit of mirth. I'll therefore present unto you a proper new love-letter of mine to the tune of *Put on the Smock o' Monday,* which in the heat of my charity I penned; and thus it begins: [The song he sings is in prose]

How like you, masters? Has any young man a desire to copy

this . . . ? Now, if I could but make a fine scurvy face, I were a king!
O nature, why didst thou give me so good a look? (*He whistles.*)
Dromo (*Re-enters*). Give us a voider! Sirrah, you must begone:
here are other men that will supply the room.
Clown. Why shall I not whistle out my whistle? Then farewell,
gentle auditors, and the next time you see me I'll make you better
sport.

In the foregoing burlesque three things are emphasized: the
essential superfluousness of the clown, his popularity, and his practice of extemporizing. Concerning the last two we have other
references.

Chapman. *M. D'Olive* (1604). IV i:

Rhoderique. Here we may strike the *plaudite* to our play; my
lord fool's gone—all our audience will forsake us.

Anon. *Parricide* (1624). Prol.:

Most like no play but such as gives large birth
To that which they judiciously call mirth;
Nor will the best works with their liking crown,
Except it be graced with part of fool or clown.

Middleton. *A Mad World* (1606). V ii:

Sir Bounteous. . . . they put all their fools to the constable's part
still.

Ibid. *Mayor of Quinborough* (1596). V i:

2nd Player.   *The Cheater and the Clown.*
Simon.   Is that come up again?
That was a play when I was apprentice first.
2nd Player.   Ay, but the cheater has learn'd more tricks of late,
And puts the clown to new additions.

Nash. *Pierce Penniless* (1592). Collier ed., p. 44:

Tarlton at the theater made jest at him [Gabriel Harvey].

Ibid. *Will Summer's Last Will and Testament* (1592). Prol.:

Will Sum. God forgive me, I did not see my lord before! I'll set a good face on it, as though what I had talked idly all this while were my part. . . . I play no more than you hear, and some of that you heard (by your leave) was extempore.

Davenport. *City Night-Cap* (1624). IV i:

Clown. Now to our masque's name; but first be it known-a
When I name a city I mean only Verona.—
Those two lines are extempore, I protest, sir. I brought them in because here are some of other cities in the room that might snuff pepper else.

Brome. *Antipodes* (1638):

Letoy. I think all perfect
But one, that never will be perfect in any thing
He studies; yet he makes such shifts extempore
(Knowing his purpose what he is to speak to)
That he moves mirth in me above all the rest.

Ibid.

Quaylpipe. But you, sir, are incorrigible, and
Take license to yourself to add unto
Your parts your own free fancy; and sometimes
To alter, or diminish what the writer
With care and skill compos'd! And when you are
To speak to your co-actors in the scene,
You hold interlocutions with the audience.
By-Play. That is a way, my lord, has been allow'd
On elder stages to move mirth and laughter.
Letoy. Yes, in the days of Tarlton and Kemp,
Before the stage was purg'd from barbarism,
And brought to the perfection it now shines with,
The fools and jesters spent their wits, because
The poets were wise enough to save their own
For profounder uses.

Perhaps we should not lose sight of the fact that that perio<

of barbarism, not this period of perfection, was the period of Shakespeare.

Aside from the inartistic intrusion of the clown, the inclusion of comic elements in serious matter was favorably regarded. Indeed, it was defended by Gager in a letter to Rainolds (1592),[1] and had the blessing of Sidney, who advances a curious argument in its favor:

> . . . some poesies have coupled together two or three kinds; as the tragical and comical, whereupon is risen the tragicomical; some have mingled matters heroical and pastoral; but that cometh all to one in this question; for, if severed they be good, then conjunction cannot be hurtful.

For a century and a half dramatists were articulate on the subject of mixture of types, yet the result is disappointing; for no higher esthetic principle was developed in its defense than that the audience demanded it; although examples were produced from which such a principle might have been induced.

Henry Medwell. *Fulgens and Lucres* (1497). Pt. 2, 21:

All be it that there was
Dyvers toyes mengled yn the same
To styre folke to myrthe and game
And to do them solace;
The which tryfyllis be impertinent
To the matter principall,
But never the lesse they be expedient
For to satisfye and content
Many a man withall.
For some there be that lokis & gapys
Only for suche tryfles and Iapys,
And some there be amonge
That forceth lytyll of such madness
But delytyth them in matter of sadnes
Be it never so longe.
And euery man must haue hys mynde,
Ellis thay will many fautys fynde

---

[1] In Karl Young. *An Elizabethan Defence of the Stage,* p. 123. Shakespeare Studies. University of Wisconsin, 1916.)

And say the play was nought.
But no force I care not,
For god knoweth my thought:
It is the mynde and intent
Of me and my company to content
The leste that stondyth here,
And so I trust ye wyll it alowe.

Rastell. *Gentleness and Nobility*:

. . . compiled in the maner of an interlude with divers toys and gestes addyt thereto to make mery pastyme and disport.

In *The Conflict of Conscience* (1560), as the Prologue explains, Nathaniel Woodes introduces comedy out of consideration for his audience, but with proper decorum:

And though the history of itself be too-too dolorous,
And would constrain a man with tears of blood his cheeks to wet,
Yet to refresh the minds of them that be the auditors,
Our author intermixed hath, in places fit and meet,
Some honest mirth, yet always 'ware decorum to exceed.

Edwards. *Damon and Pythias* (1564). Prol.:

Which matter mixed with mirth and care, a just name to apply,
As seems most fit, we have it termed a tragical comedy.

Fulwell. *Like Will to Like* (1568). Prol.:

And because divers men of divers minds be,
Some do matters of mirth and pastime require;
Other some are delighted with matters of gravity;
To please all men is our author's chief desire;
Wherefore mirth with measure to sadness is annexed,
Desiring that none here at our matter will be perplexed . .
And sith mirth for sadness is a sauce most sweet,
Take mirth then with measure that best sauceth it.

Preston. *Lamentable Tragedy of Cambises* (pr. 1570). Title page:

A lamentable tragedy mixed full of pleasant mirth.

Common Conditions (1570). Prol.:

But this I show most strange it is, and pitiful beside,
Mixt both with mirth and pleasant shows.

Whetstone. *Promos and Cassandra* (1578). Ded.:

. . . intermingling all these actions in such sort as the grave matter
may instruct and the pleasant delight; for without this change the
attention would be small, and the liking less.

Lyly. *Midas* (1589). Prol.:

. . . all cometh to this pass, that what heretofore hath been served in
several dishes for a feast, is now minced in a charger for a gallimaufry. If we present a mingle-mangle, our fault is to be excused,
because the whole world is become an hodge-podge.

Greene. *James IV* (1590). Chorus after III:

The rest is ruthful; yet, to beguile the time,
'Tis interlac'd with merriment and rhyme.

Drayton. *Merry Devil* (1600). Prol.:

Sit with a pleased eye, until you know
The comic end of our sad tragic show.

Webster. *White Devil* (1612). III ii:

Francisco.   My tragedy must have some idle mirth in 't,
Else it will never pass.

Middleton. *No Wit, No Help, like a Woman's* (1613). Prol.:

We shall both make you sad and tickle ye.

Middleton, Rowley. *World Tost at Tennis* (1619). Prol.:

This our device we do not call a play,
Because we break the stage's laws today

Of acts and scenes: sometimes a comic strain
Hath hit delight home in a master-vein,
Thalia's prize; Melpomene's sad style
Hath shook the tragic hand another while;
The Muse of History hath caught your eyes,
And she that chants the pastoral psalteries:
We now lay claim to none, yet all present,
Seeking out pleasure to find your content.

Thomas May. On Shirley's *Wedding* (1629):

> ... high-raised passion
> Temper'd with harmless mirth.

Ford. *Broken Heart* (1629). III v:

Penthea.   ... on the stage
Of my mortality my youth hath acted
Some scenes of vanity, drawn out at length
By varied pleasures, sweeten'd in the mixture,
But tragical in the issue.

Kirke. *Seven Champions of Christendom* (pr. 1638). Ded.:

The nature of the work being history, it consists of many parts; not walking in one direct path of comedy or tragedy, but having a larger field to trace; which, methinks, should yield more pleasure to the reader, novelty and variety being the only objects these our times are taken with: the tragedy may be too dull and stolid, the comedy too sharp and bitter; but a well mixed portion of either would make the sweetest harmony.

Fletcher. *Loyal Subject*. Prol. (not by Fletcher):

The mirth join'd with grave matter, and intent
To yield the hearers profit with delight.

There are several dissenting voices, though rather mild ones

Gascoigne. *Certain Notes* (1575). ed. Arber, p. 32:

... to intermingle merry jests in a serious matter is an indecorum

Fletcher, Massinger. *Custom of the Country* (1619). Prol.:

A well-drawn piece, which gave a lawful birth
To passionate scenes, mix'd with no vulgar mirth.

Ford. *Perkin Warbeck* (1635). Prol.:

     ... nor is here
Unnecessary mirth forc'd to endear
A multitude.

NAMING A PLAY

An amused interest was shown in titles. The available utterances would indicate that the playwrights were interested, not in
their appropriateness, but in their publicity value.

Heywood. *Four Prentices of London* (1594). Prol.:

I come to excuse the name of the play.

Marston. *Histriomastix* (bef. 1599). II 216:

Usher.   One of you answer. The names of your plays?
Post-Hast.   *Mother Gurton's Neddle* (a tragedy), . . .
Usher.   I promise ye, pretty names.

Marston. *What You Will* (1601). Ind.:

Atticus.   What's the Play's Name?
Phylomuse.   *What You Will.*
Doricus.   Is 't comedy, tragedy, pastoral, moral, nocturnal, or
history?
Phy.   Faith, perfectly neither, but even *What You Will.*

R. Tailor. *The Hog Hath Lost His Pearl* (1613). I i:

Player.   . . . I pray you, sir, what is the title you bestow upon it?
Haddit.   Marry, that which is full as forcible as *Garlic*: the name
of it is, *Who Buys My Four Ropes of Hard Onions?* by which four
ropes, is meant. . . .

Middleton. *The Witch.* IV i:

Almachildes. . . . If I trust her as she's a woman, let one of her long hairs wind about my heart, and be the end of me: which were a piteous lamentable tragedy, and might be entitled, *A Fair Warning for All Hair-Bracelets.*

Shirley. *Bird in a Cage* (1633). Dedication, to Wm. Prynne:

I take delight to think (not without imitation of yourself, who have ingeniously fancied such elegant apposite names for your own compositions, as *Health's Sickness, The Unloveliness of Love-Locks,* &c.) how aptly I may present you at this time with *The Bird in a Cage.*

Ibid. IV i:

Donella. . . . imagine our scene expressed, and *The New Prison,* the title, advanced in form.
Eugenia. *The New Prison!* Why?
Donella. O, 'tis an excellent name.

Shirley. *Doubtful Heir* (originally entitled *Rosania, or Love's Victory)* (1640) . 1st Prol.:

Rosania? methinks I hear one say,
What's that? 'Tis a strange title to a play,
One asks his friend who late from travel came,
What 'tis, supposing it some country's name;
Who, rather than acknowledge ignorance,
Perhaps says 'tis some pretty town in France,
Or Italy, and wittily discloses
'Twas call'd Rosania for the store of roses.
A witty comment:—others, that have seen,
And fashionably observ'd the English scene,
Say (but with less hope to be understood)
Such titles unto plays are now the mood,
Aglaura, Claricilla,—names that may
 (Being ladies) grace, and bring guests to the play.

Davenant. *The Platonic Lovers.* (1635). Prol.:

'Tis worth my smiles to think what enforc'd ways
And shifts each poet hath to help his plays.

Ours now believes the title needs must cause
From the indulgent court a kind applause. . . .
And then, forsooth, he says because 'tis new
'Twill take. . . .
But all these easy hopes I'd like t'have marr'd,
With witnessing his title was so hard
'Bove half our city audience would be lost,
That know not how to spell it on the post.
Nay, he was told some critics lately spent
Their learning to find out it nothing meant.

An exception must be made in the case of Nathaniel Woodes.
In the Prologue to *The Conflict of Conscience* he affirms that it is
obvious that the title must fit the play:

And for because we see by proof, that men do soon forget
Those things for which to call them by no name at all they know,
Our author, for to help short wits, did think it very meet
Some name for this his comedy in preface for to show.
Now names to natures must agree, as every man do know,
A fitter name he could in mind no where excogitate,
Than *The Conflict of Conscience* the same to nominate.

PROLOGUE, EPILOGUE, CHORUS, DUMB SHOW

Comments on these features are numerous, and usually of a derogatory nature. Only a few of the more individual ones are worth quoting. An objective comment which probably represents public opinion, is found in J. Barbier's *Ianua Linguarum Quadralinguis, or, A Mess of Tongues* (1617) :

> . . . in a comedy the prologue, or in a tragedy the chorus, is not for the most acute spectator; able (and more delighted) of himself to discern the pretension of every act presented.

Return from Parnassus, Pt. 1 (1601) . Prol.:

Prologue. Gentle—
Stage Keeper. How, gentle? say, you cringing parasite,
That scraping leg, that dropping curtsy,
That fawning bow, those sycophant smooth terms,
Gained our stage much favor, did they not? . . .
Sirrah, begone! you play no prologue here,
Call no rude hearer *gentle, debonaire.*
We'll spend no flattering on this carping crowd,
Nor with gold terms make each rude dullard proud.

Fletcher. *Humorous Lieutenant* (1619). Prol.:

Wou'd some man wou'd instruct me what to say:
For this same prologue, usual to a play,
Is tied to such an old form of petition,
Men must say nothing now beyond commission.
The cloaks we wear, the legs we make, the place
We stand in, must be one; and one face,
Nor alter'd nor exceeded; if it be,
A general hiss hangs on our levity.

In the prologue to *The Goblins* (1638), Suckling declaims against the recent demand for prologues and epilogues that in themselves have literary value:

Wit in a prologue poets justly may
Style a new imposition on a play.

Massinger. *Unnatural Combat* (pr. 1639). Ded.:

I present you with this old tragedy, without prologue or epilogue, it being composed in a time (and that too, peradventure, as knowing as this) when such by-ornaments were not advanced above the fabric of the whole work.

Fletcher, Massinger. *Custom of the Country* (1619) . Epil.:

Why there should be an epilogue to a play,
I know no cause. . . . The old and usual way,
For which they were made, was to entreat the grace
Of such as were spectators. In this place,
And time, 'tis to no purpose; for, I know,
What you resolve already to bestow
Will not be alter'd, whatsoe'er I say
In the behalf of us and of our play.

The same thought is expressed in the epilogues to Massinger's *Very Woman* and *Bashful Lover*. Other references: Fulwell, *Like Will to Like*, Prol.; Nash, *Will Summer*, Prol.; Marston, *Histriomastix*, II; Beaumont, *Woman Hater*, Prol.; Massinger, *Fatal Dowry*, IV iii; Fletcher, *Nice Valor*, Prol.; Massinger, *Believe as You List*, Epil.; Heywood, *Four Prentices*, Prol.; Shirley, *Birds in a Cage*, IV ii; *Imposture*, Prol.; Kyd, *Spanish Tragedy*, IV 340; Middleton, *Mayor of Quinborough*, II i Chorus; Fletcher, *Prophetess*, IV i Chorus; Munday, *Downfall of Huntington*, I iii; Middleton, *Mad World*, V (Dods. 349) .

ACTING

As we would expect, acting, the medium through which the playwright contacts his public, is the related topic on which the playwrights expressed themselves most frequently. This of course is a subject on which the academic critic would have little to say.

In recent years the attempt has been made to demonstrate that Elizabethan acting was formal and artificial. The citations here given prove overwhelmingly that the aim was to reproduce life as closely as possible.

Edwards. *Damon and Pythias* (1564). Prol.:

With speeches well pronounced, with action lively framed.

Kyd. *Spanish Tragedy* (1583). IV 279:

King.　　How well he acts his amorous passion.

Marston. *Histriomastix* (bef. 1599) . V:

Soldier.　'Slid, how do you march?
Sirrah, is this you would rend and tear a cat
Upon a stage, and now march like a drown'd rat?
Look up and play the Tamburlaine, you rogue, you.

The Induction to Marston's *Antonio and Mellida* (1600) , is a delightful chat among the actors, giving much information regarding the careful fitting of parts and the training of actors, even in such details as accent and gesture. It is too long to be included here, but it will be quoted in the proper place.

In his *History of the University of Cambridge,* Thomas Fuller gives an entertaining description of a performance there in 1600, of the university play, *Club Law*. The town officials against whom the students have a grudge, have been invited to a play which turns out to be a satire on themselves:

> A convenient place was assigned to the towns-folk (rivetted in with scholars on all sides) where they might see and be seen. Here they did behold themselves in their own best clothes (which the scholars had borrowed) so lively personated—their habits, gestures, language, lieger-jests and expressions, that it was hard to decide which was the true Townsman, whether he that sat by, or he who acted on the stage. Sit still they could not from chafing, go out they could not for crowding, but impatiently patient were fain to attend till dismissed at the end of the comedy.

It would seem, would it not? that if formal acting prevailed anywhere it would at the university.

Chapman. *Gentleman Usher* (1601). I i 199:

Sarpego.   When I in Padua school'd it,
I play'd in one of Plautus' comedies,
Namely, *Curculio,* where his part I acted,
Projecting from the poor sum of four lines
Forty fair actions.
Alphonso.   Let's see that, I pray.
Sarp.   Your Highness shall command.
But pardon me if in my action's heat,
Entering in post post haste, I chance to take up
Some of your honor'd heels. . . .
You must imagine, lords, I bring good news,
Whereof being princely proud I scour the street,
And overtumble every man I meet. . . .
Alph.   How like you, lords, this stirring action?
Strozza.   In a cold morning it were good, my lord,
But something harsh upon repletion.

Ibid. I i 228:

Medice.   My lord, away with these scholastic wits;
Lay the invention of your speech on me.
And the performance too; I'll play my part
That you shall say, Nature yields more than Art.

Alph.   Be't so resolv'd, unartificial truth
An unfeign'd passion can decipher best.

Ibid. I i 234:

Vincentio.   But 'twill be hard, my lord, . . .
          . . . to make a speech
As a pretended actor, without clothes
More gracious than your doublet and your hose.
Alph.   What, think you, son, we mean t'express a speech
Of special weight without a like attire?

Ibid. I ii 15:

Bassiolo.   Are all parts perfect?
Sarpego.   One I know there is.
Lasso.   And that is yours . . .
Bas.   Nay, he will be perfection itself
For wording well, and dextrous action too.
Las.   And will these waggish pages hit their songs?
Pages.   *Re, mi, fa, sol, la.*
Las.   Oh they are practicing; good boys, well done.
But where is Poggio? There y'are overshot,
To lay a capital part upon his brain,
Whose absence tells me plainly he'll neglect him.
Bas.   Oh no, my lord, he dreams of nothing else,
And gives it out in wagers he'll excel.

Ibid. II i 169:

Bassiolo.   Hence, ye brats!
You stand upon your tire; but for your action
Which you must use in singing of your songs
Exceeding dextrously and full of life,
I hope you'll then stand like a sort of blocks,
Without due motion of your hands and heads,
And wresting your whole bodies to your words.

Chapman. *May-Day* (1602). III iii 73:

Lodovico.   Coz, coz, thou hast acted thy dissembling part long enough, in the most modest judgment, and passing naturally.

Marston. *What You Will* (1601). II i:

Pedagogue. I was solicited to grant him leave to play the lady in comedies presented by children; but I knew his voice was too small, and his stature too low.

2 Return from Parnassus (1601) . IV iii:

Burbage. Now, Will Kemp, if we can intertain these scholars at a low rate, it will be well. They have oftentimes a good conceit in a part.
Kemp. It's true indeed, honest Dick; but the slaves are somewhat proud. Besides, it is good sport in a part to see them never speak in their walk, but at the end of the stage; just as though in walking with a fellow we should never speak but at a stile, a gate, or a ditch, where a man can go no further. I was once at a comedy in Cambridge, and there I saw a parasite make faces and mouths of all sorts on this fashion.
Bur. A little teaching will mend these faults.

A passage in John Tomkis' *Lingua* (1603) , IV ii, illustrates in what estimation stereotyped acting was held by Common Sense. Comedus starts reciting the prologue to Plautus' *Menaechmi,* but is interrupted by Phantastes, who wants an exhibition of action:

Phan. Pish, pish, this is a speech with no action. Let's hear Terence: *Quid igitur faciam,* etc.
Com. *Quid igitur faciam? non eam? ne nunc quidem,*
Cum arcessor ultro?
Phan. Fie, fie, fie, no more action! Lend me your bays.
Do it thus. *Quid igitur,* etc.
    [*He acts it after the old kind of pantomimic action.*]
Communis Sensus. I should judge this action, Phantastes, most absurd; unless we should come to a comedy, as gentlewomen to the Commencement, only to see men speak.
Phan. In my imagination 'tis excellent; for in this kind the hand, you know, is harbinger to the tongue, and provides the words a lodging in the ears of the auditors.

Chapman. *Widow's Tears* (1605). III ii:

Tharsalio. Is he perfect in's part? Has not his tongue learned of the Sylvans to trip o'th' toe?

Argus.   Sir, believe it, he does it preciously for accent and action, as if he felt the part he played. He ravishes all the young wenches in the palace.

Dekker, Webster. *Northward Ho* (1605):

Doll.   Hornet, now you play my father, take heed you be not out of your part, and shame your adopted daughter.

The importance of preparation for apparently spontaneous acting is brought out in the following from the same play, IV i:

Tharsalio.   ... thou wept'st. So have I seen many a moist auditor do at a play, when the story was a mere fiction. And didst act the Nuntius well? Would I had heard it! Could'st thou dress thy looks in a mournful habit?
Lycus.   Not without preparation, sir, no more than my speech; 'twas a plain acting of an interlude to me to pronounce the part.

And in the same scene (line 106) overdoing a part is decried:

Thar.   This strain of mourning wi'th' sepulchre, like an overdoing actor, affects grossly, and is indeed so far forced from the life, that it bewrays itself to be altogether artificial.

Fletcher. *Nice Valor* (1614). Epil.:

Our poet ... fears our overacting passions may,
As not adorn, deface his labor'd play.

Puritan Widow (1606). III v 84:

Py-bord.   ... have you never seen a stalking, stamping, player, that will raise a tempest with his tongue, and thunder with his heels?
Captain.   O yes, yes, yes; often, often.

Beaumont. *Knight of the Burning Pestle* (1607-10). II iii:

Citizen.   ... for clean action and good delivery, they may all cast their caps at him.
Wife.   ... the twelve companies of London cannot match him, timber for timber.

Barry. *Ram-Alley* (1609). Prol.:

> . . . to show
> Things never done, with that true life,
> That thoughts and wits should stand at strife
> Whether the things now shown be true,
> Or whether we ourselves now do
> The things we but present.

Heywood. *Apology* (1912). ed. Collier, p. 20:

> . . . to see a soldier shaped like a soldier, walk, speak, act like a soldier.

For the sake of realism, Heywood approves the practice of the Roman emperors of actually having people killed on the stage, the actors thus killed being criminals condemned to death. (ed. Collier, p. 45):

> And these were tragedies naturally performed.

Ibid. p. 56:

> The like use [i. e., as horrible examples] may be gathered of the drunkards so naturally imitated in our plays, to the applause of the actor, content of the auditory, and reproving of the vice.

Ibid. p. 29:

> And this is the action behooveful in any that profess this quality: not to use any impudent or forced motion in any part of the body, nor rough or other violent gesture; nor, on the contrary, to stand like a stiff, starcht man, but to qualify everything according to the nature of the person personated; for, in overacting tricks, and toiling too much in the antic habits of the humors, men of the ripest desert, greatest opinions, and best reputations, may break into the most violent absurdities.[1]

---

[1] This opinion is echoed by T. G. in *The Rich Cabinet* (1616): "Player must take heed of wrested and enforced action; for if there be not a facility in his deliverance, and, as it were, a natural dexterity, it must needs sound harsh to the auditor, and procure his distaste and displeasur." (*Eng. Drama and Stage.* p. 230. Roxb. Lib.)

Ibid. p. 53:

If we present a tragedy, we include the fatal and abortive ends of such as commit notorious murders, which is aggravated and acted with all the art that may be to terrify men from the like abhorred practices.

In the same work Heywood gives an example of the effect of good acting on the spectator:

To turn to our domestic histories, what English blood seeing the person of any bold Englishman presented and doth not hug his fame, . . . offers to him in his heart all prosperous performance, as if the personator were the man personated; so bewitching a thing is lively and spirited action that it hath power to new mold the hearts of the spectators and fashion them to the shape of any noble and notable attempt.

Massinger. *City Madam* (1619). II iii:

   Lord Lacy.   I will do my part
To set it off to the life.

May. *Heir* (1620). I i:

   Polymetes.   . . . now, Roscio,
Follows my part. I must express a grief
Not usual; not like a well-left heir
For his dead father, or a lusty widow
For her old husband, must I counterfeit:
But in a deeper, a far deeper strain,
Weep like a father for his only son.
Is that not hard to do, ha! Roscio?
   Ros.   O no, my lord;
Not for your skill. Has not your lordship seen
A player passionate Hieronimo?
   Pol.   By the mass, 'tis true. I have seen the knave paint grief
In such a lively color, that for false
And acted passion he has drawn true tears
From the spectators. Ladies in the boxes
Kept time with sighs and tears to his sad accents,
As he had truly been the man he seem'd.

Nero (1623). III ii:

> *Nero.* Come, sirs, i' faith, how did you like my acting? . .
> Did I not do it to the life?
> *Epaphroditus.* The very doing never was so lively
> As was this counterfeiting.
> *Nero.*   And when I came
> To th' point of Agripp—Clytemnestra's death,
> Did it not move the feeling auditory?
> *Epaph.* They had been stones whom that could not have moved.
> *Nero.* Did not my voice hold out well to the end?

Massinger. *New Way* (1625). IV iii:

> *Marg.* And though but a young actor, second me
> In doing to the life what he has plotted.

Ibid. *Roman Actor* (1626). I iii 89:

> *Paris.* ... If done to the life, ...
> All that have any spark of Roman in them
>   ... contend to be
> Like those they see presented.

Ibid. IV ii 221:

> *Caesar.*   Who presents
> The injured lord?
> *Æsopus.*   'Tis my part, sir.
> *Caes.*   Thou didst not
> Do it to the life; we can perform better.

Tho. Carew. On Davenant's *Just Italian.* (1630) :

> ... the true brood of actors, that alone
> Keep natural, unrestrain'd action in her throne,
> Behold their benches bare, though they rehearse
> The terse Beaumont's or great Johnson's verse.

Herrick, a "son of Ben," in his lines on Ben Jonson in *Hesperides*, draws a picture of the unnatural acting that followed the death of Jonson; the implication being that Jonson had something to do with the natural style of acting that prevailed in his time.

> After the rare arch-poet Jonson died,
> The sock grew loathsome, and the buskin's pride,
> Together with the stage's glory, stood
> Each like a poor and pitied widowhood.
> The cirque profaned was; and all postures rackt:
> For men did strut, and stride, and stare, not act.
> Then temper flew from words; and men did squeak,
> Look red, and blow, and bluster, but not speak:
> No holy rage, or frantic fires, did stir,
> Or flash about the spacious theater.

Randolph. To his friend Thomas Riley [who acted in *Jealous Lovers*] (1632) :

> When thou dost act, men think it not a play,
> But all they see is real.

Richard Brome. In praise of Fletcher's *Monsieur Thomas* (1639):

> 'Tis both the life of action and of wit,
> When actors so the fancied humors hit,
> As if 'twixt them and th' author there were strife
> How each to other should give mutual life.

Massinger. *Maid of Honor* (1622). V i 87:

> *Adorni.*   When good men pursue
> The path marked out by virtue, the blest saints
> With joy look on it, and seraphic angels
> Clap their celestial wings in heavenly plaudits
> To see a scene of grace so well presented.

Davenport. *City Night-Cap* (1624). II i:

> *Francisca.* If Pambo now comes off with his part neatly, the comedy passes bravely.

Glapthorne. *Lad's Privilege* (1640) . II i:

Corimba. . . . I have play'd a woman's part about twenty years ago in a court masque; and, though I say it, as well as some o' them.

Massinger. *Picture* (1629) . II i:

> *Hilario.*   You like my speech?
> *Corisca.*   Yes, if you give it action
> In the delivery.
>   *Hil.*   If! I pity you.
> I have play'd the fool before; this is not the first time. . . .
> If I do not
> Appear, and what's more, appear perfect, hiss me. . . .
>   *Hil.*   I am out.
>   *Cor.*   Recover, dunderhead.
>   *Hil.*   How he escaped I should have sung, not died. . . .
>   *Cor.*   You have made
> A fine piece of work on 't! How do you like the quality?
> You had a foolish itch to be an actor,
> And may stroll where you please. . . .
>   *Hil.*   Have I sweat
> My brains out for this quaint and rare invention,
> And am I thus rewarded? I could turn
> Tragedian, and roar now.

Nash, in his prologue to *Will Summer's Last Will and Testament*, speaks like one who has sweated much as a producer:

> Actors, you rogues, come away; clear your throats, blow your noses, and wipe your mouths, ere you enter, that you may take no occasion to spit or cough when you are *non plus*. And this I bar, over and besides, that none of you stroke your beards to make action, play with your codpiece points, or stand fumbling on your buttons, when you know not how to bestow your fingers. Serve God and act cleanly.

His understanding of how a play ought to be produced is further exemplified by his description of a bad academic performance at Wittenberg.

The Unfortunate Traveler (1593) (Percy Repr. p. 46):

> The Duke . . . was bidden to one of the chief schools to a comedy handled by scholars. *Acolastus, the Prodigal Child,* was the name

of it, which was so filthily acted, so leathernly set forth, as would have moved laughter in Heraclitus. One, as if he had been planing a clay floor, stampingly trod the stage so hard with his feet, that I thought verily he had resolved to do the carpenter that set it up some utter shame. Another flung his arms like cudgels at a pear tree, insomuch that it was mightily dreaded that he would strike the candles that hung above their heads out of their sockets, and leave them all dark. Another did nothing but wink and make faces. There was a parasite, and he with clapping his hands and thripping his fingers seemed to dance an antic to and fro. The only thing they did well was the prodigal child's hunger, most of their scholars being hungerly kept; and surely you would have said they had been brought up in hog's academy to learn to eat acorns, if you had seen how sedulously they fell upon them. Not a jest had they to keep the audience from sleeping but of swill and draff; yet now and then the servant put his hand into the dish before his master, and almost choked himself, eating slovenly and ravenously to cause sport.

Dekker. *Honest Whore* (1604). III i 75:

> *Candido.*   Trust me, you are not wise in my own house
> And to my face to play the antic thus.
> If you'll needs play the madman, choose a stage
> Of lesser compass, where few eyes may note
> Your action's error: but if you still miss,
> As here you do, for one clap, ten will hiss.
> *Fustigo.*   Zounds, cousin, he talks to me as if I were a scurvy tragedian.

Massinger. *Believe as You List* (1630). V i 131:

> *Cornelia.*   You disgrace your courtship
> By overacting it, my lord.

The entrance and the exit are critical moments for the actor. Here is a comment on a good exit. (Middleton. *Mad World*, V ii):

> *Sir Bounteous.*   Ay, that's the grace of all—when they go away well.

There was an awareness of subtleness of delivery.

The Actors' Remonstrance (1634):

. . . we will not entertain any comedian that shall speak his part in a tone as if he did it in derision of some of the pious.

To show that I possess the scholar's impartiality, here are two references that the formalists can make much of. In V i of Webster's *White Devil*, there is a stage direction which reads:

These speeches are several kinds of distractions, and in the action should appear so.

and in the following scene:

Cornelia doth this in several forms of distraction.

Incidentally, in the former scene there is a stage direction which shows what skill was expected of the Elizabethan actor:

Brachiano seems here near his end.

Stage directions alone would supply material for an article on Elizabethan acting.

Munday. *Downfall of Huntington* (1598) . I iii:

Marian.　Speak not so hollow then;
So sigh and sadly speak true-sorrowing men.
　Robert.　. . . My first scene tragic is, therefore tragic speech
And accents filling woful action
I strive to get. . . .
And thou shalt see me with a lofty verse
Bewitch the hearers' ears, and tempt their eyes,
To gaze upon the action that I use.

The author's helpless dependence upon the actor is feelingly pointed out by Dekker in his address to the readers of *The Whore of Babylon*:

How true Fortune's dial hath gone, whose players, like so many clocks, have struck my lines, and told the world how I have spent my hours, I am not certain, because mine ears stood not within reach of their larums. But of this my knowledge cannot fail, that in such consorts many of the instruments are for the most part out of tune. And no marvel; for let the poet set the note of his numbers even to Apollo's own lyre, the players will have his own crotchets, and sing false notes, in despite of all the rules of music. It fares with these two as it does with good stuff and a bad tailor: it is not marred in the wearing, but in the cutting out. The labors therefore of writers are as unhappy as the children of a beautiful woman, being spoiled by ill nurses within a month after they come into the world. What a number of throes do we endure ere we be delivered! and yet even then, tho that heavenly issue of our brain be never so fair and so well limd, is it made lame by the bad handling of them to whom it is put to learn to go. If this of mine be made a cripple by such means, yet despise him not for that deformity which stuck not upon him at his birth, but fell upon him by misfortune; and in recompense of such favor you shall (if your patience can suffer so long) hear how he himself can speak.

In Act II, Scene ii, of Brome's *Antipodes* (1638) we find what is obviously a conscious elaboration of the advice to the players by Hamlet and Quince. The following passage is instructive:

> *Letoy.* But you, sir, are incorrigible, and
> Take license to yourself to add unto
> Your parts your own free fancy; and sometimes
> To alter, or diminish what the writer
> With care and skill composed: and when you are
> To speak to your coactors in the scene,
> You hold interlocutions with the audients.
> *By-play.* That is a way, my lord, has been allowed
> On elder stages, to move mirth and laughter.
> *Letoy.* Yes, in the days of Tarlton and Kempe,
> Before the stage was purged from barbarism,
> And brought to the perfection it now shines with.
> Then fools and jesters spent their wits, because
> The poets were wise enough to save their own
> For profitabler uses.

Richard Flecknoe, writing his thoughts down after the Restoration, vividly recalls the fine acting of the past, especially that of Richard Burbage:

> It was the happiness of the actors of those times to have such poets as these to instruct them, and write for them; and no less of

223

those poets to have such docile and excellent actors to act their plays, as a Field and Burbidge; of whom we may say, that he was delightful Proteus, so wholly transforming himself into his part, and putting off himself with his clothes, as he never (not so much as in the tyring-house) assum'd himself again until the play was done: there being as much difference between him and one of our common actors, as between a ballad-singer who only mouths it, and an excellent singer, who knows all his graces, and can artfully vary and modulate his voice, even to know how much breath he is to give to every syllable. He had all the parts of an excellent orator, (animating his words with speaking, and speech with action) his auditors being never more delighted then when he spoke, nor more sorry then when he held his peace. Yet even then he was an excellent actor still, never falling in his part when he had done speaking; but with his looks and gesture, maintaining it still unto the heighth, he imagining *Age quod agis,* only spoke to him: so as those who call him a player do him wrong, no man being less idle than he, whose life is nothing else but action; with only this difference from other men's, that as what is but a play to them is his business; so their business is but a play to him.

Finally, it seems to me that the quotation from *Pierce Penniless* on page 143 proves conclusively that as early as 1592 the actor's ideal aim was to produce the effect of naturalness; particularly as Nash was not concerned at the moment with this or that kind of acting. He was thinking simply of the theater; and in that theater the spectator was led to imagine that he beheld, not a symbol, not a representation, of Talbot, but Talbot himself, his very self.

CASTING

The selection of players to fit the roles was part of the inherited theatrical tradition.

In John Heywood's *Play of the Weather,* the last item in "The Players' Names" reads: "A boy, the least that can play."

2 Return from Parnassus (1602). IV iii:

> *Kemp.* Now for you, methinks you should belong to my tuition, and your face, methinks, would be good for a foolish mayor, or a foolish justice of peace.

Was he alluding to Simon, the mayor of Quinborough, and Justice Shallow? Burbage, who is not represented as moronic as Kemp, would cast differently:

> *Bur.* I like your face, and the proportion of your body, for Richard the 3. I pray you, M. Philomuse, let me see you act a little of it.

Middleton. *Mad World* (1606). V:

> *Sir Bounteous.* . . . they put all their fools to the constable's part still.

Shirley. *Bird in a Cage* (1633). IV i:

> *Donella.* . . . we are all perfect in the plot, I think.
> *Eugenia.* You shall dispose the rest.
> *Don.* You will not be ambitious then, and quarrel about the parts, like your spruce actor, that will not play out of the best clothes, and the fine young prince, who, if he fight, 'tis six to four he kills all, and gets the lady.

Randolph. *Muses' Looking Glass* (1634). I i:

> *Deformed Fellow.* Roscius, I hear you've a new play today.
> *Ros.* We want you to play Mephistopheles.
> A pretty natural vizard!

Marston. *Antonio and Mellida* (1599). Ind.:

> *Antonio.* I was never worse fitted since the nativity of my actorship. I shall be hissed at, on my life now . . . I a voice to play a lady! . . .
> *Felice.* I have a part alloted me which I have neither able apprehension to conceit, nor what I conceit gracious ability to utter.
> *Galeazzo.* Whoop, in the old cut!

In this Induction the interpretation of several parts is discussed.

Massinger. *Emperor of the East* (1631). Epil.:

> We have reason to be doubtful whether he
> On whom (forced to it from necessity)
> The maker did confer his emperor's part,
> Hath given you satisfaction, in his art
> Of action and delivery; 'tis sure truth,
> The burthen was too heavy for his youth
> To undergo.

Shirley. *Duke's Mistress* (1636). Epil.:

> I have but played the part which was most against my genius of any that ever I acted in my life.

Middleton, Rowley. *Spanish Gypsy* (1623). IV ii:

> *Fernando.* What parts dost use to play?
> *Sancho.* If your lordship has ever a coxcomb, I think I could fit you.

In the same scene is presented the assignment of all the roles in a play.

Rowley *et al. Witch of Edmonton* (1621). III i:

Cuddy. But hark you; Poldavis, the baker's boy, for the witch, because he can do his art better than another.

Wilkins. *Miseries of Enforced Marriage* (1605). I:

Bartley. 'Sfoot, the knight would have made an excellent zany in an Italian comedy.

In his *Second Blast of Retreat from Plays and Theaters* Gosson, who had been a playwright, gives us an intimate peep into the procedure of casting:

> . . . doth not the talk on the stage declare the nature of their disposition? doth not everyone take that part which is proper to his kind? . . . Ask them, if in their laying out of their parts, they choose not those parts which is most agreeing to their inclination, and that they can best discharge? And look what every of them doth most delight in, that he can best handle to the contentment of others.

THE ACTOR

Heywood. *Apology.* (Shak. Soc. p. 43) :

. . . actors should be men pick'd out personable, according to the parts they present. They should be rather scholars, that, though they cannot speak well, know how to speak, or else to have that volubility that they can speak well, though they understand not what, and so both imperfections may by instructions be helped and amended: but where a good tongue and a good conceit both fail, there can never be good actor.

The printer of Whetstone's *Promos and Cassandra* (1578) complains of the difficulty of printing "so difficult a work, being full of variety, both matter, speech, and verse: for that every sundry actor hath in all these a sundry grace."

Sir Thomas More (1590). V iv 78:

More. . . . and my offense to his highness makes me of a state pleader a stage player (though I am old, and have a bad voice) to act this last scene of my tragedy.

Middleton. *Mayor of Quinborough* (1596). V i:

Simon. Now, sir, are you comedians?
2nd Player. We are, sir; comedians, tragedians, tragi-comedians, comi-tragedians, pastorists, humorists, satirists; we have them, sir, from the hug to the smile, from the smile to the laugh, from the laugh to the handkerchief.

Massinger. *Believe as You List* (1630). III i:

Flaminious. I am on the stage,
And if now, in the scene imposed upon me,

So full of changes, . . . I show not myself
A protean actor, varying every shape
With the occasion, it will hardly poise
The expectation.

Peele (?). *Wily Beguiled* (bef. 1595). Prol.:

What ho! where are these paltry players? still poring in their papers,
and never perfect? For shame, come forth; your audience stay so
long, their eyes wax dim with expectation.

Tomkis. *Lingua* (1603). III vi:

   Communis Sensus.   Leave jesting; you'll put the fresh actor out
of countenance.

Dekker. *Satiromastix* (1602). (ed. Hawkins, p. 177):

   Sir Quintilian.   Out of thy part already? fail'd the scene?
Disfrank'd the lines? disarm'd the action?

Middleton. *Women Beware Women* (1612). II ii:

   Livia.   Now comes in the heat of your part.
   Guardiano.   True, I know it, lady; and if I be out,
May the duke banish me from all employments.

Middleton, Rowley. *Spanish Gypsy* (1623). II ii:

   Pedro.   Wilt thou ever play the coxcomb?
   Sancho.   If no other parts be given me, what would you have
me do?

The epilogue to Chapman's *Bussy D'Ambois* tells us that an
actor must be given an opportunity to develop, assisted by the
encouragement of the public:

With many hands you have seen D'Ambois slain;
Yet by your grace he may revive again,
And every day grow stronger in his skill
To please, as we presume he is in will.
The best deserving actors of the time
Had their ascents; and by degrees did climb

To their full height,—a place to study due.
To make him tread in their path lies in you.

In IV ii of Massinger's *Roman Actor* (1626) the point is made that the actor need not possess the qualities of the character he impersonates:

    Domitia.   We . . . cannot find
In reason but that thou, whom oft I have seen
To personate a gentleman, noble, wise,
Faithful, and gainsome, and what virtues else
The poet pleases to adorn you with,
But that—as vessels still partake the odor
Of the sweet precious liquors they contained—
Thou must be really, in some degree,
The thing thou dost present. Nay, do not tremble.
We seriously believe it, and presume
Our Paris is the volume in which all
Those excellent gifts the stage hath seen him graced with
Are curiously bound up.
    Paris.   The argument
Is the same, great Augusta, that I, acting
A fool, a coward, a traitor, or cold cynic,
Or any other weak and vicious person,
Of force I must be such. O gracious madam,
How glorious soever, or deformed,
I do appear in the scene, my part being ended,
And all my borrowed ornaments put off,
I am no more, nor less, than what I was
Before I entered.

Of course, the clown was the strongest attraction on the stage. *Taming of a Shrew* (1588). End of I:

    Sly.   Sim, when will the fool come again?

Ibid. Beginning of IV:

    Sly.   Look, Sim, the fool is come again now.

Chapman (?). *Alphonsus* (1590). II ii:

> *Mentz.*   I am the jester.
> *Edward.*   O excellent! Is your Holiness the Vice?
> Fortune hath fitted you, i' faith, my lord;
> You'll play the Ambidexter cunningly.

The speaker here has touched on several phases in the development of the Fool. Evidently the various names were still familiar to the audience.

Middleton. *Mayor of Quinborough* (1596). V i:

> *Simon.*   I'll teach thee to understand to play the clown; thou shalt know every man is not born to it.

Ibid.:

> *1st Player.*   This is our clown, sir.
> *Sim.*   Fie, fie, you fall upon him and beat him: he's too fair, i' faith, to make the people laugh.
> *1st Player.*   Not as he may be dressed, sir.
> *Sim.*   Faith, dress him how you will, I'll give him that gift, he will never look half scurvily enough. O, the clowns that I have seen in my time! The very peeping out of one of them would have made a young heir laugh, though his father lay a-dying; a man undone in law the day before (the saddest case that can be) might for his two-pence have burst himself with laughing, and ended all his miseries. Here was a merry world, my masters!
> Some talk of state, of puling stuff;
> There's nothing in a play to a clown, if he
> Have the grace to hit on't; that's the thing indeed:
> The king shows well, but he sets off the king.

Ibid.:

> *Sim.*   O, neighbors, here's the part now that carries away the play! If the clown miscarry, farewell my hopes forever; the play's spoiled.

Chapman. *M. D'Olive* (1605). IV ii 170:

> *Roderigue.*   Here we may strike the *Plaudite* to our play; my lord Fool's gone; all our audience will forsake us.

John Cooke. *Green's Tu Quoque* (1609). Dodsley XI, 240:

Rash. . . . But what shall's do when we have dined? Shall's go see a play?

Scat. Yes, faith, brother, if it please you: let's go see a play at the Globe.

Bubble. I care not; any whither, so the clown have a part; for, i' faith, I am nobody without a fool.

Geraldine. Why, then, we'll go to the Red Bull: They say Green's a good clown.

Bubble. Green! Green's an ass.

Scat. Wherefore do you say so?

Bubble. Indeed, I ha' no reason; for they say he is like me as ever he can look.

Scat. Well, then, to the Bull.

To appreciate the joke, we must know that the part of Bubble is being played by Green.

COMMENTS ON ACTORS

Nash. *Pierce Penniless* (1592) . (Shak. Soc., p. 62):

Not Roscius nor Esop, those tragedians admired before Christ was born, could ever perform more in action than famous Ned Allen. I must accuse our poets of sloth and partiality, that they will not boast in large impressions what worthy men (above all nations) England affords. Other countries cannot have a fiddler break a string but they will put it in print. . . . if I ever write anything in Latin (as I hope one day I shall) not a man of any desert here amongst us, but I will have up. Tarlton, Ned Allen, Knell, Bentley, shall be made known to France, Spain, and Italy; and not a part that they surmounted in more than other, but I will there note and set down, with the manner of their habits and attire.

(Pity he burned away his life before he had a chance to accomplish this project.)

Heywood. *Apology* (1612). (Shak. Soc., p. 43):

. . . to do some right to our English actors, as Knell, Bentley, Mils, Wilson, Crosse, Lanam, and others, these, since I never saw them, as being before my time, I cannot (as an eye-witness of their desert) give them that applause which no doubt they worthily merit, yet by the report of many judicial auditors their performance of many parts have been so absolute, that it were a kind of sin to drown their worths in Lethe, and not commit their (almost forgotten) names to eternity. Here I must needs remember Tarlton, in his time gracious with the queen, his sovereign, and in the people's general applause; whom succeeded Wil. Kemp, as well in the favor of her majesty, as in the opinion and good thoughts of the general audience. Gabriel, Singer, Pope, Phillips, Sly; all the right I can do them is but this, that, though they be dead, their deserts yet live in the remembrance of many.

(How can one explain his omission of Burbage?)

Nash. *Almond for a Parrot*:

Coming from Venice this last summer, and taking Bergamo in my way homeward to England, it was my hap, sojourning there some four or five days, to light in fellowship with that famous Francatrip harlequin, who, perceiving me to be an Englishman by my habit of speech, asked me many particulars of the order and manner of our plays, which he termed by the name of *representations*. Amongst other talk, he inquired of me if I knew any such *Parabolano* here in London as Signior Charlatano Kempino? Very well (quoth I) and have been often in his company. He hearing me say so, began to embrace me anew, and offered me all the courtesy he could for his sake, saying, although he knew him not, yet for the report he had of his plesance, he could not but be in love with his perfections, being absent.

Above, we heard the mayor of Quinborough boast of the clowns he had seen in his time, and of the explosive effect of "the very peeping out of one of them." Nash, in *Pierce Penniless* (Shak. Soc., p. 36), describes an extraordinary occasion of that kind that ended rather tragically for the laughing audience. The story is too good not to broadcast:

Amongst other choleric wise justices he was one that, having a play presented before him and his township by Tarlton and the rest of his fellows, Her Majesty's Servants, . . . the people began exceedingly to laugh when Tarlton first peeped out his head. Whereat the justice, not a little moved, and seeing with his becks and nods he could not make them cease, he went with his staff, and beat them round about unmercifully on the bare pates, in that they, being but farmers and poor country hinds, would presume to laugh at the Queen's men, and make no more account of her cloth, in his presence.

Regarding the actors who played in Shirley's *Grateful Servant* (pr. 1630), the reader is informed that they were

. . . most of them deserving a name in the file of those that are eminent for graceful and unaffected action.

MISCELLANEOUS OBSERVATIONS

Day. *Parliament of Bees.* I (Mermaid ed., p. 221, note):

... this proud buskined actor
That smiles and kills. ...

Drayton. *Mistress Shore to Edward* IV:

Or passionate tragedian, in his rage
Acting a love-sick passion on the stage.

Chapman (?). *Alphonsus* (1590). V i 354:

  Saxon.   Methinks I now present Mark Antony,
Folding dead Julius Caesar in mine arms.

Kyd. *Spanish Tragedy* (1583). IV 160:

  Hieronimo.   The Italian tragedians were so sharp of wit,
That in one hour's meditation
They would perform anything in action.
  Lor.   And well it may; for I have seen the like
In Paris 'mongst the French tragedians.

Middleton, Rowley. *Spanish Gypsy* (1623). IV ii:

  Fernando.   ... there is a way
Which the Italians and the Frenchmen use,
That is, on a word given, or some slight plot,
The actors will extempore fashion out
Scenes neat and witty.

2 Return from Parnassus (1602). IV iii:

Studioso.   Let's learn to act that tragic part we have.
Philomuse.   Would I were silent actor in my grave.

Armin. *Two Maids of More-clacke* (1608) . (ed. Grosart, p. 68):
Enter Lady, Mistress Mary, Mistress Tabitha, and some other women for show.

Brome. *Antipodes* (1638) . II i:

By-Play.   Only we want a person for a mute.
Letoy.   Blaze when he comes shall serve.

Glapthorne. *Revenge for Honor* (1624). III ii 123:

Enter Abilqualit. Mutes, *whispering, seem to make protestations.*

The absurdity of the convention of concealing identity by a change of dress could not of course escape the perpetrators thereof. Chapman. *May-Day* (1601). II i 472:

Lorenzo.   . . . for the safeguard of her honor I would do much; methinks a friar's weed were nothing.
Angelo.   Out upon't; that disguise is worn threadbare upon every stage, and so much villainy committed under that habit that 'tis grown as suspicious as the vilest. If you will harken to any, take such a transformance as you may be sure will keep you from dis- covery; for though it be the stale refuge of miserable poets by a change of a hat or a cloak to alter the whole state of a comedy, so as the father must not know his own child, forsooth, nor the wife her husband, yet you must not think they do in earnest carry i away so; for say you were stuffed into a motley coat, crowded in the case of a base viol, or buttoned up in a cloak-bag even to you face, I am able to say, 'This is Signor Lorenzo,' and therefore unles your disguise be such that your face bear as great a part in it as th rest, the rest is nothing.

B. and F. *Scornful Lady* (1609) . III i 260:

E. Loveless.   Why, then, he lives still; I am he, your Loveles
[*Throws off his disguise.*]
Lady.   Alas, I knew it, sir, and for that purpose
Prepar'd this pageant! Get you to your task,
And leave these players' tricks.

Fletcher. *Women Pleased* (1620). V ii near end:

> *Claudio.*   I must use a player's shift. [*Throws off his disguise.*]
> Do you know me now, lady?

Dekker. *Satiromastix* (1602) (Hawkins, p. 177):

> *Sir Quintilian.* ... begin the scene; who shall speak first?
> O, I; I play the king, and kings speak first.

Middleton. *Mad World* (1606). In the play-within-the-play in V ii, a constable sits tied and gagged for some time. One of the "audience" remarks:

> But what follows all this while, sir? methinks some should pass by before this time, and pity the constable.

Webster. *Duchess of Malfi* (1614). IV ii (Mermaid ed., p. 213) :

> *Ferdinand.* ... we observe in tragedies
> That a good actor many times is cursed
> For playing a villain's part.

Brome. *Antipodes* (1638). I v:

> *Letoy.*   These lads can act the emperor's love all over,
> And Shakespeare's chronicled histories to boot;
> And were that Caesar or that English earl
> That loved a play and player now living,
> I would not be outvied in my delights.

This was after the full flowering of the Elizabethan theater. Less han a century earlier an author could not foresee what "these lads" vere capable of. The author of *Jack Juggler* (1553) avers in the rologue that only light comedies were suitable for performance y boys.

In the first scene of the next act Letoy pays a special tribute to ne of his lads, and takes issue with Hamlet:

> Well, sir, my actors
> Are all in readiness; and I think all perfect,

But one, that never will be perfect in a thing
He studies; yet he makes such shifts extempore,
(Knowing the purpose what he is to speak to)
That he moves mirth in me 'bove all the rest.
For I am none of those poetic furies
That threats the actor's life, in a whole play
That adds a syllable, or takes away.
If he can fribble through, and move delight
In others, I am pleased.

Wilkins. *Miseries of Enforced Marriage* (1605). I:

> *Bartley.* 'Sfoot, the knight would have made an excellent zany
> in an Italian comedy.

This passage and the following reference to the *Commedia del Arte* in the last act of *The Spanish Tragedy* are evidence that the English playwrights were aware of the dramatic activity fostered on the continent:

> *Hier.* The Italian tragedians were so sharp of wit,
> That in one hour's meditation
> They would perform anything in action.
> *Lor.* And well it may; for I have seen the like
> In Paris 'mongst the French tragedians.

A complaint apt to be rendered today is to the effect that the play is no longer the thing, that its primary position has been usurped by the production. It seems that the same complaint was in order as early as 1582, when Gosson wrote *Plays Confuted,* in which he murmurs:

> The preparation of plays, apparel, and such like as setteth out
> our plays in shows of pomp and state, is it that we wonder and gaze
> at. By Tully it is outed and laughed to scorn. The stateliness of the
> preparation drowns the delight which the matter affords.

STATUS OF THE ACTING PROFESSION

The Elizabethan actor was classed with rogues and vagabonds, and I believe that classification still holds on the English statute books. Heywood in his *Apology* works loyally to improve public opinion of actors, one of the three books into which the work is divided being devoted to "their ancient dignity." The low status assigned them by society is indicated in the following quotations.

Kyd. *Spanish Tragedy* (1583). IV i:

> *Balthazar.* What, would you have us play a tragedy?
> *Hieronimo.* Why, Nero thought it no disparagement,
> And kings and emperors have ta'en delight
> To make experience of their wits in plays.

Narcissus (1602) 1. 125:

> We are no vagabones, we are no arrant
> Rogues that run with plays about the country. . .
> We are no saucy common playing skipjacks,
> But town born lads, the king's own lovely subjects.

To the Cambridge author of *2 Return from Parnassus* (1602) he reputation of Kemp and Burbage affords an opportunity for nobbish jesting. IV iii:

> *Studioso.* God save you, M. Kemp; welcome, M. Kemp, from dancing the morrice over the Alps.
> *Kemp.* Well, you merry knaves, you may come to the honor of it one day. Is it not better to make a fool of the world, as I have done, than to be fooled of the world, as you scholars are? But be merry, lads; you have happened upon the most excellent vocation in the world for money. They come north and south to bring it to

239

our playhouse; and for honors, who of more report than Dick Burbage and Will Kemp? He is not counted a gentleman that knows not Dick Burbage and Will Kemp. There's not a country wench that can dance Sellenger's Round, but can talk of Dick Burbage and Will Kemp.

But the two young men are no sooner left alone than they express their own opinion of the profession into which they have been forced by necessity:

Philomuse.   And must the basest trade yield us relief?
Must we be practis'd to those leaden spouts,
That nought do vent but what they do receive?
Some fatal fire hath scorcht our fortune's wing,
And still we fall, as we do upward spring:
As we strive upward to the vaulted sky,
We fall and feel our hateful destiny.

Evidently, from the following speech by Studioso in the next scene, there was one profession ranked even lower than that of the actor:

Better it is mongst fiddlers to be chief,
Than at a player's trencher beg relief.
But is't not strange, these mimic apes should prize
Unhappy scholars at a hireling rate?
Vile world, that lifts them up to high degree,
And treads us down in groveling misery.
England affords those glorious vagabonds,
That carried erst their fardels on their backs,
Coursers to ride on through the gazing streets,
Sooping it in their glaring satin suits,
And pages to attend their maisterships.
With mouthing words that better wits have framed,
They purchase lands, and now esquires are named.

There were other envious souls that could not accept wit equanimity the material prosperity of the player. For exampl Greene, in his *Groatsworth of Wit*:

"A player!" quoth Roberto, "I took you rather for a gentleman great living; for if by outward habit men should be censured,

240

tell you you would be taken for a substantial man." "So am I where I dwell" quoth the player "reputed able at my proper cost to build a windmill."

Gosson. *School of Abuse* (Arber ed., p. 29):

Overlashing in apparel is so common a fault, that the very hirelings of some of our players, which stand at reversion of 6s. by the week, jet under gentlemen's noses in suits of silk.

His strictures are directed to the hirelings; regarding the master players he admits that

it is well known that some of them are sober, discreet, properly learned, honest householders, and citizens well thought on among their neighbors at home, though the pride of their shadows (I mean those hangbys whom they succor with stipend) cause them to be somewhat ill talked of abroad.

A similar description is made by Heywood in his *Apology* (p. 44). Despite his unenviable position in the social scale, the actor possessed a glamor which he has not lost to this day. It was not acting, but acting for a living, that was degrading. Royalty loved to parade in masques. Add to the glamor the fact that we like to pet those beneath us, and we can understand why it was a popular practice to throw parties for actors.

Middleton. *Mad World* (1606) V:

Courtesan. . . . I could find it in my heart to fall in love with that player now, and send for him to supper. I know some in town that have done as much.

Barry. *Ram-Alley* (1609) V:

Constantia. . . . what do you say
To a citizen's daughter that never was in love
With a player, that never learnt to dance, . .
Might not she in time prove an honest wife?

ekker reports that it is the ambition of dandies who would be ought men of fashion to give banquets to actors, and Jonson ornfully says of courtiers that "their glory is to invite players to suppers." To the veracity of these utterances we have the testimony of John Earle, who informs us that actors were the chief guests of the gentlemen of the Inns of Court, and the favorites of fine ladies. So ancient is the institution of the "matinee idol."

I wonder how many actors would really have thought of making the following declaration from Massinger's *Roman Actor* (I i):

Our aim is glory, and to leave our names
To aftertimes.

III. SHAKESPEARE

It were astonishing to a degree could it be proved that Shakespeare, the myriad-minded, indulged in little reflection on the art which he was practicing. On the contrary, a careful reading of his utterances reveals the fact that the greatest of poets fully understood the technique of his art. Nevertheless he did not realize the greatness of his own work; otherwise how explain his unconcern about its preservation? It is hard for us to understand such lack of perception. But isn't it just as hard to understand how a man like Pepys could call *Othello* a "mean thing" alongside of Tuke's *Adventures of Five Hours*?—harder, for the evaluation of one's own creation is beset with peculiar difficulties. This very problem Shakespeare was aware of, for it is the theme of an important dialogue in *Troilus and Cressida* (III iii 95):

Achilles. What are you reading?
Ulysses. A strange fellow here
Writes me that man, how dearly ever parted,
How much in having, or without or in,
Cannot make boast to have that which he hath,
Nor feels not what he owes, but by reflection;
As when his virtues shining upon others
Heat them and they retort that heat again
To the first giver.
Achil. That is not strange, Ulysses.
The beauty that is borne here in the face
The bearer knows not, but commends itself
To others' eyes; nor doth the eye itself,
That most pure spirit of sense, behold itself,
Not going from itself; but eye to eye oppos'd
Salutes each other with each other's form;
For speculation turns not to itself,

Till it hath travell'd and is mirror'd there
Where it may see itself. This is not strange at all.
   Ulys.   I do not strain at the position,—
It is familiar,—but at the author's drift;
Who, in his circumstance, expressly proves
That no man is the lord of anything,
 (Though in and of him there is much consisting,)
Till he communicate his parts to others;
Nor doth he of himself know them for aught
Till he behold them formed in th'applause
Where they're extended; who, like an arch, reverb'rate
The voice again, or, like a gate of steel
Fronting the sun, receives and renders back
His figure and his heat. I was much wrapt in this.

Well, Shakespeare surely beheld his parts "formed in th' applause where they're extended:" but there was another factor that could not be overlooked: the unreliability of that applause. He goes on:

Nature, what things there are
Most abject in regard and dear in use!
What things again most dear in the esteem
And poor in worth!

Thus, if he was thinking of himself, he found himself at the end just where he was at the beginning; so he did not publish his works,—despite the example set him by his dogmatic adversary in the Mermaid debates, Ben Jonson (who called his plays *works*). It simply remains for us to send up daily prayers of thanksgiving for the miracle of their survival. However, the dialogue quoted confronts us with a Shakespeare who was an analytic thinker

[1] It will be easier for us to comprehend Shakespeare's apparent indifference if we pause to realize that the mental attitude toward work for the theater has changed little since his time. How many of the plays today, even of the successful ones, reach the printer—except, perhaps, in French's edition, which is not intended for the general reading public? Playwrights simply think of Broadway, not posterity.

"CENSURE"

If Shakespeare is the author of Sonnet VIII in *The Passionate Pilgrim,* which includes a warm appreciation of Spenser (quoted in Chapter I) then we have from his pen three references to a contemporary writer. The second is his tender tribute in *As You Like It* to Christopher Marlowe, who was of the same age as Shakespeare, yet who at the time of his death had produced greater work than he; who, therefore, was the only contemporary that could challenge his preeminence. Yet what a feeling of sincere esteem one can read in the line, "Dead shepherd, now I find thy saw of might." The third is his acknowledgment of the superiority of the rival poet in Sonnet 86.

THE ART OF POETRY

Shakespeare's critical utterances are enabled to escape sounding like an intrusion of the voice of the author, by having their manner of delivery characteristic of the person who speaks them. For instance, his most important statement on the process of poetic creation comes from the mouth of Theseus, who speaks the truth, but contemptuously, and without approval; for he is a soldier. Likewise Holofernes speaks the truth, but in the manner of the conceited pedant and pedagogue.

M. N. D. V i 1:

> *Hippolyta.* 'Tis strange, my Theseus, that these lovers speak of.
> *Thes.* More strange than true; I never may believe
> These antique fables, nor these fairy toys.
> Lovers and madmen have such seething brains,
> Such shaping fantasies, that apprehend
> More than cool reason ever comprehends.
> The lunatic, the lover, and the poet
> Are of imagination all compact.
> One sees more devils than vast hell can hold;
> That is, the madman. The lover, all as frantic,
> Sees Helen's beauty in a brow of Egypt.
> The poet's eye, in a fine frenzy rolling,
> Doth glance from heaven to earth, from earth to heaven;
> And as imagination bodies forth
> The forms of things unknown, the poet's pen
> Turns them to shapes, and gives to airy nothing
> A local habitation and a name.

One instinctively hears other speeches on the power of the imagination to create, speeches that sometimes sound like echoes, paraphrases of this one; for instance, Mercutio's discourse on dreams in *Romeo and Juliet*, I iv 95:

> *Romeo.*   Peace, peace, Mercutio, peace!
> Thou talk'st of nothing.
> *Mer.*   True, I talk of dreams,
> Which are the children of an idle brain,
> Begot of nothing but vain fantasy,
> Which is as thin of substance as the air
> And more inconstant than the wind.

And the two speeches in his last play in which he reviews his creation, and publishes the termination of his career as a creator (*Tempest*, IV i 148):

> *Prospero.*   Our revels now are ended. These our actors,
> As I foretold you, were all spirits, and
> Are melted into air, into thin air;
> And, like the baseless fabric of this vision,
> The cloud-capp'd towers, the gorgeous palaces,
> The solemn temples, the great globe itself,
> Yea, all which it inherit, shall dissolve
> And, like this insubstantial pageant faded,
> Leave not a rack behind. We are such stuff
> As dreams are made on, and our little life
> Is rounded with a sleep.

Ibid. V i 33:

> *Pros.*   Ye elves, . . . by whose aid
> Weak masters though ye be, I have bedimm'd
> The noontide sun, call'd forth the mutinous winds,
> And 'twixt the green sea and azur'd vault
> Set roaring war; to the dread rattling thunder
> Have I given fire, and rifted Jove's stout oak
> With his own bolt; the strong-bas'd promontory
> Have I made shake, and by the spurs pluck'd up
> The pine and cedar; graves at my command
> Have wak'd their sleepers, op'd, and let 'em forth
> By my so potent art. But this rough magic
> I here abjure, and . . . I'll break my staff,
> Bury it certain fathoms in the earth,

And deeper than did ever plummet sound
I'll drown my book.

Which so strongly expressed resolution he, alas, adhered to.

Poetry's independence of external phenomena is again affirmed
in *Timon of Athens*. It is presented characteristically by a poet
who as a man is contemptible, I i 19:

> *Painter.*   You are rapt, sir, in some work, some dedication
> To the great lord.
> *Poet.*   A thing slipp'd idly from me.
> Our poetry is as a gum, which oozes
> From whence 'tis nourish'd. The fire i' th' flint
> Shows not till it be struck; our gentle flame
> Provokes itself and, like the current, flies
> Each bound it chafes.

He wants to dissipate the painter's notion that he was "rapt;" he
prefers to give the impression that writing poetry comes easily and
naturally to him. His description of the process, however, is in
keeping with the romantic conception of poetic creation, and is
to be accepted as Shakespeare's own view; except that he probably
would not deny the value of external stimulus, (read, for instance,
Sonnet 38) as suggested by Berowne's semi-serious speech in *Love's
Labor's Lost*, IV iii 346:

> Never durst poet touch a pen to write
> Until his ink were temp'red with love's sighs;
> O, then his lines would ravish savage ears
> And plant in tyrants mild humility.

In the second scene of the same act Holofernes improvises an
intricate piece of alliteration, pun, and rhyme, which evokes
Nathaniel's admiration:

> *Nath.*   A rare talent!
> *Hol.*   This is a gift that I have, simple, simple; a foolish extrava-
> gant spirit, full of forms, figures, shapes, objects, ideas, apprehen-
> sions, motions, revolutions. These are begot in the ventricle of
> memory, nourisht in the womb of pia mater, and delivered upon
> the mellowing of occasion. But the gift is good in those in whom it
> is acute, and I am thankful for it.

A general statement made by the princess in *Love's Labor's Lost* (V ii 517) would give preeminence to the unconscious element in art:

> *Prin.* That sport best pleases that doth least know how;
> Where zeal strives to content, and the contents
> Dies in the zeal of that which it presents.
> Their form confounded makes most form in mirth,
> When great things laboring perish in their birth.

The core of this passage is obscure, but the first and last lines (the important ones) are clear.

Related ideas are expressed in the last act of *A Midsummer-Night's Dream* (V i 81):

> *Theseus.*　　　　　I will hear that play;
> For never anything can be amiss
> When simpleness and duty tender it. . . .
> *Hip.* I love not to see wretchedness o'er-charged,
> And duty in his service perishing.
> *The.* Why, gentle sweet, you shall see no such thing.
> *Hip.* He says they can do nothing in this kind.
> *The.* The kinder we, to give them thanks for nothing.
> Our sport shall be to take what they mistake;
> And what poor duty cannot do, noble respect
> Takes it in might, not merit.

And a little later he says:

> The best in this kind are but shadows, and the worst no worse, if imagination amend them.

which is a fore-echo of the famous passage in *The Tempest* already quoted. Noble sentiments are these expressed by Theseus and Hippolyta, but when it came to it they behaved in such a way as to merit Holofernes' sensitive rebuke under similar circumstances: "This is not generous, not gentle."

The implication in the foregoing passage is that the receiving end is a factor in art creation, a fact that nearly broke Touchstone's heart (A. Y. L. I., III iii 12). Rosaline, in *Love's Labor's Lost* (V ii 871) states this principle directly:

249

> A jest's prosperity lies in the ear
> Of him that hears it, never in the tongue
> Of him that makes it;

which would apply to any form of artistic communication. Difference in public attitude is illustrated in *1 Henry* IV, III i 123:

> *Glendower.*   I framed to the harp
> Many an English ditty lovely well
> And gave the tongue a helpful ornament,
> A virtue that was never seen in you.
> *Hotspur.*   Marry,
> And I am glad of it with all my heart.
> I had rather be a kitten and cry mew
> Than one of these same meter ballad-mongers.
> I had rather hear a brazen canstick turn'd,
> Or a dry wheel grate on the axle-tree,
> And that would set my teeth nothing on edge,
> Nothing so much as mincing poetry.
> 'Tis like the forc'd gait of a shuffling nag.

King Henry V, another soldier, feels about the same way about poetry (*Henry* V. V ii 137):

> *K. Hen.*   Marry, if you would put me to verses or to dance for your sake, Kate, why you undid me; for the one, I have neither words nor measure, and for the other I have no strength in measure, yet a reasonable measure in strength. . . . And while thou liv'st, dear Kate, take a fellow of plain and uncoined constancy; for he perforce must do thee right, because he hath not the gift to woo in other places; for these fellows of infinite tongue, that can rhyme themselves into ladies' favors, they do always reason themselves out again. What! a speaker is but a prater; a rhyme is but a ballad.

How successfully Shakespeare, in the following extract, makes the statement of an important principle of literary criticism seem a natural part of the play, by having it issue from the lips of Holofernes! (*Love's Labor's Lost*, IV ii 126):

> Ovidius Naso was the man! and why, indeed, Naso, but for smelling out the odoriferous flowers of fancy, the jerks of invention? *Imitari* is nothing; so doth the hound his master, the ape his keeper, the tired horse his rider.

Ibid. IV ii 156:

> *Hol.* . . . But to return to the verses: did they please you, Sir Nathaniel?
> *Nath.* Marvellous well for the pen.
> *Hol.* . . . I will prove those verses to be very unlearned, neither savoring of poetry, wit, nor invention.

Shakespeare dodges giving us a lesson in *explication de texte* by having Holofernes put off his proof to their next meeting at dinner.

Earlier Holofernes had pointed out that meter does not make poetry; that there are other physical characteristics that are more important. IV ii 124:

> . . . let me supervise the canzonet. Here are only numbers ratified; but, for the elegancy, facility, and golden cadence of poesy, *caret*.

Like his contemporaries, Shakespeare played with the humorous distortion of Aristotle's explanation that poetry was a kind of feigning.

A. Y. L. I. III iii 16:

> *Touchstone.* . . . Truly, I would the gods had made thee poetical.
> *Audry.* I do not know what "poetical" is. Is it honest in deed and word? Is it a true thing?
> *Touch.* No, truly; for the truest poetry is the most feigning; and lovers are given to poetry, and what they swear in poetry may be said as lovers they do feign.
> *Aud.* Do you wish then that the gods had made me poetical?
> *Touch.* I do, truly; for thou swearest to me thou art honest. Now, if thou wert a poet, I might have some hope thou didst feign.

T. N. I v 202:

> *Viola.* . . . I will on with my speech in your praise, and then show you the heart of my message.
> *Olivia.* Come to what is important in't. I forgive you the praise.
> *Vio.* Alas, I took great pains to study it, and 'tis poetical.
> *Oliv.* It is the more like to be feigned.

T. of A. I i 220:

Apemantus.   How now, poet!
Poet.   How now, philosopher!
Apem.   Thou liest.
Poet.   Art not one?
Apem.   Yes.
Poet.   Then I lie not.
Apem.   Art not a poet?
Poet.   Yes.
Apem.   Then thou liest.

There was one popular quip concerning poetry that Shakespeare did not indulge in; namely, that poetry is inspired by wine —and clearly Shakespeare had a healthy interest in wine. Even when Falstaff calls for a cup of sack in preparation for his acting the part of the unhappy father, it is not to make him more eloquent, or a better actor; it is to make his eyes look red, to give him the appearance of having wept.

Jaques, in *As You Like It*, humorously alludes to the custom of young lovers to write woeful ballads on their mistresses' eyebrows, and Orlando adorns the trees of the Forest of Arden with bad poetical fruit. But Shakespeare realized that these effeminate practices were only degenerations occasioned by a genuine and healthy power possessed by poetry. This is illustrated in the following dialogue from *The Two Gentlemen of Verona* (III ii 67) :

Proteus.   But you, Sir Thurio, are not sharp enough.
You must lay lime to tangle her desires
By wailful sonnets, whose composed rhymes
Should be full-fraught with serviceable vows.
Duke.   Ay,
Much is the force of heaven-bred poesy.
Pro.   Say that upon the altar of her beauty
You sacrifice your tears, your sighs, your heart;
Write till your ink be dry, and with your tears
Moist it again, and frame some feeling line
That may discover such integrity:
For Orpheus' lute was strung with poets' sinews,
Whose golden touch could soften steel and stones,
Make tigers tame, and huge leviathans
Forsake unsounded deeps to dance on sands.
After your dire-lamenting elegies,

Visit by night your lady's chamber-window
With some sweet consort; to their instruments
Tune a deploring dump. The night's dead silence
Will well become such sweet-complaining grievance.
This, or nothing else, will inherit her.

Shakespeare thus affirms the inextricable relation between
poetry and music, and his comments on the latter, with their
philosophical implications, are among his most quoted lines.
T. of S. I i 31:

> *Trania.* I am . . .
> Glad that you thus continue your resolve
> To suck the sweets of sweet philosophy.
> Only, good master, while we do admire
> This virtue and this moral discipline,
> Let's be not Stoics nor no stocks, I pray,
> Or so devote to Aristotle's checks
> As Ovid be an outcast quite abjur'd . . .
> Music and poetry use to quicken you . . .
> No profit grows where is not pleasure ta'en.

M. of V. i 69:

> *Jessica.* I am never merry when I hear sweet music.
> *Lorenzo.* The reason is, your spirits are attentive;
> For do but note a wild and wanton herd,
> Or race of youthful and unhandled colts,
> Fetching mad bounds, bellowing and neighing loud,
> Which is the hot condition of their blood,
> If they but hear perchance a trumpet sound,
> Or any air of music touch their ears,
> You shall perceive them make a mutual stand,
> Their savage eyes turn'd to a modest gaze
> By the sweet power of music; therefore the poet
> Did feign that Orpheus drew trees, stones, and floods;
> Since nought so stockish, hard, and full of rage,
> But music for the time doth change his nature.
> The man that hath no music in himself,
> Nor is not mov'd with concord of sweet sounds,
> Is fit for treasons, stratagems, and spoils.
> The motions of his spirit are dull as night

And his affections dark as Erebus.
Let no such man be trusted.

Caesar distrusts Cassius because of his indifference to music. What applies to poetry applies to the other arts, including music; namely, that its operation is a relative, not an absolute thing: M. of V. V i 97:

> *Portia.*   Music! Hark!
> *Nerissa.*   It is your music, madam, of the house.
> *Por.*   Nothing is good, I see, without respect;
> Methinks it sounds much sweeter than by day.
> *Ner.*   Silence bestows that virtue on it, madam.
> *Por.*   The crow doth sing as sweetly as the lark
> When neither is attended; and I think
> The nightingale, if she should sing by day,
> When every goose is cackling, would be thought
> No better a musician than the wren.
> How many things by season season'd are
> To their right praise and true perfection.

The last two lines imply that the quality of a work of art is not relative, but absolute; the proper combination of circumstances, however, is required to make that quality operative. The absoluteness of quality is insisted on by Hector (*T. and C.* II ii 52):

> *Troilus.*   What is aught, but as 'tis valu'd?
> *Hector.*   But value dwells not in particular will;
> It holds his estimate and dignity
> As well wherein 'tis precious of itself
> As in the prizer.

R. and J. II ii 166:

> *Rom.*   How silver-sweet sound lovers' tongues by night.
> Like softest music to attending ears!

M. A. II iii 39:

> *D. Pedro.*   Come, shall we hear this music?
> *Claudio.*   Yes, my good lord. How still the evening is,
> As hush'd on purpose to grace harmony!

254

Ibid. II iii 60:

> *Benedick.* Now, divine air! now is his soul ravish'd! Is it not strange that sheeps' guts should hale souls out of men's bodies?

1 Henry IV. III ii 208:

> *Mortimer.*   . . . thy tongue
> Makes Welsh as sweet as ditties highly penn'd,
> Sung by a fair queen in a summer's bower,
> With ravishing division, to her lute.

T. A. II iv 48:

> *Marcus.* . . . had he heard the heavenly harmony
> Which that sweet tongue hath made,
> He would have dropp'd his knife, and fell asleep
> As Cerberus at the Thracian poet's feet.

One would wish Shakespeare to have been a little more specific when he had the Duke in *Measure for Measure* (IV i 14) affirm:

> . . . music oft hath such a charm
> To make bad good, and good provoke to harm.

Unlike Ben Jonson and Milton, Shakespeare was careful to distinguish between the artist and his art. He knew that the good artist need not necessarily be a good man. The poet in *Timon of Athens* is a repulsive flatterer and time-server, eager to prostitute his art. We see him planning to win the favor of Timon (V i 34):

> I am thinking what I shall say I have provided for him. It must be a personating of himself; a satire against the softness of prosperity, with a discovery of the infinite flatteries that follow youth and opulency.

Shakespeare drops him to the lowest level of the despicable by making him the author of the following lines (I i 15):

> When we for recompense have prais'd the vile,
> It stains the glory of that happy verse
> Which aptly sings the good.

His companion, the painter, is as contemptible as he. Throughout Shakespeare's plays, poets, wherever they appear, do not occupy any noble station either intrinsically or conventionally. Like another, though lesser, genius nearer our own day, Nathaniel Hawthorne, he saw in the poet not the embodiment of the ideal, but only the man who had the power to embody the ideal.

Did the vast difference between the poetry of his time and that of the period immediately preceding, as well as between his own later and earlier work, suggest to Shakespeare that poetry underwent a continuous process of improvement, so that the future would see still better poetry? That is the opinion he expresses in Sonnets 32 and 76.

Art must be free. One of the things that made him cry for restful death in Sonnet 66, was that he saw "art made tongue-tied by authority." Censorship of plays is the form in which the exercise of that authority would touch Shakespeare most nearly. It is important to bear in mind that his opinion was not the prevailing one. No less a thinker than Francis Bacon thought that the existing regulation of the theater was not adequate (*Advancement*, Bk. II, Ch. 13):

Dramatic poetry, which has the theater for its world, would be of excellent use if it were sound; for the discipline and corruption of the theater are of very great consequence. And the corruptions of this kind are numerous in our times, but the regulation quite neglected. The action of the theater, though modern states esteem it but ludicrous, unless it be satirical and biting, was carefully watched by the ancients, that it might improve mankind in virtue: and indeed many wise men and great philosophers have thought it to the mind as the bow to the fiddle; and certain it is, though a great secret in nature, that the minds of men in company are more open to affections and impressions than when alone.

ART AND NATURE

How these terms were used by the Elizabethans is explained on page 47. As to their bearing on the question of poetic creation Shakespeare recorded nothing. To be sure, Lear comes out with the statement, "Nature's above art in that respect." But he does it in the scene in which he utters "matter and impertinency mix'd." It doesn't mean anything where it stands. It is an echo of Marston's "Art above nature, judgment above art," and Chapman's contradiction: "Nature is far above art or judgment." Its presence merely proves that Shakespeare was cognizant of the dispute. Is it, perhaps, assigned to a man out of his senses to give a hint at the author's attitude toward unprofitable academic discussion?

We saw that on the question of the relation of art to nature, in the sense in which the terms are used today, the Elizabethans did not get beyond a realistic conception, especially as applied to pictorial art. In three instances Shakespeare seems to have conceived the idea that the artist's aim ought to be to idealize, not to copy. Two occur in *Venus and Adonis*:

l. 11:   Nature that made thee with herself at strife,
            Saith that the world hath ending with thy life.

l. 289:   Look, when a painter would surpass the life
             In limning out a well-proportioned steed,
             His art with nature's workmanship at strife,
             As if the dead the living should exceed.

The third occurs in *Timon of Athens* (I i 30) :

Poet.   Admirable! How this grace
Speaks his own standing! What a mental power

This eye shoots forth! How big imagination
Moves in this lip! To th' dumbness of the gesture
One might interpret.
    Painter. It is a pretty mocking of the life . . .
    Poet.   I will say of it,
It tutors nature. Artificial strife
Lives in these touches, livelier than life.

In all his other references, however, he is at one with his contemporaries. A painting is to be admired for its approximation
to reality. In *The Rape of Lucrece*, for two hundred lines beginning with line 1366, he gives us a long series of amazingly detailed descriptions of a painting, emphasizing that approximation.

T. of S. Ind. ii 51:

    2. Servant. Dost thou love pictures? We will fetch thee straight
Adonis painted by a running brook,
And Cytherea all in sedges hid,
Which seem to move and wanton with her breath
Even as the waving sedges play with wind.
    Lord. We'll show you Io as she was a maid,
And how she was beguiled and surpris'd,
As lively painted as the deed was done.
    3. Serv. Or Daphne roaming through a thorny wood,
Scratching her legs that one shall swear she bleeds,
And at that sight shall sad Apollo weep,
So workmanly the blood and tears are drawn.

M. of V. III ii 116:

    Bass. Fair Portia's counterfeit! What demi-god
Hath come so near creation? Move these eyes?
Or whether, riding on the balls of mine,
Seem they in motion? Here are sever'd lips,
Parted with sugar breath; so sweet a bar
Should sunder such sweet friends. Here in her hairs
The painter plays the spider, and hath woven
A golden mesh t'entrap the hearts of men
Faster than gnats in cobwebs. But her eyes,—
How could he see to do them? Having made one,
Methinks it should have power to steal both his

And leave itself unfurnish'd. Yet look, how far
The substance of my praise doth wrong this shadow
In underprizing it, so far this shadow
Doth limp behind the substance . . .

Pericles. V Chorus 5:

> . . . with her neeld composes
Nature's own shape of bud, bird, branch, or berry,
That even her art sisters the natural roses.
Her inkle, silk, twin with the rubied cherry.

Cymb. II iv 68:

> *Iach.* . . . it was hang'd
With tapestry of silk and silver; the story
Proud Cleopatra, when she met her Roman,
And Cydnus swell'd above the banks, or for
The press of boats or pride; a piece of work
So bravely done, so rich, that it did strive
In workmanship and value; which I wonder'd
Could be so rarely and exactly wrought,
Since the true life on't was—

Ibid. II iv 81:

> *Iach.* . . . the chimney-piece
Chaste Diana hunting. Never saw I figures
So likely to report themselves. The cutter
Was as another Nature, dumb, outwent her,
Motion and breath left out.

Shakespeare's opinion of Julio Romano (W. T. V ii 105):
. . . that rare Italian master, Julio Romano, who, had he himself
eternity and could put breath into his work, would beguile Nature of her custom, so perfectly he is her ape.

There is one passage that has been cited to prove that Shakespeare believed in the complete subjection of art to nature
(*Winter's Tale* IV iv 79):

> *Perdita.*   Sir, the year growing ancient,
> Not yet on summer's death, nor on the birth
> Of trembling winter, the fairest flowers o' th' season
> Are our carnations and streak'd gillyflowers,
> Which some call Nature's bastards. Of that kind
> Our rustic garden's barren; and I care not
> To get slips of them.
> *Polixenes.*   Wherefore, gentle maiden,
> Do you neglect them?
> *Per.*   For I have heard it said
> There is an art which in their piedness shares
> With great creating Nature.
> *Pol.*   Say there be;
> Yet Nature is made better by no mean
> But Nature makes that mean; so, over that art
> Which you say adds to Nature, is an art
> That Nature makes . . . . This is an art
> Which does mend Nature, change it rather, but
> The art itself is Nature.

But sweet, unsophisticated Perdita cannot grasp his explanation. Illogically enough, she sees an analogy in the painted face. Well, our sophisticated generation employs the same logic, and sees the same analogy, when it defends its practice with the contention that it is "assisting nature."

The argument employed by Polixenes, and even the example, Shakespeare found in Richard Puttenham's *Art of English Poesy*:

> In some cases we say art is an aid and coadjutor to nature, and a furtherer of her actions to good effect. . . . And the gardener by his art will not only make an herb, or flower, or fruit, come forth in his season without impediment, but also will embellish the same in virtue, shape, odor, and taste, that nature of herself would never have done; as to make single gillyflower, or marigold, or daisy, double, and the white rose red, yellow, or carnation . . . he (the poet) doth as the cunning gardener that, using nature as a coadjutor furthers her conclusions, and many times makes her effects more absolute and strange.

In the same context Puttenham states the Elizabethan view of the relation of painting and sculpture to nature; and states it as if it were an obvious fact.

In another respect we say art is neither an aider nor a surmounter, but only a bare imitator of nature's works; following and counterfeiting her actions and effects; . . . of which sort are the arts of painting and carving, whereof one represents the natural by light, color, and shadow in the superficial flat, the other in a body massive, expressing the full and empty, even, extant, rabbated, hollow, or whatsoever other figure and passion of quantity.

DICTION

To Shakespeare, we can readily conceive, language was a passion. The mere sound of words, apart from their meaning, could send him into ecstasy, as illustrated in *HIV*, Part I, III ii 208ff.·

>   . . . thy tongue
> Makes Welsh as sweet as ditties highly penn'd,
> Sung by a fair queen in a summer's bower,
> With ravishing division, to her lute.

The imagery and the diction inspired by the thought seem like a fore-echo of the lines by Keats inspired by the song of the nightingale:

>   The same that ofttimes hath
>   Charmed magic casements, opening on the foam
>   Of perilous seas, in faery lands forlorn.

Doing violence to the instrument that served as his medium partook of the nature of blasphemy (*M.W.* I iv 5) : "Here will be an old abusing of God's patience and the King's English." And Falstaff expresses the bottom depths of humiliation in the words (*M.W.* V v 152): "Have liv'd to stand the taunt of one that makes fritters of English?"

He made it his business to know the language through and through (*2HIV*. IV iv 69) :

>   *Warwick.*   . . . to gain the language,
> 'Tis needful that the most immodest word
> Be look'd upon and learn'd; which once attain'd,
> Your Highness knows, comes to no further use
> But to be known and hated.

When Shakespeare arrived in London, England was language-conscious, as explained earlier (pp. 53ff.). His first play, *Love's Labor's Lost*, is given over to an exposure of the artificialities of diction for which that consciousness was responsible. The play was produced in the winter of 1588. That makes Shakespeare a pioneer in this field of criticism. Three of the characters, Armado, Nathaniel, and Holofernes, are representative of the most absurd of the linguistic aberrations that prevailed. Other vicious practices are assigned to the less "humorous" characters. Of Armado the king has this to say (I. i. 171):

This child of fancy, that Armado hight,
For interim to our studies shall relate,
In high-born words, the worth of many a knight
From tawny Spain.

and Berowne adds:

Armado is a most illustrious wight,
A man of fire-new words.

Concerning all three Moth says (V i 39):

They have been at a great feast of languages, and stol'n the scraps.

This was after they had engaged in the "skew kind of language" which Memory, in Tomkis' *Lingua*, remembers having been popular "about the year 1602," (see p. 64) which was more than a dozen years later. But the craze must have been continuous, the year 1602 being picked because that was probably the year in which the play was being written.

Amusingly enough, the pot calls the kettle black. Holofernes does not approve of Armado: he calls him a "racker of orthography," and describes him as "too spruce, too affected, too odd, as it were, too peregrinate, as I may call it." Nathaniel pounces on the word *peregrinate*: "A most singular and choice epithet," and promptly takes out his notebook to record it. It reminds one of Polonius' "That's good; 'mobled queen' is good," after having condemned "beautified" as "a vile phrase." He hangs on Holofernes' lips with worshiping admiration. "Truly, Master Holofernes, the epithets are sweetly varied, like a scholar at the least."

The affectations to be taken seriously are those that afflict the main characters, and the exposure of these is assigned to Berowne.

IV ii 238:

Lend me the flourish of all gentle tongues,—
Fie, painted rhetoric! O, she needs it not.

V ii 763:

Honest plain words best pierce the ear of grief.

V ii 402:

O, never will I trust to speeches penn'd, . . .
Taffeta phrases, silken terms precise,
Three-piled hyperboles, spruce affectation,
Figures pedantical; these summer-flies
Have blown me full of maggot ostentation.
I do forswear them, and I here protest, . . .
Henceforth my wooing mind shall be express'd
In russet yeas and honest kersey noes;
And, to begin, wench,— so God help me, la!—
My love to thee is sound, sans crack or flaw.
      Rosaline.   Sans sans, I pray you.
      Berowne.   Yet I have a trick
Of the old rage. Bear with me, I am sick;
I'll leave it by degrees.

2 Henry IV. III ii 72:

      Bardolph.   Sir, pardon; a soldier is better accommodated than with a wife.
      Shallow.   It is well said, in faith, sir; and it is well said indeed too. Better accommodated! it is good; yea, indeed, is it. Good phrases are surely, and ever were, very commendable. Accommodated! it comes of *accommodo*, very good; a good phrase.

M. W. of W. I i 150:

Pistol. He hears with ears.
Evans. The tevil and his tam! what phrase is this, "He hears with ear"? Why, it is affectations.

And in the same play (II i 142) Nym's "humorous" speech prompts Page to remark: "Here's a fellow frights English out of his wits."

M. A. II iii 18:

Benedick. He was wont to speak plain and to the purpose, like an honest man and a soldier; and now is he turn'd orthography; his words are a very fantastical banquet, just so many strange dishes.

R. and J. II iv 29:

Mercutio. The pox of such antic, lisping, affecting fantasticoes; these new tuners of accent!

T. N. I v 181:

Viola. Most radiant, exquisite, and unmatchable beauty,—I pray you, tell me if this be the lady of the house, for I never saw her. I would be loath to cast away my speech, for besides that it is excellently well penn'd, I have taken great pains to con it.

Ibid. III i 24:

Viola. Thy reason, man.
Clown. Troth, sir, I can yield you none without words: and words are grown so false, I am loath to prove reason with them . . . who you are and what you would are out of my welkin; I might say "element," but the word is overworn . . .
Viola. Most excellent accomplished lady, the heavens rain odors on you!
Sir Andrew. That youth's a rare courtier. "Rain odors!"
Viola. My matter hath no voice, lady, but to your own most pregnant and vouchsafed ear.
Sir And. "Odors," "pregnant," and "vouchsafed": I'll get 'em all three all ready.

Hamlet. I iii 107:

> *Polonius.* . . . Tender yourself more dearly,
> Or,—not to crack the wind of the poor phrase,
> Running it thus—you'll tender me a fool.

Ibid. II ii 461:

> *Ham.* I remember one said there was . . . no matter in the
> phrase that might indict the author of affectation; but call'd it an
> honest method, as wholesome as sweet, and by very much more
> handsome than fine.

Needless rhetoric is the theme of Sonnets 82 and 83.

In the second scene of the last act Hamlet mimics and holds
up to ridicule the affected speech of Osric.

In II ii of *King Lear*, when Cornwall is displeased with Kent's
blunt manner of speaking, the latter assumes an affected tone:

> Sir, in good sooth, in sincere verity,
> Under the allowance of your great aspect,
> Whose influence, like the wreath of radiant fire
> On flickering Phoebus' front,—
>   *Corn.*   What mean'st by this?
>   *Kent.*   To go out of my dialect, which you discommend so much.

There are several references pertaining specifically to verbosity.
Well known is Hamlet's "Words, words, words." Another is
Polonius' prolix report on the cause of Hamlet's madness. It is
one of the characteristics that Holofernes objects to in Armado.

L. L. L. V i 18:

> *Hol.* He draweth out the thread of his verbosity finer than the
> staple of his argument. I abhor such fanatical phantasimes.

1 Henry VI. IV vii 72:

> *La Pucelle.* Here's a silly stately style indeed!
> The Turk, that two and fifty kingdoms hath,
> Writes not so tedious a style as this.

Bottom's improvisations in *A Midsummer-Night's Dream*, as
well as the play, *Pyramus and Thisbe*, constitute a satire on the

bombast joined with excessive alliteration characteristic of the earlier plays.

For bombast we also have besides all of Pistol, Falstaff's statement in *1 Henry IV*, II iv:

> . . . I must speak in passion, and I will do it in King Cambises' vein.

Trite similes are listed in *Troilus and Cressida*, III iii 179:

> *Tro.*   True swains in love shall in the world to come
> Approve their truths by Troilus. When their rhymes
> Full of protest, of oath and big compare,
> Want similes, truth tir'd with iteration,
> As true as steel, as plantage to the moon,
> As sun to day, as turtle to her mate,
> As iron to adamant, as earth to th' center,
> Yet, after all comparisons of truth,
> As truth's authentic author to be cited,
> "As true as Troilus" shall crown up the verse,
> And sanctify the numbers.

The principle of "decorum" is affirmed in *Winter's Tale*, II i 82:

> *Leontes.*   O thou thing!
> Which I'll not call a creature of thy place,
> Lest barbarism, making me the precedent,
> Should a like language use to all degrees,
> And mannerly distinguishment leave out
> Betwixt the prince and beggar.

That a writer's style ought to change and improve with time is implied in Sonnet 76:

> Why is my verse so barren of new pride,
> So far from variation or quick change?
> Why with the time do I not glance aside
> To new-found methods and to compounds strange?
> Why write I still all one, ever the same,
> And keep invention in a noted weed,
> That every word doth almost tell my name,
> Showing their birth and where they did proceed?

Sonnet 86 suggests that the example of superior work might have a repressive effect upon a writer:

Was it the proud full sail of his great verse,
Bound for the prize of all-too-precious you,
That did my ripe thoughts in my brain inhearse,
Making their tomb the womb wherein they grew?
Was it his spirit, by spirits taught to write
Above a mortal pitch, that struck me dead?

Matter is more important than form.
R. and J. II vi 30:

Juliet. Conceit, more rich in matter than in words,
Brags of his substance, not of ornament.

M. of V. III v 70:

Lorenzo. O dear discretion, how his words are suited!
The fool hath planted in his memory
An army of good words; and I do know
A many fools, that stand in better place,
Garnish'd like him, that for a tricksy word defy the matter.

Hamlet. II ii 95:

Queen.   More matter, with less art.
Polonius. Madam, I swear I use no art at all.
That he is mad, 'tis true; 'tis true 'tis pity,
And pity 'tis 'tis true. A foolish figure!
But farewell it, for I will use no art.

T. of. A. V i 87:

Timon. Why, thy verse swells with stuff so fine and smooth
That thou art even natural in thine art.

A. Y. L. I. IV i 31:

Jaques. Nay, then, God buy you, an you talk in blank verse.

There is one passage to be considered which in some respects is the most important of all that enter into this study, because it presents a problem which cannot be easily solved.

In the second act of *Hamlet* Shakespeare cites a play and gives us a direct criticism of it, loading it with praise. He then quotes what he considers a particularly fine speech. Here we have no abstractions to work with. There is the criticism, and the illustration is an example of unwholesome imagery and unnatural writing. It has been suggested that the whole thing is a satire on Marlovian bombast; but the context forces us to dismiss the notion. Shakespeare even emphasizes its merit by having Polonius dislike it. It has also been suggested that Shakespeare did not wish Hamlet's views to be considered his own. This too seems beside the mark. Hamlet's dramaturgic remarks are distinct digressions. They have nothing to do with the play.

To complicate matters, Coleridge thinks very highly of the speech. There is nothing half-hearted about his opinion. He says:

> The fancy that a burlesque was intended sinks below criticism: the lines as epic narrative are superb. In the thoughts, and even in the separate parts of the diction, this description is highly poetical: in truth, taken by itself, that is its fault, that it is too poetical!

Can we afford to dismiss lightly the opinion of Coleridge, perhaps the greatest of English critics, and himself the purest of poets? Is it not that we are repelled by the narrative because of its adjacency to Shakespeare's great poetry? I admit that I do not find it as bad as I did at first, and certainly not after reading Marlowe's *Dido*, where the same event is narrated. When it comes to judging a piece of poetry like the one under consideration, Shakespeare had an advantage over us. His experience gave him a perspective which we lack. He had watched the steady improvement in English style, in himself as well as in others, and Sonnets 32 and 76 indicate that he expected the process of improvement to continue. He proved his skill by successfully recreating the style that was considered good, even by himself, a dozen years back. The speech obviously purports to be the Messenger's speech from a play constructed along Senecan lines, and as such it fulfills its function effectively, and must be adjudged good.

PROSODY

In *Love's Labor's Lost*, IV ii 123, Holofernes finds fault with the way Nathaniel has read Berowne's verses to Rosaline, missing the rhythm; at the same time he finds that the verses themselves are merely metrically correct, but are not poetry:

> You find not the apostrophas, and so miss the accent: let me supervise the canzonet. Here are only numbers ratified; but, for the elegancy, facility, and golden cadence of poesy, *caret*.

Ibid. V ii 34:

> *Rosaline.* Nay, I have verses too, I thank Berowne;
> The numbers true, and were the numb'ring too,
> I were the fairest goddess on the ground.

M. A. V ii 30:

> *Benedick.* Leander, . . . Troilus, . . . and a whole bookful of these quandum carpet-mongers, whose names yet run smoothly in the even road of a blank verse, why, they were never so truly turn'd over and over as my poor self in love. Marry, I cannot show in rhyme. I have tried. I can find out no rhyme to "lady" but "baby," an innocent rhyme; for "scorn," "horn," a hard rhyme; for "school," "fool," a babbling rhyme; very ominous endings. No, I was not born under a rhyming planet.

A. Y. L. I. III ii 101:

> *Touchstone.* I'll rhyme you so eight years together, dinners and suppers and sleeping-hours excepted. It is the right butter-woman's rank to market. . . . This is the very false gallop of verses.

Ibid. V ii 172:

> *Celia.* Did'st thou hear these verses?
> *Rosalind.* O yes, I heard them all, and more too; for some of them had in them more feet than the verses would bear.
> *Cel.* That's no matter. The feet might bear the verses.
> *Ros.* Ay, but the feet were lame and could not bear themselves without the verse, and stood lamely in the verse.

J. C. IV iii 133:

> *Cassius.* Ha, ha! how vilely doth this cynic rhyme!

Hamlet. II ii 338:

> *Ham.* . . . the lady shall say her mind freely, or the blank verse shall halt for't.

M. N. D. III i 17:

> *Bot.* I have a device to make all well. Write me a prologue; and let the prologue seem to say we will do no harm with our swords and that Pyramus is not kill'd indeed; and, for the more better assurance, tell them that I Pyramus am not Pyramus, but Bottom the weaver. This will put them out of fear.
> *Quince.* Well, we will have such a prologue; and it shall be written in eight and six.

But the soaring Bottom is not satisfied with so little:

> *Bot.* No, make it two more; let it be written in eight and eight.

In point of fact, when this prologue does appear, it is written in the usual ten and ten.

To receive justice a poem must be read correctly. One must not miss the accent, as Nathaniel did, and as Jaques did metaphorically when Orlando asked him not to mar his verses by reading them ill-favoredly (A.Y.L.I. III ii 278) .

FUNCTION OF THE DRAMA

Cicero's doctrine that the drama was *imitatio vitae, speculum consuetudinis*, was made familiar to us through Hamlet's advice to the players (III ii 22):

> ... any thing so overdone is from the purpose of playing, whose end, both at the first and now, was and is, to hold, as 'twere, the mirror up to nature; to show virtue her own feature, scorn her own image, and the very age and body of the time his form and pressure.

This deliberate elaboration of Cicero's simple phrase shows how seriously Shakespeare accepted the principle. Yet he nowhere suggests that the aim is a didactic one. The aim is to give pleasure. The line in *The Taming of the Shrew* (I i 39),

> No profit grows where is no pleasure ta'en,

has no reference to the drama. It is the reason advanced by Tranio for his advice to Lucentio not to overdo his interest in mathematics and metaphysics.

M. N. D. V i 35:

> *Theseus.* Where is our usual manager of mirth?
> What revels are in hand? Is there no play
> To ease the anguish of a torturing hour? ...
> Say, what abridgement have you for this evening?
> What masque? what music?

T. of S. Ind. ii 131:

> *Messenger.* Your honor's players, hearing your amendment,
> Are come to play a pleasant comedy;

For so the doctors hold it very meet,
Seeing too much sadness hath congeal'd your blood
And melancholy is the nurse of frenzy.
Therefore they thought it good you hear a play
And frame your mind to mirth and merriment,
Which bars a thousand harms and lengthens life.[1]

To be sure, the poem on the fickleness of Fortune outlined by the poet in *Timon of Athens* (I i 63) is intended as a lesson for Timon; but the poet here is a time-server, who prostitutes his art. It is undisputed, of course, that lessons will be derived from literature. Any form of art that reflects life will teach if life teaches. The question is one of intention. The painter in *Timon* will not be outdone by the poet. When it comes to teaching, he insists, the painter has the advantage (I i 90) :

A thousand moral paintings I can show
That shall demonstrate these quick blows of Fortune's
More pregnantly than words.

That the poet might properly glorify the good when embodied in a particular person is implied in a passage, already quoted, in *Timon of Athens* (I i 15):

When we for recompense have prais'd the vile,
It stains the glory of that happy verse
Which aptly sings the good.

However, the contrary, to take upon oneself to attack the vile embodied in a particular person, would be personal satire, and that Shakespeare, unlike so many of his contemporaries, disavowed only once, incidentally (T. of A., I i 45) :

Poet.   My free drift
Halts not particularly, but moves itself
In a wide sea of wax. No levell'd malice
Infects one comma in the course I hold;
But flies an eagle flight, bold and forth on,
Leaving no tract behind.

---

[1] Gower, at the opening of *Pericles,* states the intention "to glad your ear and please your eyes," but that speech is not Shakespeare's.

Even impersonal satire was distasteful to him. Among the items from which Theseus is to choose his "abridgement" is one that reads (*M. N. D.*, V i 52):

"The thrice three Muses mourning for the death
Of Learning, late deceas'd in beggary."

a title that describes Spenser's *Tears of the Muses*. Theseus' comment is:

That is some satire, keen and critical,
Not sorting with a nuptial ceremony.

An important utterance on the practice of satire is found in *As You Like It*, beginning with II vii 42:

   Jaques.   O that I were a fool!
I am ambitious for a motley coat.
   Duke S.   Thou shalt have one.
   Jaq.   It is my only suit;—
Provided that you weed your better judgments
Of all opinion that grows rank in them
That I am wise. I must have liberty
Withal, as large a charter as the wind,
To blow on whom I please; for so fools have;
And they that are most galled with my folly,
They most must laugh. And why, sir, must they so?
The "why" is plain as way to parish church.
He that a fool doth very wisely hit
Doth very foolishly, although he smart,
Not to seem senseless of the bob; if not,
The wise man's folly is anatomiz'd
Even by the squand'ring glances of the fool.
Invest me in my motley. Give me leave
To speak my mind, and I will through and through
Cleanse the foul body of th' infected world,
If they will patiently receive my medicine.
   Duke S.   Fie on thee! I can tell what thou wouldst do.
   Jaq.   What, for a counter, would I do but good?
   Duke S.   Most mischievous foul sin, in chiding sin.

For thou thyself hast been a libertine,
As sensual as the brutish sting itself;
And all th' embossed sores and headed evils
That thou with license of free foot hast caught,
Wouldst thou disgorge into the general world.
  Jaq. Why, who cries out on pride
That can therein tax any private party?
Doth it not flow as hugely as the sea,
Till that the wearer's very means do ebb?
What woman in the city do I name,
When that I say that the city woman bears
The coat of princes on unworthy shoulders?
Who can come in and say that I mean her,
When such a one as she such is her neighbor?
Or what is he of basest function,
That says that his bravery is not on my cost,
Thinking that I mean him, but therein suits
His folly to the mettle of my speech?
There then; how then? what then? Let me see wherein
My tongue hath wrong'd him. If it do him right,
Then he hath wrong'd himself. If he be free,
Why then my taxing like a wild-goose flies,
Unclaim'd of any man.

Shakespeare here, in the person of Duke Senior, expresses his disapproval of the self-righteous attitude and procedure adopted by Ben Jonson; for the position taken by Jaques is precisely that of Jonson. However, not to limit the reference exclusively to the latter, he assigns to Jaques characteristics that nobody would think of tacking on to Jonson. It is important to note that Jaques' reply to the duke has no bearing on anything the duke has said. It simply rewords the common arguments advanced by the playwrights, including Jonson, who indulged in satire.

In *Anglia* VII Fleay tries to explain why Shakespeare refrained from casting satirical reflections on the Puritans. His explanation is that Shakespeare early in his career had committed himself against the enemies of Puritanism and so could not consistently take their side later. *Love's Labor's Lost*, he maintains, contains a satire against six of his enemies. To pass no judgment on Fleay's identifications, that Shakespeare failed to ridicule the Puritans because he dreaded inconsistency is inconceivable. A truer explanation probably is that he did not see in Puritanism an institution that ought to be ridiculed. One must refer to a significant little dialogue in *Twelfth Night* (II iii 151) :

> *Maria.*   Marry, sir, sometimes he is a kind of Puritan.
> *Sir Andrew.*   O, if I thought that I'd beat him like a dog.
> *Sir Toby.*   What, for being a Puritan? Thy exquisite reason, dear knight?
> *Sir And.*   I have no exquisite reason for't, but I have reason good enough.
> *Mar.*   The devil a Puritan he is, or anything constantly, but a time-pleaser.

Satire there is in *Love's Labor's Lost,* but good-natured satire, with no venom or bitterness in it; and not personal satire. In this, his first play after he got to London, he ridiculed the various artificialities of written and spoken English that he found current there. That was his only significant venture in satire.

PLAYMAKING

A play must be properly proportioned and suitably cast:

M. N. D. V i 61:

> *Phil.* A play there is my lord, some ten words long,
> Which is as brief as I have known a play;
> But by ten words, my lord, it is too long,
> Which makes it tedious; for in all the play
> There is not one word apt, one player fitted.

Material drawn from history must be modified for dramatic
purposes.

V. T. III ii 34:

> *Hermione.* ... my past life
> Hath been as continent, as chaste, as true,
> As I am now unhappy; which is more
> Than history can pattern, though devis'd
> And play'd to take spectators.

Details of story for stage presentation must be selected.

T. and C. Prol. 26:

> ... our play
> Leaps o'er the vaunt and firstlings of those broils,
> Beginning in the middle, starting thence away
> To what may be digested in a play.

Pericles. III Chorus 53:

And what ensues in this fell storm
Shall for itself itself perform.
I nill relate; action may
Conveniently the rest convey,
Which might not what by me is told.

Ibid. V. Chorus 22:

Of heavy Pericles think this his bark,
Where what is done in action, (more, if might)
Shall be discover'd.

Henry V. V Chorus 1:

Vouchsafe to those that have not read the story,
That I may prompt them; and of such as have,
I humbly pray them to admit th' excuse
Of time, of numbers, and due course of things,
Which cannot in their huge and proper life
Be here presented.

The story must have the appearance of probability.

T. N. III iv 140:

Fabian. If this were played upon a stage now, I could condemn
it as an improbable fiction.

A delightful trick this to disarm the audience, a trick whic
Fletcher borrowed in *The Captain* (See p. 129). This *is* bein
played upon a stage now, and he makes the audience believe th
improbable by telling them that if he were one of them he woul
not swallow it. He realized the principle of romantic art that
is only necessary to have your audience willing for the time bein
to accept what you present.

A play must be well constructed.

Hamlet. II ii 457:

Ham. . . . it was—as I receiv'd it, and others, whose judgme
in such matters cried in the top of mine—an excellent play, w
digested in the scenes, set down with as much modesty as cunnin

If we remember that *digested* means *disposed in due method,* and that *modesty* means *absence of exaggeration,* we can appreciate the significance of the statement.

Technique of the old comedy.

Lear I ii 146:

> *Edmund.* . . . pat he comes, like the catastrophe of the old comedy. My cue is villainous melancholy, with sigh like Tom o' Bedlam.

Here too Shakespeare resorts to a trick—making the audience accept the unlikely entrance of Edgar just at the dramatically effective moment, by calling attention to its unlikelihood. Later in the same play he calls attention to the melodramatic character of the situation he so elaborately presents (V iii 84):

> *Albany.*   For your claim, fair sister,
> I bar it in the interest of my wife.
> 'Tis she is sub-contracted to this lord,
> And I, her husband, contradict your banns.
> If you will marry, make your loves to me;
> My lady is bespoke.
> *Goneril.*   An interlude!

Shakespeare believed with Aristotle that the theme of a play should be of sufficient magnitude. Rosaline in *Love's Labor's Lost* (V ii 305) speaks of "their shallow shows." His other allusions to the subject show his predilection for the "imperial theme" or "swelling act" made popular by Marlowe.

J. C. III i 111:

> *Cassius.*   How many ages hence
> Shall this our lofty scene be acted over
> In states unborn and accents yet unknown!

Shakespeare here cannily prophesies the production of his own play, as he does in *Antony and Cleopatra.*

Macbeth I iii 127:

> *Mac.*   Two truths are told
> As happy prologues to the swelling act
> Of the imperial theme.

Henry V Prol.:

> O for a Muse of fire, that would ascend
> The brightest heaven of invention,
> A kingdom for a stage, princes to act,
> And monarchs to behold the swelling scene!

W. T. V ii 86:

> *1. Gent.*   The dignity of this act was worth the audience of kings
> and princes, for by such was it acted.

The full scene that the Elizabethans were fond of is also alluded to in Richard III, IV iv 91, where Margaret speaks of herself as "A queen in jest, only to fill the scene."

Following are other suggestive illustrations of Shakespeare's penchant for thinking in terms of stage production. Jaques' famous "All the world's a stage" does not need to be quoted.

2 Henry VI I ii 66:

> *Duchess.*   . . . being a woman, I will not be slack
> To play my part in Fortune's pageant.

Ibid. III i 147:

> *Gloucester.*   I know their complot is to have my life,
> And if my death might make this island happy
> And prove the period of their tyranny,
> I would expend it with all willingness;
> But mine is made the prologue to their play.

3 Henry VI V vi 10:

> *K. Henry.*   What scene of death hath Roscius now to act?

280

Rich. III II ii 38:

> *Duchess.* What means this scene of rude impatience?
> *Q. Eliz.* To make an act of tragic violence.

John II i 374:

> *Bast.* And stand securely on their battlements
> As in a theater, whence they gape and point
> At your industrious scenes and acts of death.

Rich. II V iii 78:

> *Duch.* A beggar begs that never begg'd before.
> *Boling.* Our scene is alt' red from a serious thing,
> And now chang'd to "The Beggar and the King."

2 Henry IV IV v 196:

> *King.* All these bold fears
> Thou see'st with peril I have answered;
> For all my reign hath been but as a scene
> Acting that argument.

R. and J. IV iii 18:

> *Jul.* Nurse!—What should she do here?
> My dismal scene I needs must act alone.

Ham. V ii 30:

> *Ham.* Ere I could make a prologue to my brains,
> They had begun the play.

THE QUESTION OF AUTHORITY

The keynote of Shakespeare's attitude on this question is struck in Sonnet 66, in which he complains bitterly that art is made tongue-tied by authority. This is one of the things that tend to make him pessimistic. He cannot brook restraint of any sort—neither that which is exacted by present social conditions nor that imposed by tradition. He insists on independent thinking. In *Love's Labor's Lost* (I i 86) he speaks sneeringly of the continual plodders who have won little save base authority from others' books.

The objection to yielding to the dictates of the past could not be better worded than it is by Coriolanus (II iii 125):

> What custom wills, in all things should we do't,
> The dust on antique time would lie unswept,
> And mountainous error be too highly heapt
> For truth to o'er-peer.

But his memorable declaration of independence is proclaimed by Time, the prologue to the fourth act of *The Winter's Tale*. It was the one final answer which he deigned to give toward the end of his career to those who objected to his free violation of the dignified classic laws:

> Impute it not a crime
> To me or my swift passage, that I slide
> O'er sixteen years and leave the growth untri'd
> Of that wide gap, since it is in my power
> To o'erthrow law and in one self-born hour
> To plant and o'erwhelm custom.

Shakespeare rejected the validity of the sacred unities, the violation of which he acknowledges in the foregoing quotation, because he realized that the appeal of art is not to the reason but to the imagination. This truth he imbedded in Theseus' overstatement, "The best in this kind are but shadows, and the worst no worse if imagination amend them," and extended its application in Hamlet's "Nothing is either good or bad but thinking makes it so." Its proclamation by the chorus in *Henry V*, in diction seldom accorded to its species, peals out like a trumpet-blast from the camp of Romanticism:

> But pardon, gentles all,
> The flat unraised spirits that hath dar'd
> On this unworthy scaffold to bring forth
> So great an object. Can this cockpit hold
> The vasty fields of France? Or may we cram
> Within this wooden O the very casques
> That did affright the air at Agincourt?
> O, pardon! since a crooked figure may
> Attest in little place a million;
> And let us, ciphers to this great accompt,
> On your imaginary forces work.
> Suppose within the girdle of these walls
> Are now confin'd two mighty monarchies,
> Whose high upreared and abutting fronts
> The perilous narrow ocean parts asunder;
> Piece out our imperfections with your thoughts;
> Into a thousand parts divide one man,
> And make imaginary puissance;
> Think, when we talk of horses, that you see them
> Printing their proud hoofs i' th' receiving earth.
> For 'tis your thoughts that now must deck our kings,
> Carry them here and there, jumping o'er times,
> Turning the accomplishment of many years
> Into an hour-glass.

Ibid. II Chorus 31:

> Linger your patience on, and we'll digest
> The abuse of distance, force a play . . . the scene
> Is now transported, gentles, to Southampton.
> There is the playhouse now, there must you sit;

And thence to France shall we convey you safe,
And bring you back, charming the narrow seas
To give you gentle pass; for, if we may,
We'll not offend one stomach with our play.

Ibid. III Chorus:

Thus with imagin'd wing our swift scene flies
In motion of no less celerity
Than that of thought. Suppose that you have seen . . .
Play with your fancies, and in them behold . . . O, do but think
You stand upon the rivage and behold . . . Follow, Follow!
Grapple your minds to sternage of this navy,
And leave your England . . .
Work, work your thoughts, and therein see . . . Still be kind,
And eke out our performance with your mind.

Ibid. IV Chorus:

Now entertain conjecture of a time
When creeping murmur and the poring dark
Fills the wide vessel of the universe . . .
And so our scene must to the battle fly,
Where—O for pity!—we shall much disgrace
With four or five most vile and ragged foils,
Right ill-dispos'd in brawl ridiculous,
The name of Agincourt.

Here Shakespeare runs head-on into Sidney's

. . . two armies fly in, represented by four swords and bucklers
and what hard heart will not receive it for a pitched field?

Ibid.:

              Yes sit and see,
Minding true things by what their mockeries be.

Ibid. V Chorus:

              So let him land,
And solemnly see him set on to London.
So swift a pace hath thought that even now
You may imagine him upon Blackheath . . . But now behold,

In the quick forge and working-house of thought,
How London doth pour out her citizens! . . .
Then brook abridgement, and your eyes advance
After your thoughts, straight back again to France.

Shakespeare reiterates the principle through the person of
Gower, the Chorus in *Pericles*:

III:
                    Be attent,
And time that is so briefly spent
With your fine fancies quaintly eche . . .
In your imagination hold
This stage the ship, upon whose deck
The sea-tost Pericles appears to speak.

IV

Imagine Pericles arriv'd at Tyre,
Welcom'd and settled to his own desire . . .
Only I carry winged time
Post on the lame feet of my rhyme;
Which never could I so convey,
Unless your thoughts went on my way.

IV iv:

Thus time we waste, and longest leagues make short;
Sail seas in cockles, have a wish but for't;
Making, to take your imagination,
From bourn to bourn, region to region.

V:

In your supposing once more put your sight.
Of heavy Pericles think this his bark,
Where what is done in action, (more, if might)
Shall be discover'd. Please you, sit and hark.

An amusing reference to the unities is Polonius' "scene individ-
ble or poem unlimited," to denote the wide area in which the
visiting players excelled. "For the law of writ and the liberty,
hese are the only men."

Immediately after the production of *A Winter's Tale,* in which the classic rules are most drastically violated, Shakespeare wrote *The Tempest,* in which those rules are observed in a way to satisfy the most orthodox, and produced one of his greatest works. He thus proved to his classically minded fellows that he ignored those rules as a matter of choice, not necessity; and that Cartwright's later tribute to Fletcher (see p. 166) could fit him perfectly:

> . . . thou couldst thine own free fancy bind
> In stricter numbers, and run so confined
> As to observe the rules of art which sway
> In the contrivance of a true-born play;

except that he would deny the last clause.

We must not lose sight of the fact that *The Tempest* is not the only play in which Shakespeare stuck to the rules. *The Comedy of Errors,* the first of his plays to be written, is another. I say to be *written,* not to be *produced;* for Professor Baldwin has shown that that distinction belongs to *Love's Labor's Lost.* I assume, of course, that Shakespeare wrote it before he left Stratford. Is it conceivable that he decided to wait till he got to London before yielding to the inner urge? What young genius regulates his life so methodically? Like Samuel Johnson later, when he left for London he had on his person at least part of a play that he hoped to see produced in the great metropolis. When he got there he found a theme that was more timely, so he seized upon it. But *The Comedy of Errors* is just the kind of play that a young schoolmaster would practice with.

In both *The Comedy* and *The Tempest,* be it noted, Shakespeare ostentatiously calls attention to the passing of the hours.

CONVENTIONS

Like all other arts the art of the theater has its conventions. One of the most elusive of these is the fact that no matter where the scene is laid the characters speak the language of the audience. Gower, who acts as chorus in *Pericles*, speaks of this (IV iv 5) :

By you being pardoned, we commit no crime
To use one language in each several clime
Where our scene seems to live.

In other words, the justification for the convention, as for all artistic conventions, is willingness to accept them, because the appeal is to the imagination, not to the reason. It must be admitted that Shakespeare errs here artistically in calling attention to the convention, thus disturbing the illusion, as he does in *Julius Caesar,* when he lets Caesar come out with three Latin words.

PROPRIETY

One passage serves to show how Shakespeare felt regarding wanton surrender to vulgarity for the sake of immediate popular appeal (*Hamlet,* II ii 461):

I remember, one said there were no sallets in the lines to make the matter savory.

What he thought of the spectator who favored the "sallets" is indicated by Hamlet's comment on Polonius's taste (II iii 422):

. . . he's for a jig or a tale of bawdry, or he sleeps.

STANDARD OF JUDGMENT

It can be demonstrated that Shakespeare did not have contempt for the common people as human beings, but he certainly had contempt for their capacity to judge plays. He speaks distinctly on the subject, and not too often. It was not a pet gripe with him, as it was with some of his companions.

In the Induction to *The Taming of the Shrew* Sly is delighted at the thought of witnessing either a tumbling-trick or some lascivious household stuff.

J. C. I ii 260:

> *Casca.* If the tag-rag people did not clap him and hiss him, according as he pleas'd and displeas'd them, as they use to do the players in the theater, I am no true man.

Ham. II ii 456:

> *Ham.* . . . the play, I remember, pleas'd not the million; 'twas caviare to the general; but it was—as I received it, and others, whose judgment in such matters cried in the top of mine—an excellent play.

Ibid. III ii 12:

> *Ham.* . . . the groundlings, who, for the most part, are capable of nothing but inexplicable dumb shows and noise. . . . .
> . . . . Now this overdone or come tardy off, though it make the unskilful laugh, cannot but make the judicious grieve; the censure of which one must, in your allowance, o'erweigh a whole theater of others.

The Prologue to *Pericles* ends with the lines,

What now ensues to the judgment of your eye
I give, my cause who best can justify.

If there were no other evidence, these two lines alone would be sufficient to prove that Shakespeare did not write the prologue.

We see that there was nothing snobbish about Shakespeare's attitude. He simply recognized a fact. Hamlet admits that there are those whose opinion is worth more than his. And surely Polonius, whose daughter might have ascended the throne, did not belong to the masses; yet Hamlet says of him: "he's for a jig or a tale of bawdry, or he sleeps." And even regarding the "groundlings," Hamlet does not make a sweeping statement. He declares that they are incapable only "for the most part," conceding, therefore, that there are among them such as are capable of judging intelligently.

At the same time we cannot overlook the fact that very early in his literary career he did make a sweeping statement. The motto prefixed to *Venus and Adonis* is taken from Ovid:

Vilia miretur vulgus; mihi flavus Apollo
Pocula Castalia plena ministret aqua.

However, with a poem dedicated to a nobleman, this quotation may be interpreted as implied flattery, of the kind characteristic of dedications.

TYPES OF DRAMA

Most of Shakespeare's references to the variety of dramatic types have a comic twist. Best known is Polonius's enumeration:

tragedy, comedy, history, pastoral, pastoral-comical, historical-pastoral, tragical-historical, tragical-comical-historical-pastoral.

M. N. D. V i 66:

Philostrate. And tragical, my lord, it is,
For Pyramus therein doth kill himself.

This agrees with the prevailing conception of what constituted a tragedy. On the other hand, a play would popularly not be considered a comedy unless the sympathetic characters attained their desires.

L. L. L. Vii 884:

Berowne. Our wooing doth not end like an old play;
Jack hath not Jill. These ladies' courtesy
Might well have made our sport a comedy.

Shakespeare was evidently having fun with these terms.

We saw that there was a tendency to associate comedy and history as two species ranked below the dignity of tragedy. Perhaps this association is indicated in the second scene of the Induction to *The Taming of the Shrew:*

Messenger. Your honor's players, hearing your amendment,
Are come to play a pleasant comedy....

>*Sly.* Marry, . . . let them play it. Is not a comonty a
>Christmas gambold, or a tumbling-trick?
>*Page.* No, my good lord; it is more pleasing stuff.
>*Sly.* What, household stuff?
>
>*Page.* It is a kind of history.

That comedy in Shakespeare's mind was not the unworthy form of entertainment that Hieronimo estimated it, is indicated by the following in *3 Henry VI,* V vii 42:

>*K. Edw.* And now what rests but that we spend the time
>With stately triumphs, mirthful comic shows,
>Such as befits the pleasure of the court?

The chronicle play was thought of as a succession of fascinating events.

A. Y. L. I. II vii 163:

>*Jaques.* . . . Last scene of all,
>That ends this strange eventful history.

What Shakespeare thought of the melodramatic type of play may be gathered from the following:

M. N. D. V i 365:

>*Theseus.* . . . if he that writ it had played Pyramus and hanged himself in Thisbe's garter, it would have been a fine tragedy.

It is hard to imagine a more delightful choice of a single incident for the satire.

MIXTURE OF TYPES

Shakespeare has nothing directly to say about the propriety of mixing types; but Polonius's enumeration shows that he was interested in the question, apparently in an amused way. Perhaps it is significant that the mixing of the two main types, the tragic and the comic, is not included in that enumeration. Probably to Shakespeare, free from academic domination, the question presented no problem. His function was to hold the mirror up to life, and life was not sorted out. That the mingling might be done badly he knew from the examples presented by the earlier plays such as *Damon and Pythias* and *Appius and Virginia*. These he burlesqued in *Pyramus and Thisbe,* including the title: *The Most Lamentable Comedy and Most Cruel Death of Pyramus and Thisbe,* and the description submitted to Philostrate: "A tedious brief scene of young Pyramus and his love Thisbe; very tragical mirth." That this was truly not an exaggeration is proved by the oldest extant playbill of an English play, produced in Nuremberg in 1628, which reads:

ZU WISSEN SEI JEDERMAN DASZ ALLHIER ANGEKOMMEN EINE GANZ

newe Compagni Comoedianten / so niemals zuvor hier zu Land gesehen / mit einem sehr lustigen Pickelhering / welche täglich agirn werden / shöne Comoedien / Tragoedien / Pastorellen / (Schaeffereyn) vnd Historien / vermengt mit lieblichen vnd lustigen interludien / und zwar heut Mitwochs den 21. Aprilis werden sie praesentirn eine sehr lustige Comoedi / genant.

DIE LIEBES SUESSIGKEIT VERAENDERT SICH IN TODES BITTERKEIT.

Nach der Comoedi soll præsentirt werden ein schoen Ballet / vnd lacherliches Possenspiel / Die Liebhaber solcher Schauspiele wollen sich nach Mittags Glock 2. einstellen vffm Fechthausz / allda vmb die bestimbte Zeit præcise soll angefangen werden.

It is difficult for us, to whom the practice of mingling seems rational, to comprehend the repugnance of others toward it. It is therefore instructive to learn that the others find our attitude even less comprehensible. An example is offered by the publisher's preface to the 1764 edition of Corneille—two centuries after the birth of Shakespeare, with the example of Shakespeare's achievement before the world. We read:

Il est vrai que dans presque toutes ces tragédies espagnoles, il y avait toujours quelques scènes de bouffonerie. Cet usage infecta l' Angelterre. Il n'y a guère de tragédie de Shakspear où l'on ne trouve des plaisanteries d'hommes grossiers à côté du sublime des héros. *A quoi attribuer un mode si extravagante & si honteuze pour l'esprit humain. . . ? . . .* Jamais ce vice n'avilit la scène française.

Perhaps the last statement explains why the French theater never produced a Shakespeare. The gentleman is mistaken, however, when he says that the practice of mingling was imported into England from Spain. It was a native product, never having been absent from the time that plays were produced in the English language.

PROLOGUE, EPILOGUE, Etc.

Shakespeare liked to use the word prologue in a metaphorical sense. When he refers to the prologue or the epilogue in a technical sense it is apt to be in a tone of mild contempt, as useless appendages. Prologues were always superfluous. When they were obscure they were not understood; when they were understood they merely give information that the audience would acquire in good time. In *Othello* he speaks of "an index and obscure prologue," and one recalls what fun he makes in *Midsummer Night's Dream* of the practice of explaining all details beforehand. Their usual wretchedness from the literary standpoint is noted in *Love's Labor's Lost* (V ii 305):

> *Ros.* Their shallow shows and prologue vilely penn'd.

The following extracts bear on the point.
L. L. L. V i 140:

> *Hol.* He shall present Hercules in minority; his enter and exit shall be strangling a snake; and I will have an apology for that purpose.

2 Henry VI. III i 151:

> *Glou.* But mine is made the prologue to their play;
> For thousands more, that yet suspect no peril,
> Will not conclude their plotted tragedy.

Hamlet describes dumb-shows as inexplicable, and an instance is presently provided immediately after the dumb-show in the third act:

> *Oph.* What means this, my lord?
> *Ham.* Marry, this is miching mallecho; that means mischief.
> *Oph.* Belike this show imports the argument of the play?
> *Ham.* We shall know by this fellow [the Prologue]. The players cannot keep counsel; they'll tell all.
> *Oph.* Will they tell us what this show meant?

Ibid. III ii 162:

> *Ham.* Is this a prologue, or the posy of a ring?

Ibid. V ii 30:

> *Ham.* Ere I could make a prologue to my brains,
> They had begun the play.

A. Y. L. I. Epilogue:

> If it be true that good wine needs no bush, 'tis true that a good play needs no epilogue.

M. N. D. V i 362:

> *Theseus.* No epilogue, I pray you; for the play needs no excuse. Never excuse; for when the players are all dead, there need none to be blamed.

Shakespeare himself occasionally has a song at the end of a play, but he seems to ridicule the practice in the following:

M. N. D. IV i 219:

> *Bot.* I will get Peter Quince to write a ballad of this dream, . . . and I will sing it in the latter end of a play, before the Duke; peradventure, to make it the more gracious, I shall sing it at her death.

The playwrights had reason to hate the jig that commonly followed the play proper: It cut into time that could have been allotted to the play. Shakespeare's contempt for it and the spectator that favored it, is expressed in his remark on Polonius's taste (II ii 422):

> . . . he's for a jig or a tale of bawdry, or he sleeps.

ACTING

That Shakespeare felt keenly the social degradation entailed by the actor's calling is suggested in Sonnet 29. In Sonnet 111 he declaims bitterly against it for the moral degradation to which it inevitably brings its follower. In *Hamlet,* in a passage in which he steps out to rebuke his contemporaries who wrote for children's companies, for ruining the public theaters, he speaks commiseratingly of the likelihood of the boy actors continuing in the profession after they have grown up. Nowhere does he point out the essential dignity of the profession as an art, though his comments on acting are quite numerous.

Shakespeare's utterances on the subject give evidence decidedly against the formalist theory.

T. of S. Ind. i 83:

> *Lord.*　　　　　　This fellow I remember
> Since once he play'd a farmer's eldest son.
> 'Twas where you woo'd the gentlewoman so well.
> I have forgot your name; but, sure, that part
> Was aptly fitted and naturally perform'd.
> 　*Player.*　I think 'twas Soto your honor means.
> 　*Lord.*　'Tis very true; thou didst it excellent.

The suggestion that this passage is not Shakespeare's, but a late insertion referring to Fletcher's *Women Pleased,* dated 1620, is not tenable. There is a Soto in that play; but he is a farmer's only son, not eldest son (an important point in the play), and he plays the clown, and woos no gentlewoman, or any other woman. Shakespeare here invented a situation the reverse of the one in *Friar Bacon and Friar Bungay;* and it may very well be that Flet-

297

cher made use of the name and the description that he found in this play.

T. G. of V. IV iv 170:

> *Julia.*   And at that time I made her weep agood,
> For I did play a lamentable part.
> Madam, 'twas Ariadne passioning
> For Theseus' perjury and unjust flight;
> Which I so lively acted with my tears
> That my poor mistress, moved therewithal,
> Wept bitterly.

Surely it is not necessary to quote Hamlet's advice to the players. It suffices to note that what is stressed is his detestation of unnatural acting and delivery.

Cor. III ii 105:

> *Cor.*   You have put me now to such a part which never I shall discharge to th' life.

Tempest. III iii 83:

> *Pros.*   Bravely the figure of this harpy hast thou
> Perform'd, my Ariel; a grace it had, devouring.
> Of my instruction hast thou nothing bated
> In what thou hadst to say; so, with good life
> And observation strange, my meaner ministers
> Their several kinds have done.

Polonius is so overcome by the suffering of the actor that he cannot endure any more (*Hamlet* II ii 542):

> Look whe'er he has not turn'd color, and has tears in his eyes.
> Pray you, no more.

He appreciates Hamlet's good delivery (II ii 497):

> 'Fore God, my lord, well spoken! with good accent and good discretion.

The power of the good actor over himself (II iii 577) :

Hamlet. Is it not monstrous that this player here,
But in a fiction, in a dream of passion,
Could force his soul so to his own conceit
That from her working all his visage wan'd
Tears in his eyes, distraction in's aspect,
A broken voice, and his whole function suiting
With forms to his conceit?
The power of the good actor over the audience (II ii 588):

Hamlet. He would drown the stage with tears
And cleave the general ear with horrid speech,
Make mad the guilty and appal the free,
Confound the ignorant and amaze indeed
The very faculties of eyes and ears.

The antics of the poor actor illustrated:

T. and C. I iii 149:

Ulyss. . . . with ridiculous and awkward action
(Which, slanderer, he imitation calls)
He pageants us. Sometime, great Agamemnon
Thy topless deputation he puts on,
And, like a strutting player whose conceit
Lies in his hamstring, and doth think it rich
To hear the wooden dialogue and sound
'Twixt his stretch'd footing and the scaffoldage,—
Such to-be-pitied and o'er-wrested seeming
He acts thy greatness in.

Macbeth. V v 24:

Macb. Life's but a walking shadow, a poor player
That struts and frets his hour upon the stage
And then is heard no more.

Rich. III. III v 1:

Glou. Come, cousin, canst thou quake and change thy color,
Murder thy breath in middle of a word
And then again begin, and stop again,
As if thou were distraught and mad with terror?
    Buck. Tut, I can counterfeit the deep tragedian,
Speak and look back, and pry on every side,
Tremble and start at wagging of a straw,
Intending deep suspicion. Ghastly looks
Are at my service, like enforced smiles;
And both are ready in their offices
At any time to grace my stratagems.

Hamlet. III ii 262:

    Ham. . . . Begin, murderer; pox, leave thy damnable faces, and
begin.

Cor. II i 82:

    Men. . . . if you chance to be pinch'd with the colic, you make
faces like mummers.

How to deliver curses (*Henry VI.* III ii 310) :

    Suffolk. Would curses kill, as doth the mandrake's groan,
I would invent as bitter searching terms,
As curst, as harsh and horrible to hear,
Deliver'd strongly through my fixed teeth,
With full as many signs of deadly hate,
As lean-faced Envy in her loathsome cave.
My tongue should stumble in mine earnest words;
Mine eyes should sparkle like the beaten flint;
Mine hair be fix'd on end, as one distract;
Ay, every joint should seem to curse and ban.

The queen describes Hamlet as he looks when the ghost appears in the chamber (III iv 119):

Forth at your eyes your spirits wildly peep,
And, as the sleeping soldiers in th' alarm,
Your bedded hair, like life in excrements,
Start up and stand on end.

1 Henry IV. II iv 421:

> *Falstaff.* Well, an the fire of grace be not quite out of thee, now shalt thou be moved. Give me a cup of sack to make my eyes look red, that it may be thought I have wept; for I must speak in passion, and I will do it in King Cambyses' vein . . .
> *Hostess.* O Jesu, he doth it as like one of these harlotry players as ever I see!

Falstaff's device is matched in ingenuity by the Lord's in the Induction to *The Taming of the Shrew:*

> And if the boy have not a woman's gift
> To rain a shower of commanded tears,
> An onion will do well for such a shift,
> Which in a napkin being close convey'd,
> Shall in despite enforce a watery eye.

The problem of casting: Philostrate reports that in all the plays of *Pyramus and Thisbe* there is not one player fitted, and Coriolanus complains that he will never be able to act the part assigned to him effectively. In *Love's Labor's Lost* (V ii 587) Costard finds Nathaniel "a little o'erparted" in the role of Alexander. In *The Taming of the Shrew* (Ind. i 83) the lord remembers one of the visiting players in a part in which he was "aptly fitted."

Speech graced by gesture:

T. And. V ii 17:

> *Tit.* . . . how can I grace my talk,
> Wanting a hand to give it action?

Entrance and exit are critical moments in an actor's performance.

L. L. L. V ii 599:

> *Holofernes.* Keep some state in thy exit, and vanish.

The inexperienced actor may forget his lines and be "out":

Cor. V iii 40:

> *Cor.*   Like a dull actor now
> I have forgot my part, and I am out,
> Even to a full disgrace.

L. L. L. V ii 561:

> *Cost.* . . . I hope I was perfect. I made a little fault in "Great."

Holofernes was not so lucky: he had to admit that he had been put "out" by the teasing of his audience.

Sonnet 23:

> As an unperfect actor on the stage
> Who with his fear is put besides his part.

R. and J. I iv 4:

> We'll have no Cupid hoodwink'd with a scarf, . . .
> Nor no without-book prologue, faintly spoke
> After the prompter.

These lines were probably conceived in pleasant memories of Holofernes, Quince, and Bottom.

M. W. of W. III iii:

> *Mrs. Ford.* Mistress Page, remember you your cue.
> *Mrs. Page.* I warrant thee; if I do not act it, hiss me.

The skillful can "cover up" in case anything goes wrong, there is a humorous reference to the practice in *Love's Labor's Lost,* V i 140:

> *Hol.* . . . He shall present Hercules in minority; his enter and exit shall be strangling a snake; and I will have an apology for that purpose.
> *Moth.* An excellent device! so, if any of the audience hiss, you

may cry, "Well done, now thou crushest the snake!" This is the way to make an offense gracious, though few have the grace to do it.

A play needs sufficient rehearsing:

M. W. of W. IV iv 64:

> *Ford.*   The children must
> Be practis'd well in this, or they'll ne'er do't.

Hamlet objects to the clown's extemporizing. An example of the kind of extemporizing they might do is given in *Antony and Cleopatra,* V ii 216:

> *Cleo.*   The quick comedians
> Extemporally will stage us, and present
> Our Alexandrian revels; Antony
> Shall be brought drunken forth, and I shall see
> Some squeaking Cleopatra boy my greatness
> I' th' posture of a whore.

Another practice by the clowns that Hamlet objects to is indicated in the 1603 Quarto only:

> And then you have some again that keeps one suit
> Of jests, as a man is known by one suit of
> Apparel, and gentlemen quote his jests down
> In their tables, before they come to the play.

The importance of appropriate costume to the actor is suggested in *Winter's Tale,* IV iv 133:

> *Per.* Methinks I play as I have seen them do
> In whitsun pastorals. Sure this robe of mine
> Does change my disposition.

How thoroughly Shakespeare studied the technique of his art is indicated by the following passage from Richard II (V ii 23):

> *York.* As in a theater, the eyes of men,
> After a well-grac'd actor leaves the stage,
> Are idly bent on him that enters next,
> Thinking his prattle to be tedious.

BALLADS

Shakespeare frequently makes disparaging allusions to the popular ballad. Making such allusions was one of the favorite diversions of the Elizabethan dramatists. Usually these ballads were wretched stuff, and so could easily be ridiculed. The inference of Dr. Hamelius that Shakespeare believed poetry to be the result of culture seems to me too violent. Shakespeare in this was merely a typical Elizabethan, whose attitude toward the ballad is well illustrated by a passage in *The Actors' Remonstrance,* depicting the dire consequences of the shutting down of the theaters.

For some of our ablest ordinary poets, instead of their annual stipends and beneficial second-days, being for mere necessity compelled to get a living by writing contemptible penny-pamphlets, . . . and feigning miraculous stories and relations of unheard of battles. Nay, it is to be feared that shortly some of them (if they have not been enforced to do it already) will be enticed to enter themselves into Martin Parker's society, and write ballads. And what a shame this is, great Phoebus, and you, sacred Sisters, for your own priests thus to be degraded of their ancient dignities.

1 Henry IV. II ii 47:

Fal. . . . An I have not ballads made on you all and sung to filthy tunes, let a cup of sack be my poison.

2 Henry IV. IV iii 50:

Fal. . . . I beseech your Grace, let it be book'd with the rest of this day's deeds; or, by the Lord, I will have it in a particular ballad else, with mine own picture on the top on't, Colville kissing

my foot; to the which course if I be enforc'd, if you do not all show
like gilt twopences to me, and I in the clear sky of fame o'ershine
you as much as the full moon doth the cinders of the element, . . .
believe not the word of the noble.

A. W. II i 172:

> *King.* Upon thy certainty and confidence
> What dar'st thou venture?
> *Hel.*   Tax of impudence,
> A strumpet's boldness, a divulged shame,
> Traduc'd by odious ballads.

A. and C. V ii 214:

> *Cleo.* . . . Saucy lictors
> Will catch at us like strumpets, and scald rhymers
> Ballad us out o' tune.

W. T. V ii 25:

> *2.Gent.* . . . Such a deal of wonder is broken out within this
> hour that ballad-makers cannot be able to express it.

What a "deal of wonder" the ballad-makers were capable of
expressing we can gather from Autolicus' stock in trade (IV iv
261 ff.).
Probably the most mortifying rap that could be inflicted on the
humble ballad is found in *Coriolanus* (IV v 233):

> *Second Serving-man.* Why, then we shall have a stirring world
> again. This peace is nothing but to rust iron, increase tailors, and
> breed ballad-makers.

ONE WORD MORE

Dr. Paul Hamelius, in his little pamphlet entitled *Was Dachte
Shakespeare über Poesie,* expresses disappointment in the end
that his quotations cannot be so arranged as to constitute a com-

plete poetic theory. Neither can the quotations I have gathered, though much greater in number, be so ordered as to constitute an organized system. No such system will be found, because Shakespeare did not put it there. He merely gave expression to his views on various questions pertaining to his art as they were suggested by the context. His utterances on those questions, however, are among the most pregnant pronounced in his age. What we have is only a notable fragment. So is Aristotle's *Poetics*.

IV. BEN JONSON

Drummond informs us in the *Conversations* (Gifford-Cunningham ed., III. 487) that Jonson "hath commented and translated Horace's *Art of Poesy:* it is in dialogue ways." The translation has come down to us, but the commentary was destroyed by the fire in which a considerable number of his works perished. As to the nature of the commentary we have two bits of evidence. One is Drummond's statement above that it was in the form of a dialogue; the other is Jonson's own meager description in his *Execration upon Vulcan:*

> But, in my desk, what was there to accite
> So ravenous and vast an appetite?
> I dare not say a body, but some parts
> There were of search, and mastery in the arts.
> All the old Venusine, in poetry,
> And lighted by the Stagerite, could spy,
> Was there made English.

We may indeed regret the loss of this dialogue, no less than that of Spenser's *The English Poet.* Had it come down to us, we should now be in possession of one systematic exposition of the poetic art by a prominent Elizabethan playwright; and a consideration of Jonson as a theorist would have been a much simpler matter.

The facts being what they are we must content ourselves with the material he *has* bequeathed us. This material is indeed more substantial than that afforded by any other dramatist of the age, and in one important respect is more satisfactory, in that it includes a substitute for the lost commentary. I refer of course to the *Timber, or Discoveries.* The substitute is not all we should like to have it, but it possesses the merit of being extra-dramatic, and therefore purely critical. The nature of the work is announced on the title-page of the first edition: *Timber; or, Discoveries; Made upon Men and Matter; as they have flow'd out of his daily Readings; or had their reflux to his peculiar Notion of the Times.* It is now conceded that the entries from other authors, even when not visibly modified, coincide with his own views, and may therefore be quoted as such.

All references to this work are to Schelling's edition.

POETIC CREATION

Art and nature—in studying Jonson's poetics one must bear in mind the sense in which these terms were used by the Elizabethans. This is explained on page 47.

Jonson's views on the subject of poetic creation contrast sharply with those of Shakespeare. Shakespeare emphasized the inspirational aspect of the process; Jonson emphasized the deliberative. The difference in attitude is the difference between the romantic and the classic. Jonson's position is fairly represented by his lines *To the Memory of my Beloved, the Author Mr. William Shakespeare*:

Yet must I not give nature all. Thy art,
My gentle Shakespeare, must enjoy a part.
For though the poet's matter nature be,
His art doth give the fashion. And that he
Who casts to write a living line, must sweat,
(Such as thine are) and strike the second heat
Upon the Muse's anvil, turn the same,
(And himself with it) that he thinks to frame;
Or, for the laurel, he may gain a scorn;
For a good poet's made, as well as born.
And such wert thou.

This poem belonging as it does to the class of conventional commendatory verses, we must be cautious about accepting as sincere expression of opinion. In fact, we know that it is not. He here conveys the idea that Shakespeare's greatness was due in part to the fact that Shakespeare labored diligently over his work, sweated and revised. What he really thought we can read in the *Discoveries* (ed. Schelling, p. 23) :

I remember the players have often mentioned it as an honor to Shakespeare that in his writing, whatsoever he penned, he never blotted out a line. My answer hath been, "Would he had blotted a thousand," which they thought a malevolent speech. I had not told posterity this but for their ignorance who chose that circumstance to commend their friend by wherein he most faulted, and to justify mine own candor, for I loved the man, and do honor his memory on this side idolatry as much as any. He was indeed honest, and of an open and free nature; had an excellent fancy, brave notions, and gentle expressions, wherein he flowed with that facility that sometime it was necessary he should be stopped. His wit was in his own power; would the rule of it had been so too. Many times he fell into those things could not escape laughter, as when he said in the person of Caesar, one speaking to him: "Caesar, thou dost me wrong." He replied: "Caesar did never wrong but with just cause;" and such like, which were ridiculous.

Jonson closes with a generous concession: "But he redeemed his vices with his virtues. There was ever more in him to be praised than to be pardoned." Really? I am afraid that, despite his protestations, the players, who associated with Jonson and knew him, had a correct estimate of his feeling toward Shakespeare. If they sensed malevolence in his criticism, it probably was there. He accuses Shakespeare of *many* times slipping into the ridiculous, and he cites *one* example which does not ever exist—which his eagerness to find fault dictated to his ear. More than a quarter of a century after the performance he could not resist a malicious allusion. "You never did wrong but with just cause," says the Prologue in the Induction to *The Staple of News.* He was no doubt sincere in his declaration of love for the man but he could not adjust himself to the dramatist's superior position in spite of his *not* having adopted the procedure with which he credits him in his tribute, when, in his belief, *he* had taught his generation how to write plays, and had so proclaimed to the world. In that tribute what he was interested in was to reaffirm the validity of the theories which he sponsored, even if he had to pretend that Shakespeare exemplified them.

It would seem that he still had Shakespeare in mind a little farther on, when he wrote the following:

But the wretcheder are the obstinate contemners of all helps and arts; such as, presuming on their own naturals, which perhaps are excellent, dare deride all diligence, and seem to mock at the terms when they understand not the things; thinking that way to get off wittily with their ignorance. These are imitated often by such as are their peers in negligence, though they cannot be in nature; and they utter all they can think with a kind of violence and indisposition, unexamined, without relation either to person, place, or any fitness else; and the more wilful and stubborn they are in it the more learned they are esteemed of the multitude, through their excellent vice of judgment, who think those things the stronger that have no art . . .

It cannot but come to pass that these men who commonly seek to do more than enough may sometimes happen on something that is good and great, but very seldom . . . Now, because they speak all they can, however unfitly, they are thought to have the greater copy; where the learned use ever election and a mean, they look back to what they intended at first, and make all an even and proportioned body.

Most of this is found in practically identical phraseology in the address to the reader prefixed to *The Alchemist*.

In reading the tribute to Shakespeare there is danger of doing Jonson an injustice. The line, "For a good poet's born, as well as made," is ambiguous. It seems to say that a man may be developed into a good poet even if he is not gifted. We know that Jonson was not guilty of such an absurd notion. What it means to say is that if a man is born with the poetic gift, it is essential to develop it. Jonson has clearly expressed himself on the subject. In the *Discoveries* (ed. Schelling, p. 75) he enumerates and elaborates the five requisites of the poet, and the first is natural ability:

First, we require of our poet . . . a goodness of natural wit, *ingenium*. For whereas all other arts consist of doctrine and precepts, the poet must be able by nature and instinct to pour out the treasure of his mind . . . it riseth higher, as by a divine instinct, when it contemns common and known conceptions. It utters somewhat above a mortal mouth. Then it gets aloft and flies away with his rider, whither before it was doubtful to ascend. This the poets understood by their Helicon, Pegasus, or Parnassus . . .

The second requisite is practice and laborious perseverance. The third is assimilative ability:

> The third requisite in our poet or maker is imitation, to be able to convert the substance or riches of another poet to his own use. To make choice of one excellent man above the rest, and so to follow him till he grow very he, or so like him as the copy may be mistaken for the principal. Not as a creature that swallows what it takes in, crude, raw, or undigested; but that feeds with an appetite, and hath a stomach to concoct, divide and turn all into nourishment.

The fourth requisite is careful general reading:

> But that which we especially require of him is an exactness of study and multiplicity of reading, *lectio*, which maketh a full man.

The fifth requisite is what the Elizabethans called art:

> And not think he can leap forth suddenly a poet by dreaming he hath been in Parnassus, or having washed his lips, as they say, in Helicon. There goes more to his making than so; for to nature; exercise, imitation, and study, art must be added to make all these perfect. *Ars coronat opus.* And though these challenge to themselves much in the making up of our maker, it is art only can lead him to perfection, and leave him there in possession, as planted by her hand.

We can see from his belief in the truth of the last emphatic statement why he insisted to the world that Shakespeare had met this fifth requisite.

> . . . but all this in vain without a natural wit and a poetical nature in chief. For no man, so soon as he knows this or reads it, shall be able to write the better; but as he is adapted to it by nature he shall grow the perfecter writer.

Also *Disc.* (ed. Schelling, p. 24) :

> There is no doctrine will do good where nature is wanting.

312

Ibid., p. 56:

But arts and precepts avail nothing, except Nature be beneficial and aiding.

Ibid., p. 78:

. . . but all this in vain without a natural wit and a poetical nature in chief.

Ibid., p. 49:

They both (poet and painter) are born artificers, not made. Nature is more powerful in them than study.

E. M. out of His H. Ind.:

> *Asper.*   O, how I hate the monstrousness of the time,
> Where every servile imitating spirit,
> Plagued with an itching leprosy of wit,
> In a mere halting fury, strives to fling
> His ulcerous body in the Thespian spring,
> And straight leaps forth a poet!

In lighter vein he derives the inspiration for poetry from the love of womankind and all things associated with it:

Poetaster. II i:

> *Chloe.*   . . . Could not one get the emperor to make my husband a poet, think you?
> *Chris.*   No lady; 'tis love and beauty make poets.

Underwoods LX:

> I do claim a right
> In all that is call'd lovely. Take my sight
> Sooner than my affection for the fair.
> No face, no hand, proportion, line, or air
> Of beauty, but the Muse hath interest in:
> There is not worn that lace, purl, knot, or pin,
> But is the poet's matter; and he must,
> When he is furious, love, although not lust.

Likewise from drink:

World in the Moon:

> *Factor.* . . . I am sure if he be a good poet he has discovered a good tavern in his time.
> *1. Herald.* That he has; I should think the worse of his verse else.
> *Printer.* And his prose too, i' faith.

In the following quotations the terms *art* and *nature* seem to be used in the conventional sense. In them, also, we hear the voice of the classicist, to whom the exercise of imagination could easily be excessive.

Alchemist. IV i:

> *Mammon.* . . . And thou shalt have thy wardrobe
> Richer than nature's, still to change thyself,
> And vary oftener, for thy pride, than she,
> Or art, her wise and almost-equal servant.

Disc. p. 26:

> The true artificer will not run away from Nature as he were afraid of her; or depart from life, or the likeness of truth, but speak to the capacity of his hearers.

Alchemist. To the Reader:

> . . . now the concupiscence of dances and antics so reigneth, that to run away from Nature and be afraid of her is the only point of art that tickles the spectators.

Tale of a Tub. V ii:

> *Medlay.* If I might see the place, and had surveyed it,
> I could say more: for all invention, sir,
> Comes by degrees, and on the view of nature;
> A world of things concur to the design,
> Which make it feasible, if art conduce.

314

An important pronouncement relating to artistic creation is found in the opening sentence of the dedication of *The Fox*:

> Never . . . had any man a wit so presently excellent as that it could raise itself; but there must come both matter, occasion, commenders, and favorers to it: . . . the fortune of all writers doth daily prove it.

In *Neptune's Triumph* Jonson joins in the popular jesting about wine being the source of poetic inspiration:

> *Cook.* . . . you must begin at the kitchen. There the art of poetry was learn'd, and found out, or nowhere; and the same day with the art of cookery.
> *Poet.* I should have given it rather to the cellar, if my suffrage had been ask'd.
> *Cook.* O, you are for the oracle of the bottle, I see; hogs-head Trismegistus, he is your Pegasus. Thence flows the spring of your muses, from that hoof.[1]

Over the door at the entrance into the Apollo, his club room in the Old Devil Tavern, Jonson had an inscription placed which included these lines:

> He the half of life abuses,
> That sits watering with the Muses;
> Those dull girls no good can mean us.
> Wine it is the milk of Venus,
> And the poet's horse accounted:
> Ply it and you all are mounted.
> 'Tis the true Phoebian liquor,
> Cheers the brains, makes wit the quicker.

In *The Devil Is an Ass* he slyly presents the point of view of the Puritan (V v):

> *Gilthead.* How the devil can act!
> *Sir Paul.* He is the master of players, master Gilthead,
> And poets too: you heard him talk in rhyme.

---

[1] The masque was never produced, but Jonson liked this passage so well that two years later he lifted it bodily and incorporated it in *The Staple of News* (IV i).

NATURE OF POETRY

Disc. ed. Schelling, p. 73:

What is a Poet? —A poet is . . . a maker, or a feigner: his art, an art of imitation or feigning; expressing the life of man in fit measure, numbers, and harmony; according to Aristotle from the word ποίείν, which signifies to make or feign. Hence he is called a poet, not he which writeth in measure only, but that feigneth and formeth a fable, and writes things like the truth. For the fable or fiction is, as it were, the form and soul of any poetical work or poem.

Epic. 2nd Prol.:

    . . . poet never credit gain'd
By writing truths, but things like truths well feign'd.

Conversations:

. . . he thought not Bartas a poet, but a verser, because he wrote not fiction.

Disc. p. 76:

The common rimers pour forth verses, such as they are, *ex tempore;* but there never comes from them one sense worth the life of a day. A rimer and a poet are two things.

Epicœne. II ii:

Daw. Why, every man that writes in verse is not a poet; you have of the wits that write verses, and yet are no poets: they are poets that live by it, the poor fellows that live by it.

Daw is represented as a fool, and must give the correct statement a humorous twist.

Jonson's interest in the graphic and plastic arts is evidenced by fairly extensive entries in the *Discoveries*. Here is a comparison between poetry and painting (ed. Schelling, p. 49):

> Poetry and picture are arts of a like nature, and both are busy about imitation. It was excellently said of Plutarch, poetry was a speaking picture, and picture a mute poesy. For they both invent to the use and service of Nature. Yet of the two the pen is more noble than the pencil; for that can speak to the understanding, the other only to the sense. They both behold pleasure and profit as their common object.

Yet in *Underwoods* LXX, addressed to Burlase, he gives the advantage to painting:

> O, had I now your manner, mastery, might,
> Your power of handling shadow, air and spright,
> How I would draw and take hold and delight!
> But you are he can paint, I can but write:
> A poet hath no more but black and white,
> Ne knows he flattering colors, or false light.

Disc. p. 49:

> Whosoever loves not picture is injurious to truth and all the wisdom of poetry. Picture is the invention of heaven, the most ancient and most akin to Nature. It is in itself a silent work, and always of one and the same habit; yet it doth so enter and penetrate the inmost affection (being done by an excellent artificer) as sometimes it o'ercomes the power of speech and oratory.

Cynth. Rev. II i:

> *Cupid.* . . . She has a good superficial judgment in painting, and would seem to have so in poetry.

In the following quotation Jonson shows his good taste in ridiculing the practice of painting statues.

Mag. Lady. V v:

> *Rut.* I'd have her statue cut now in white marble.
> *Sir Mat.* And have it painted in most orient colors.
> *Rut.* That's right! all city statues must be painted. Else they
> be worth nought in their subtle judgment.

DIGNITY OF POETIC ART

Jonson joins in the chorus of complaint about the low estimation in which the poetic art was held in his day.

Disc. p. 22:

> Poetry, in this latter age, hath proved but a mean mistress to such as have wholly addicted themselves to her . . . she doth emulate the judicious but preposterous bounty of the time's grandees, who accumulate all they can upon the parasite or fresh-man in their friendship, but think an old client or honest servant bound by his place to write and starve.

This attitude he attributes, for one thing, to ignorance.

Epigram X. To My Lord Ignorant:

Thou call'st me poet, as a term of shame;
But I have my revenge made in thy name.

E. M. in H. H. Ded.:

> There are, no doubt, a supercilious race in the world who will esteem all office done you in this kind an injury, so solemn a vice it is with them to use the authority of their ignorance to the crying down of poetry, or the professors.

At the same time he was willing, nay, eager, to admit that justification for the attitude was provided by the multitude of unworthy followers of the art. In a passage in *Every Man in His Humor* which appeared only in the original quarto, Jonson eloquently maintained that if poesy were stripped of the base rags in which his contemporaries had clothed her, she would reveal a presence of divine splendor:

> I can refell opinion, and approve
> The state of poesy, such as it is,
> Blessed, eternal, and most true divine:
> Indeed if you will look on poesy,
> As she appears in many, poor and lame,
> Patched up in remnants and old worn-out rags,
> Half-starved for want of her peculiar food,
> Sacred invention, then I must confirm
> Both your conceit and censure of her merit;
> But view her in her glorious ornaments,
> Attired in the majesty of art,
> Set high in spirit with the precious taste
> Of sweet philosophy; and, which is most,
> Crowned with the rich traditions of a soul
> That hates to have her dignity profaned
> With any relish of an earthly thought,
> Oh then how proud a presence doth she bear!
> Then is she like herself, fit to be seen
> Of none but grave and consecrated eyes.

Some years later, in the dedication of *The Fox,* he proclaimed it his sacred office to restore poesy to her rightful throne:

> . . . if my Muses be true to me, I shall raise the despised head of poetry again, and stripping her out of those rotten and base rags wherewith the times have adulterated her form, restore her to her primitive habit, feature, and majesty, and render her worthy to be embraced and kissed of all the great and master-spirits of our world.

This was written shortly after the world had seen the production of such works as *The Fairy Queen, Hamlet, Macbeth, Othello,* and *King Lear.*

Poetaster. I i:

> *Ovid jun.* O, sacred Poesy, thou spirit of arts,
> The soul of science, and the queen of souls,

What profane violence, almost sacrilege,
Hath here been offer'd thy divinities!
That thine own guiltless poverty should arm
Prodigious ignorance to wound thee thus!
For thence is all their force of argument
Drawn forth against thee; or, from the abuse
Of thy great powers in adulterate brains:
When, would men learn but to distinguish spirits,
And set true difference 'twixt those jaded wits
That run a broken pace for common hire,
And the high raptures of a happy Muse
Borne on the wings of her immortal thought,
That kicks at earth with a disdainful heel,
And beats at heaven gates with her bright hoofs,
They would not then, with distorted faces,
And desperate censures, stab at Poesy.

Ibid., IV i:

 Gallus. Why, Cytheris, may not poets (from whose divine
spirits all the honors of the gods have been deduced) entreat so
much honor of the gods, to have their divine presence at a poetical
banquet? . . . Who knows not, Cytheris, that the sacred breath of
a true poet can blow any virtuous humanity up to deity?

Ibid., V i:

 Caesar. Sweet poesy's sacred garlands crown your gentry:
Which is, of all the faculties on earth,
The most abstract and perfect; if she be
True-born, and nurs'd with all the sciences.
She can so mold Rome and her monuments
Within the liquid marble of her lines,
That they shall stand fresh and miraculous,
Even when they mix with innovating dust;
In her sweet streams shall our brave Roman spirits
Chase, and swim after death, with their choice deeds
Shining on their white shoulders; and therein
Shall Tiber, and our famous rivers fall
With such attraction, that th' ambitious line
Of the round world shall to her center shrink,
To hear her music.

Disc. p. 74:

Now, the poesy is the habit or the art; nay, rather the queen of arts, *artium regina,* which had her original from heaven, received thence from the Hebrews, and had in prime estimation with the Greeks, transmitted to the Latins and all nations that professed civility. The study of it, if we will trust Aristotle, offers to mankind a certain rule and pattern of living well and happily, disposing us to all civil offices of society. If we will believe Tully, it nourisheth and instructeth our youth, delights our age, adorns our prosperity, comforts our adversity, entertains us at home, keeps us company abroad, travels with us, watches, divides the time of earnest and sports, shares in our country recesses and recreations; insomuch as the wisest and best learned have thought her the absolute mistress of manners and nearest kin to virtue. And whereas they entitle philosophy to be a rigid and austere poesy; they have, on the contrary, styled poesy a dulcet and gentle philosophy, which leads on and guides us by the hand to action with a ravishing delight and incredible sweetness.

Epistle to Elizabeth, Countess of Rutland (*The Forest XII*):

I . . . send you verse;
A present which, if elder writs rehearse
The truth of times, was once of more esteem
Than this our gilt, not golden, age can deem . . .
It is the Muse alone can raise to heaven,
And at her strong arm's end hold up, and even,
The souls she loves. Those other glorious notes,
Inscrib'd in touch or marble, or the coats
Painted or carv'd upon our great men's tombs,
Or in their windows, do but prove the wombs
That bred them, graves: when they were born they died
That had no Muse to make their fame abide.
How many equal with the Argive queen
Have beauty known, yet none so famous seen?
Achilles was not first that valiant was,
Or, in an army's head, that lockt in brass
Gave killing strokes. There were brave men before
Ajax, or Idomen, or all the store
That Homer brought to Troy; yet none do live:
Because they lack'd the sacred pen could give

Like life unto 'em. Who heav'd Hercules
Unto the stars? or the Tyndarides?
Who placed Jason's Argo in the sky?
Or set bright Ariadne's crown so high?
Who made a lamp of Berenice's hair?
Or lifted Cassiopeia in her chair?
But only poets, rapt with rage divine?

Staple of News. Prol.:

Great noble wits, be good unto yourselves,
And make a difference 'twixt poetic elves
And poets. All that dabble in the ink
And defile quills are not those few can think,
Conceive, express, and steer the souls of men,
As with a rudder, round thus, with their pen.
He must be one that can instruct your youth,
And keep your acme in the state of truth,
Must enterprise this work.

E. M. in H. H. V i:

   Clement. . . . They are not born every year, as an alderman.
There goes more to the making of a good poet, than a sheriff.

New Inn. Epil.:

But mayors and shrieves may yearly fill the stage;
A king's or poet's birth doth ask an age.

Disc. p. 76:

Every beggarly corporation affords the State a mayor or two bailiffs
yearly; but *solus rex, aut poeta, non quotannis nascitur.*

Epigram LXXIX. To Elizabeth, Countess of Rutland:

That poets are far rarer births than kings,
Your noblest father proved.

Evidently Jonson was found of this figure.

The idea, to which Marlowe gave eloquent utterance, that the poet cannot do full justice to his ideal,[1] is the theme of the following quotation from *The Poetaster*, V i:

> *Gallus.* And yet so chaste and tender is his ear,
> In suffering any syllable to pass
> That he thinks may become the honored name
> Of issue to his so examined self,
> That all the lasting fruits of his full merit
> In his own poems, he doth still distaste;
> As if his mind's peace, which he strove to paint,
> Could not with fleshly pencils have her right.

In the dedication of *The Fox* Jonson advances the opinion, later supported by Milton, that the good poet must be a good man. We saw that Shakespeare, with truer insight, knew better.

---

[1]Cf. p. 36.

STATUS OF THE POET

Poetaster I i:

Ovid sen. ... Name me a profest poet that his poetry did ever afford so much as a competency. Ay, your god of poets there, whom all of you admire and reverence so much, Homer, he whose worm-eaten statue must not be spewed against, but hallowed lips and grovelling adoration, what was he? What was he?

Tucca. Marry, I'll tell thee, old swaggerer. He was a poor, blind, rhyming rascal, that lived obscurely up and down in booths, and tap-houses, and scarce ever made a good meal in his sleep, the whoreson hungry beggar.

Ovid sen. He says well. Nay, I know this nettles you now, but answer me; is't not true? You'll tell me his name shall live; and that now being dead, his works have eternized him, and made him divine. But could this divinity feed him while he lived? could his name feast him?

Neptune's Triumph:

Cook. What are you, sir?

Poet. The most unprofitable of his servants, I, sir, the poet. A kind of a Christmas ingine; one that is used at least once a year, for a trifling instrument of wit, or so.

Staple: First Intermean:

Mirth. Or a begging scholar in black, or one of these beggarly poets, gossip, that would hang upon a young heir like a horseleech.

Conv. with Drummond:

He dissuaded me from poetry, for that she had beggared him, when he might have been a rich lawyer, physician, or merchant.

Disc. p. 12:

He is upbraidingly called a poet, as if it were a most comtemptible nick-name; but the professors, indeed, have made the learning cheap—railing and tinkling rimers, whose writings the vulgar more greedily read.

It would be instructive to know who the poets were that were responsible for the low estate of contemporary poetry. But the gripers never mention names. However, it is significant that the greatness of Spenser (and Chaucer) is universally acknowledged.

DICTION

About one fourth of the material in the *Discoveries,* apart from what is concerned with the drama and literature in general, would constitute a substantial little treatise on rhetoric and composition. From this, only such statements will be quoted as relate to the extracts from his other works.

Disc. p. 26:

The true artificer will not run away from Nature as he were afraid of her, or depart from life and the likeness of truth, but speak to the capacity of his hearers. And though his language differ from the vulgar somewhat, it shall not fly from all humanity, with the Tamerlanes and Tamerchams of the late age, which had nothing in them but the scenical strutting and furious vociferation to warrant them to the ignorant gapers. . . . Then in his elocution to behold what word is proper, which hath ornament, which height, . . . where figures are fit, which gentle, which strong, to show the composition manly; and how he hath avoided faint, obscure, obscene, sordid, humble, improper or effeminate phrase.

Ibid. p. 21:

But now nothing is good that is natural; right and natural language seems to have least of wit in it; that which is writhed and tortured is counted the more exquisite . . . no beauty to be had but in wresting and writhing our own tongue. Nothing is fashionable till it be deformed; and this is to write like a gentleman. All must be affected and preposterous as our gallants' clothes.

E. M. O. I i:

Fast.   'Fore heavens, his humor arrides me exceedingly.

Cor.   Arrides you!

Fast.   Ay, pleases me. A pox on it! I am so haunted at the court, and at my lodging, with your refined choice spirits, that it makes me clean of another garb, another sheaf, I know not how! I cannot frame me to your harsh vulgar phrase; 'tis against my genius.

Cor.   This is right to that of Horace, *"Dum vitant stulti vitia, in contrario currunt;"* so this gallant, laboring to avoid popularity, falls into a habit of affectation ten thousand times hatefuller than the former.

Poetaster. V i:

Virgil.   You must not hunt for wild outlandish terms
To stuff out a peculiar dialect,
But let your matter run before your words:
And if, at any time, you chance to meet
Some Gallo-Belgic phrase, you shall not straight
Rack your poor verse to give it entertainment;
But let it pass: and do not think yourself
Much damnified if you leave it out,
When nor your understanding nor the sense
Could well receive it.

Cynth. Rev. II i (Mermaid ed., p. 203):

Cupid.   . . . She is like one of your ignorant poetasters of the time, who, when they have got acquainted with a strange word, never rest till they have wrung it in, though it loosen the whole fabric of the sense.

The Prologue to *Cynthia's Revels* closes with the assertion that the play "affords matter above words"; and in *Discoveries* (p. 60) we read:

In all speech, words and sense are as the body and soul. The sense is as the life and soul of language, without which all words are dead.

Underwoods LXVII:

What though she talk, and can at once with them
Make state, religion, bawdry, all a theme;
And as lip-thirsty, in each word's expense,
Doth labor with the phrase more than with the sense!

The foregoing extracts are concerned with some of the extravagant linguistic practices of the day, and Marlowe's diction is specifically included. We cannot help recalling that in a well-known connection Jonson speaks approvingly of "Marlowe's mighty line," however we interpret the contradiction. The satire in the following extracts is directed specifically at Euphuism.

E. M. out of H. H. II i (Mermaid ed., p. 157):

Fast. Oh, it flows from her like nectar, and she doth give it that sweet, quick grace, and exornation in the composure, that, by this good air, as I am an honest man, would I might never stir, sir, but she does observe as pure a phrase, and use as choice figures in her ordinary conferences, as any be i' the *Arcadia*.
Carlo. Or rather in Green's works, whence she may steal with more security.

Ibid. V vii (Mermaid ed., p. 252):

Fallace. . . . O, Master Brisk, as 'tis in *Euphues*, "Hard is the choice, when one is compelled either by silence to die with grief, or by speaking to live with shame."

The theater made its contribution to daily speech:

Poetaster. II i (Mermaid ed., p. 290):

Albius. "At your ladyship's service." [*Aside*] I got that speech by seeing a play last day, and it did me some grace now. I see 'tis good to collect sometimes; I'll frequent these plays more than I have done.

In the last act of this play Crispinus [Marston] is made to vomit up his favorite artificial vocabulary. We must wonder, however, what objection Jonson could have had to some of the words; and note that Marston himself condemns the practice that Jonson accuses him of (p. 63).

329

Epigrams XCV:

Although to write be lesser than to do,
It is the next deed, and a great one too.
We need a man that knows the several graces
Of history, and how to apt their places:
Where brevity, where splendor, and where height,
Where sweetness is required, and where weight.

In the following he ridicules the conventional imagery of love poetry (*Cynth. Rev.* V ii) :

> *Crites.* I can do you over too. You that tell your mistress her beauty is all composed of theft: her hair stole from Apollo's goldylocks; her white and red, lilies and roses stole out of paradise; her eyes two stars, pluckt from the sky; her nose the gnomen of Love's dial, that tells you how the clock of your heart goes. And for her other parts, as you cannot reckon 'em, they are so many, so you cannot recount them, they are so manifest.

In The Poetaster, III. i. he quotes snatches of old plays to satirize their artificial devices; specifically, the trick of "too many o's," as Chapman calls it (cf. p. 69), and excessive alliteration, both of which had been rendered ludicrous by the lamenting Pyramus in *A Midsummer Night's Dream*. The ridiculous Mathew in *Every Man in His Humor* selects precisely such examples for special admiration.

PROSODY

Under this heading comes the curious jingle entitled *A Fit of Rhyme against Rhyme* (Underwoods XLVII), from which the following is quoted:

Rhyme, the rack of finest wits,
That expresses but by fits
    True conceit,
Spoiling senses of their treasure,
Cozening judgment with a measure,
    But false weight;
Wresting words from their true calling;
Propping verse for fear of falling
    To the ground;
Jointing syllables, drowning letters,
Fastening vowels, as with fetters
    They were bound!
Soon as lazy thou wert known,
All good poetry hence was flown.
    And art banish'd:
For a thousand years together
All Parnassus' green did wither,
    And wit vanish'd!

A simple way of explaining the darkness of the Dark Ages!

Ibid.:

Vulgar language that want
Words, and sweetness, and be scant
    Of true measure,
Tyrant rhyme hath so abused,
That they long since have refused
    Other censure.

Then follows a picturesque curse upon the inventor.

World in the Moon:

> *Chronicler*...Is he a man's poet or a woman's poet, I pray you?
> *2 Herald.*   Is there any such difference?
> *Factor.*   Many; as betwixt your man's tailor and your woman's tailor.
> *1 Herald.*   How, may we beseech you?
> *Factor.*   I'll show you: your man's poet may break out strong and deep i' the mouth, . . . but your woman's poet must flow and stroke the ear, and, as one of them said of himself sweetly,

> Must write a verse as smooth and calm as cream,
> In which there is no torrent, nor scarce stream.

This couplet is also used as an illustration in the *Discoveries* with this comment (p. 25):

> Others there are that have no composition at all, but a kind of tuning and rhyming fall in what they write. It runs and slides, and only makes a sound. Women's poets they are called, as you have women's tailors. You may sound these wits and find the depth of them with your middle finger. They are cream-bowl-, or but puddle-deep.

Of Samuel Daniel he thus expresses his contempt in the *Conversations with Drummond*:

> Samuel Daniel was a good, honest man, had no children; but no poet.

and in *The Forest* XII, referring to his appointment as Poet Laureate:

> . . . though she have a better verser got
> (Or poet, in the court-account) than I,
> And who doth me, though I not him envy.

> *Conv.*   . . . the translations of Homer and Virgil in long Alexandrines were but prose.

Jonson's opinion of the sonnet form is thus reported by Drummond in the *Conversations*:

> He cursed Petrarch for redacting verses to sonnets; which he said were like that tyrant's bed, where some who were too short were racked, others too long cut short.

The sonnet was not the only form to displease him; he detested all complex rhyme schemes. Drummond tells us at the opening of the *Conversations*:

> ... he had an intention to perfect an epic poem entitled *Heroologia*, of the worthies of this country roused by fame; and was to dedicate it to his country; it is all in couplets, for he detesteth all other rhymes. Said he had written a Discourse of Poesy both against Campion and Daniel, especially this last, where he proves couplets to be the bravest sort of verses, especially when they are broken, like hexameters; and that cross-rhymes and stanzas (because the purpose would lead him beyond eight lines to conclude) were all forced.

Presumably these were destroyed by the fire, although they are not mentioned in the *Execration upon Vulcan*. Probably the world can afford to spare the first from its shelf, but the other would have been a welcome addition to the too few expository works in the field based upon the concrete.

On the relation between poetry and form Jonson seems to have been unable to make up his mind.

Conversations with Drummond:

> That verses stood by sense, without either colors or accent; which yet other times he denied.

THE DRAMA

Jonson finds the same justification for the ill opinion in which he says the drama was held in his time, as that which applied to poetry in general. In the dedication of *The Fox* we read:

> ... it being an age wherein poetry, and the professors of it, hear so ill on all sides, there will a reason be lookt for in the subject. It is certain, nor can it with any forhead be oppos'd, that the too-much license of poetasters in this time, hath much deform'd their mistress; that every day their manifold and manifest ignorance doth stick unnatural reproaches upon her: ... now, especially in dramatic, or (as they term it) stage-poetry, nothing but ribaldry, profanation, blasphemy, all license of offense to God and man, is practic'd. I dare not deny a great part of this (and am sorry I dare not) because in some men's abortive features (and would they had never boasted the light) it is over-true. But that all are imbark'd in this bold adventure for hell, is a most uncharitable thought, and, utter'd, a more malicious slander. For my particular, I. ...

He himself expresses the wish that he had never enlisted in the profession, in view of the bad company he got himself into. He says so in the *Apologetical Dialogue* attached to *The Poetaster*:

> *Polyposus.* ... they say you're slow,
> And scarce bring forth a play a year.
> *Author.* 'Tis true.
> I would they could not say that I did that!
> There's all the joy that I take i' their trade,
> Unless such scribes as they might be proscrib'd
> The abused theaters.

Poetaster. I i:

334

Ovid. . . . My name shall live, and my best parts aspire.

Ovid sen. Your name shall live indeed, sir! you say true: but how infamously, how scorn'd and contemn'd in the eyes and ears of the best and gravest Romans, that you think not on: you never so much as dream of that . . . Verses? Poetry? Ovid, whom I thought to see the pleader, become Ovid the play-maker? . . . What? shall I have my son a stager now? an ingle for players? a gull, a rook, a shot-clog, to make suppers, and be laught at? . . .

Lupus. Indeed, Marcus Ovid, these players are an idle generation, and do much harm in the state, corrupt young gentry very much; I know it. I have not been a Tribune thus long and observ'd nothing.

E. M. in His H. II i:

    Kitely. He makes my house here common as a mart,
A theater, a public receptacle
For giddy humor, and diseased riot.

SCOPE AND FUNCTION OF THE DRAMA

Jonson being primarily a writer of comedies, nearly everything he has to say about the drama is said with comedy in mind.

Disc., p. 79:

The poet is the nearest borderer upon the orator, and expresseth all his virtues, though he be tied more to numbers, is his equal in ornament, and above him in his strengths. And of the kind the comic comes nearest; because in moving the minds of men, and stirring of affections, in which oratory shows, and especially approves her eminence, he chiefly excels. What figure of a body was Lysippus ever able to form with his graver, or Apelles to paint with his pencil, as the comedy to life expresseth so many and various affections of the mind? There shall the spectator see some insulting with joy, others fretting with melancholy, raging with anger, mad with love, boiling with avarice, undone with riot, tortured with expectation, consumed with fear; no perturbation in common life but the orator finds example of it in the scene.

E. M. in H. H. Prol.:

He rather prays you will be pleas'd to see
One such today as other plays should be; . . .
. . . persons, such as comedy would choose
When she would show an image of the times,
And sport with human follies, not with crimes;
Except we make 'em such by loving still
Our popular errors, when we know th' are ill.
I mean such errors as you'll all confess,
By laughing at them, they deserve no less:
Which when you heartily do, there's hope left then,
You, that have grac'd monsters, may like men.

E. M. out of H. H. Ind.:

>   . . . my soul
> Was never ground in such oily colors,
> To flatter vice, and daub iniquity:
> But, with an armed and resolved hand,
> I'll strip the ragged follies of the time
> Naked as at their birth—and with a whip of steel
> Print wounding lashes in their iron ribs.

Jonson was fond of the figure which represented the drama as a mirror. He makes use of it in the prologue to *Every Man in his Humor*, already quoted, and in the following.

Mag. Lady. Chorus after II:

> *Probee.* If I see a thing lively presented on the stage, that the glass of custom, which is comedy, is so held up to me by the poet as I can therein view the daily examples of men's lives, and images of truth, in their manners so drawn for my delight or profit, as I may, either way, use them . . .

E. M. out of H. H. Ind.:

> Well, I will scourge those apes,
> And to these courteous eyes oppose a mirror,
> As large as the stage whereon we act,
> Where they shall see the time's deformity
> Anatomiz'd in every nerve and sinew,
> With constant courage, and contempt of fear.

Ibid. After III i:

> *Mitis.* I travail with another objection, signior, which I fear will be enforced against the author ere I can be delivered of it.
> *Cor.* What's that, sir?
> *Mit.* That the argument of his comedy might have been of another nature: as of a duke to be in love with a countess, and that countess to be in love with the duke's son, and the son to love the lady's waiting-maid: some such cross-wooing, with a clown to their serving-man—better than to be thus near, and familiarly applied to the time.

Cor. You say well; but I would fain hear one of these autumn-judgments define once, *Quid sit comoedia?* If he cannot, let him content himself with Cicero's definition (till he have strength to propose to himself a better) who would have a comedy to be *Imitatio vitae, speculum consuetudinis, imago veritatis;* a thing throughout pleasant, and ridiculous, and accommodated to the correction of manners.

Jonson thus early in his career committed himself to the theory of the didactic function of the drama. This theory he never abandoned, though he did not accept it in a pure and simple state.

Fox. Ded.:

. . . it being the office of a comic poet to imitate justice, and instruct to life, as well as purity of language, or stir up gentle affections: to which I shall take occasion elsewhere to speak.

The last clause is thus worded in the quarto: "to which, upon my next opportunity toward the examining and digesting of my notes, I shall speak more wealthily, and pay the world a debt." The allusion is to his prospective edition of Horace's *Art of Poetry,* which he had promised the readers of *Sejanus.* How all his references to that lost labor makes us join in his execration upon Vulcan! In it he spoke "wealthily" on the topics now under discussion.

Ibid.:

I have labor'd, for their instruction and amendment, to reduce not only the ancient forms, but manners of the scene, the easiness, the propriety, the innocence, and last, the doctrine, which is the principal end of poesy, to inform men in the best reason of living.

When he says that instruction is the *principal* end of poetry he implies that there are possible subsidiary ends. In most of his other pertinent references delight is coupled with profit as one of the ends of the drama.

Fox. Prol.:

In all his poems still hath been this measure:
To mix profit with your pleasure.

Epic. 2nd Prol.:

The ends of all who for the scene do write,
Are, or should be, to profit and delight.

Staples of News. Epil.:

Thus have you seen the maker's double scope,
To profit and delight.

Disc. p. 49:

They both (poet and painter) behold pleasure and profit as their common object.

He scorned to accommodate himself to those who came for pleasure only.

E. M. out of H. H. Ind.:

   Cor.   We must not bear this peremptory sail,
But use our best endeavors how to please.
   Asp.   Why, therein I commend your careful thoughts,
And I will mix with you in industry
To please; but whom? attentive auditors,
Such as will join their profit with their pleasure,
And come to feed their understanding parts.
For these I'll prodigally spend myself,
And speak away my spirit into air;
For these I'll melt my brain into invention,
Coin new conceits, and hang my richest words
As polisht jewels in their bounteous ears.

Referring to Aristophanes' treatment of Socrates he says (*Disc.*, p. 83) :

This was theatrical wit, right stage jesting, and relishing a play-house, invented for scorn and laughter; whereas, if it had savored of equity, truth, perspicuity, and candor, to have tasten a wise or a learned palate,—spit it out presently! this is bitter and profitable: this instructs and informs us! what need we know anything, that are nobly born, more than a racehorse, or a hunting-match, our day to break with citizens, and such innate mysteries? This is truly leaping from the stage to the tumbril again, reducing all wit to the original dungcart.

Surely one would expect the royal masque to be exempt from the didactic imperative. Not so in the philosophy of Ben Jonson. Prefaced to *Love's Triumph through Callipolis* is the following declaration:

> All representations, especially those of this nature in court, public spectacles, either have been, or ought to be, the mirrors of man's life, whose ends, for the excellence of their exhibitors (as being the donatives of great princes to their people) ought to carry a mixture of profit with them, no less than delight.

Note the *especially*.

SATIRE IN THE DRAMA

For the employment of satire in implementing the didactic
nction of the drama, as indicated above in the quotation from
M. out of H. H. (p. 337), Jonson felt that he had the support
history.

Apologetical Dialogue:

> *Author.* If all the salt in the Old Comedy
> Should be so censur'd or the sharper wit
> Of the bold satire termed scolding rage,
> What age could then compare with those for buffoons?
> What should be said of Aristophanes,
> Persius, or Juvenal? whose names we now
> So glorify in schools, at least pretend it.
> And still 't hath been the praise of all best times,
> So persons were not touch'd, to tax the crimes.

nd he felt that it was his mission to correct "the time's de-
rmity," even if that meant the application of "a whip of steel."

E. M. out of H. H. Ind.:

> *Asper.*   . . . my soul
> Was never ground in such oily colors,
> To flatter vice, and daub iniquity:
> But, with an armed and resolved hand,
> I'll strip the ragged follies of the time
> Naked, as at their birth, and with a whip of steel
> Print wounding lashes in their iron ribs.

Ibid.:

Asper.   Who is so patient of this impious world
That can check his spirit, or rein his tongue?
Or who hath such a dead unfeeling sense
That heaven's horrid thunders cannot wake?
To see the earth crack'd with the weight of sin,
Hell gaping under us, and o'er our heads
Black rav'nous ruin, with her sail-stretcht wings,
Ready to sink us down and cover us—
Who can behold such prodigies as these,
And have his lips seal'd up? Not I . . .
       . . . my strict hand
Was made to seize on vice, and with a gripe
Squeeze out the humor of such spongy natures,
As lick up every idle vanity.

In a passage in the *Discoveries* (p. 72) he incorporates t‍
main ideas which he repeats in the course of his career whenev‍
he feels called upon to defend his policy:

Now the discredits and disgraces are many it (i.e. poetry) hath ‍
ceived of depravation or calumny; , , , and the age is grown
tender of her fame, as she calls all writings "aspersions."

Whilst I name no persons, but deride follies, why should a‍
man confess or betray himself? It is such an inexpiable crime
poets to tax vices generally, and no offense in them who by the
exception confess they have committed them particularly. Are ‍
fallen into those times that we must not *Auriculas teneras morda‍
radere vero?* If men may by no means write freely, or speak trut‍
but when it offends not, why do physicians cure with sharp med‍
cines, or corrosives? Is not the same equally lawful in the cure ‍
the mind that is in the cure of the body? Some vices, you will sa‍
are so foul that it is better they they should be done than spoke‍
But they that take offense where no name, character, or signatu‍
doth blazon them seem to me like affected as women who if the‍
hear anything ill spoken of the ill of their sex, are presently move‍
as if the contumely respected their particular; . . . If I see anythin‍
that toucheth me, shall I come forth a betrayer of myself presentl‍
No; if I be wise I'll dissemble it; if honest, avoid it, lest I publis‍
that on my own forehead which I saw there noted without a tit‍
A man that is on the mending hand will either ingenuously co‍
fess or wisely dissemble his disease. And the wise and virtuous wi‍
never think anything belongs to themselves that is written, b‍

rejoice that the good are warned not to be such. The person offended hath no reason to be offended with the writer, but with himself, so to declare that properly to belong to him which was so spoken of all men as it could be no man's several, but his that would wilfully and desperately claim it.

He thus admits the prevalence of "depravation or calumny." In the first scene of *The Poetaster* he supplies an amusing illustration, imitated by Marmion in *Fine Companion* (Cf. p. 119f.):

> *Lupus.* . . . they (the players) will rob us, that are magistrates, of our respect, bring us upon their stages, and make us ridiculous to the plebeians; they will play you, or me, the wisest men they can come by still, only to bring us in contempt with the vulgar, and make us cheap.
>
> *Tuc.* Th'art in th' right, my venerable cropshin, they will indeed: the tongue of the oracle never twanged truer. Your courtier cannot kiss his mistress's slippers in quiet for 'hem; nor your innocent gallant pawn his revelling suit, to make his punk a supper. An honest decayed commander cannot skelder, cheat, nor be seen in a bawdy-house, but he shall be straight in one of their wormwood comedies. They are grown licentious, the rogues; libertines, flat libertines. They forget they are i' the statute, the rascals; they are blazoned there; there they are tricked, they and their pedigrees; they need no other heralds, I wiss.

and again in III i:

> *Tucca.* I hear you'll bring me o' the stage there; you'll play me, they say; I shall be presented by a sort of copper-laced scoundrels of you. Life of Pluto, an you stage me, stinkard, your mansions shall sweat for't, your tabernacles, varlets, your Globes, and your Triumphs.

What exercized him most, however, was that *he* was accused of personal satire. He took pains, therefore, to publish denials that he had any part in the practice. Of course he did have part in it; and in one daring instance the personal reference was so patent that Jonson all but announced his victim's name. I refer to the masque, *Time Vindicated,* half of which consists of a withering satire on the poet George Wither.

Fox. Ded.:

I would ask of these supercilious politics, what nation, society, or general order or state, I have provoked? What public person? Whether I have not in all these preserved their dignity as mine own person, safe? My works are read, allowed (I speak of those that are entirely mine); look into them: what broad reproof have I used? where have I been particular? where personal? except to a mimic, cheater, bawd, or buffoon-creatures, for their insolencies, worthy to be taxed? yet to which of these so pointingly, as he might not either ingenuously have confessed, or wisely dissembled his disease? . . . Application is now grown a trade with many; and there are that profess to have a key for the deciphering of everything: but let wise and noble persons take heed how they be too credulous.

Poetaster. III ii (Near end) :

   Treb. No, Horace; I of force must yield to thee;
Only take heed, as being advised by me,
Lest thou incur some danger: better pause
Than rue thy ign'rance of the sacred laws:
There's justice, and great action may be sued
'Gainst such, as wrong men's fame with verses lewd.
   Hor. Ay, with lewd verses, such as libels be,
And aimed at persons of good quality.
I rev'rence and adore that just decree:
But if they shall be sharp, yet modest rhymes,
That spare men's persons, and but tax their crimes,
Such shall in open court find current pass,
Were Caesar judge, and with the maker's grace.
   Treb. Nay, I'll add more; if thou thyself being clear,
Shalt tax in person a man fit to bear
Shame and reproach, his suit shall quickly be
Dissolved in laughter, and thence sit free.

Ibid. V i:

   Virgil. 'Tis not the wholesome sharp morality,
Or modest anger of a satiric spirit,
That hurts or wounds the body of state;
But the sinister application

Of the malicious, ignorant, and base
Interpreter: who will distort, and strain
The general scope and purpose of an author
To his particular and private spleen.

Apologetical Dialogue:

   Author.   My books have still been taught
To spare the persons, and to speak the vices.

Staple. Interlude after II:

   Censure.   Ay, therein they abuse an honorable princess, it is
thought.
   Mirth.   By whom is it so thought? or where lies the abuse?
   Censure.   Plain in the styling her Infanta, and giving her three
names.
   Mirth.   Take heed it lie not in the vice of your interpretation.

Barth. Fair. Ind.:

In consideration of which, it is finally agreed by the aforesaid
hearers and spectators, That they neither in themselves conceal,
nor suffer by them to be concealed, any state-decypherer, or politic
picklock of the scene, so solemnly ridiculous as to search out who
was meant by the gingerbread-woman, who by the hobby-horse
man, who by the costermonger, nay, who by their wares. Or that
will pretend to affirm on his own inspired ignorance, what Mirror
of Magistrates is meant by the justice, what great lady by the pig-
woman, what concealed statesman by the seller of mouse-traps, and
so of the rest.

The prologue to the same play touches on the subject, and the
interlude following the second act of *The Magnetic Lady* elaborates on it.

Epigram II:

             . . . let men know
Thou art not covetous of least self-fame
Made from the hazard of another's shame.

As indicated in the words of Virgil quoted above from *The Poetaster,* Jonson insisted that the satiric spirit as such, that steers clear of personal allusion, is a wholesome thing. He reaffirms this view in the prologue to *The Alchemist,* and, further, advances the naive notion that those in need of his treatment will be grateful to him for administering it:

> But when the wholesome remedies are sweet,
> And in their working gain and profit meet,
> He hopes to find no spirit so much diseased,
> But will with such fair correctives be pleased.

repeating the conviction which he had already expressed in the Induction to *E. M. out of H. H.*:

> Do not I know the time's condition?
> Yes, Mitis, and their souls, and who they be,
> That either will, or can, except 'gainst me.
> None but a sort of fools, so sick in taste
> That they contemn all physic of the mind,
> And, like galled camels, kick at every touch.
> Good men, and virtuous spirits, that loathe their vices,
> Will cherish my free labors, love my lines,
> And, with the fervor of their shining grace,
> Make my brain fruitful to bring forth more objects,
> Worthy their serious and intensive eyes.

But his patients were not pleased, with the result that he finally decided to quit helping the ungrateful creatures.

Underwood's XLI:

> And since our dainty age
> Cannot endure reproof,
> Make not thyself a page
> To that strumpet the stage,
> But sing high and aloof,
> Safe from the wolf's black jaw, and the dull ass's hoof.

THE DRAMA AS LITERATURE

In the original form of this compilation I ventured the opinion that Jonson's plays were poor acting plays. In this view I should still be supported by the following informative lines by Leonard Diggs, relating to a performance of Shakespeare's *Julius Caesar*:

> . . . Oh how the audience
> Were ravish'd, with what wonder they went thence,
> When some new day they would not brook a line
> Of tedious (though well-labor'd) *Catilines*.
> *Sejanus* too was irksome. They priz'd more
> Honest Iago, or the jealous Moor.
> And though the Fox and subtile Alchemist,
> Long intermitted, could not quite be mist,
> Though these have sham'd all the ancients, and might raise
> Their author's merit with a crown of bays,
> Yet these sometimes, even at a friend's desire,
> Acted, have scarce defray'd the sea-coal fire
> And door-keepers.

I have since had the opportunity to witness performances of several of Jonson's plays and have found them actable. Jonson had a genuine dramatic gift. The failure of so many of his plays was probably due to the fact that he preferred to look upon his products, not as stage-plays, but as literary masterpieces. Witness his solicitude concerning their transmission to posterity. He prefers to call his audience *auditors,* and again and again he insists on their keeping their ears open.

E. M. out of H. H. Ind.:

> *Cordatus.* We must . . . use our best endeavors how to please.

347

Asper.   Why, therein I commend your careful thoughts,
And I will mix with you in industry
To please; but whom? attentive auditors,
Such as will join their profit with their pleasure,
And come to feed their understanding parts.
For these I'll prodigally spend myself,
And speak away my spirit into air;
For these I'll melt my brain into invention,
Coin new conceits, and hang my richest words
As polish'd jewels in their bounteous ears.

Ibid.:

Asper.   Only vouchsafe me your attentions,
And I will give you music worth your ears.

Ibid.:

Carlo.   Marry, if any here be thirsty . . . their best way (that I know) is, sit still, seal up their lips, and drink so much of the play in at their ears.

Cynth. Rev. Prol.:

       . . . his muse . . .
. . . proves new ways to come to learned ears.
. . . his poesy, . . . he knows, affords
Words above action, matter above words.

Epic. 2nd Prol.:

Then, in this play which we present tonight,
And make the object of your ear and sight, . . .

Staple of News. Prol. (for the stage) :

For your own sakes, not his, he bade me say,
Would you were come to hear, not see, a play.
Though we his actors must provide for those
Who are our guests here in the way of shows,
The maker hath not so. He'd have you wise
Much rather by your ears than by your eyes.

Jonson's view could not be more directly stated. The theatrical aspect of the play is only a concession. What he thinks of the "guests" to whom he has to concede is unmistakenly expressed in the prologue written for the court performance of the same play:

> We hope it may produce delight;
> The rather being offer'd as a rite
> To scholars that can judge and fair report
> The sense they hear, above the vulgar sort
> Of nut crackers, that only come for sight.

New Inn. Prol.:

> Hear for your health, then, but at any hand,
> Before you judge, vouchsafe to understand.

Jonson wrote a second epilogue to this play, in which he appealed to "men that have more of ears than eyes to judge," "but," we are told, "the play lived not in opinion to have it spoken."

Mag. Lady. Ind.:

> *Boy.* I . . . will undertake for them that they shall know a good play when they hear it.

In the first scene of *The Case Is Altered* Anthony Munday, for whom Jonson had no high regard, in the person of Antonio Balladino, is made to express contempt for good writing:

> *Ant.* . . . no matter for the pen, the plot shall carry it.
> *Onion.* Indeed, that's right; you are in print already for the best plotter. (Meres had so characterized Munday.)

And Jonson here indicates what he thinks of mere plot.

Even in the masque, where the text would be expected (as in the modern musical comedy) to serve merely as a vehicle for the spectacle and music, Jonson insisted that the literary element was the more important. This is what caused the rupture between him and Inigo Jones. He presents a cogent argument in a statement preceding *Hymenaei*:

It is a noble and just advantage that the things subjected to understanding have of those which are objected to sense: that the one sort are but momentary, and merely taking; the other impressing, and lasting. Else the glory of all these solemnities had perish'd like a blaze, and gone out in the beholder's eyes. So short-liv'd are the bodies of all things in comparison with their souls. And though bodies oft-times have the ill luck to be sensually preferr'd, they find afterwards the good fortune (when souls live) to be utterly forgotten. This it is hath made the most royal princes and greatest persons (who are commonly the personators of these actions) not only studious of riches and magnificence in the outward celebration, or show (which rightly becomes them) but curious after the most high and hearty inventions, to furnish the inward parts; and those grounded upon antiquity, and solid learning, which, though their voice be taught to sound to present occasions, their sense or doth, or should, always lay hold on more remov'd mysteries.

In the description of the *Masque of Queens* we read:

. . . a writer should always trust somewhat to the capacity of the spectator, especially at these spectacles; where men, beside inquiring eyes, are understood to bring quick ears, and not those sluggish ones of porters and mechanics, that must be bored through, at every act, with narrations.

The final clause sheds a side-light on Jonson's numerous inductions and choruses.

THE QUESTION OF AUTHORITY

The basis for Jonson's attitude toward this question may be found in a passage in the *Discoveries* (p. 80):

> Whatsoever nature at any time dictated to the most happy, or long exercise to the most laborious, that the wisdom and learning of Aristotle hath brought into an art, because he understood the causes of things; and what other men did by chance or custom he doth by reason; and not only found out the way not to err, but the short way we should take not to err.

In his view, the trouble with most of his contemporaries was that they had not taken the trouble to learn that "short way."

Mag. Lady (1633) Ind.:

> *Boy.* Where it is not at all known how should it be observed? The most of those your people call authors never dreamt of any decorum, or what was proper in the scene; but grope at it in the dark, and feel or fumble for it.

However, for a correct estimate of Jonson's attitude toward Aristotle and ancient authority one must also read the beginning of the paragraph from which the passage quoted from the *Discoveries* is taken:

> I am not of that opinion to conclude a poet's liberty within the narrow limits of laws which either the grammarians or philosophers prescribe. For before they found out those laws there were many excellent poets that fulfilled them, amongst whom none more perfect than Sophocles, who lived a little before Aristotle. Which of the Greeklings durst ever give precepts to Demosthenes? or to Peri-

cles, whom the age surnamed Heavenly, because he seemed to thunder and lighten with his language? or to Alcibiades, who had rather nature for his guide than art for his master?

Disc. p. 7:

I know nothing that can conduce more to letters than to examine the writings of the ancients, and not to rest in their sole authority, or take all upon trust from them . . . For to all the observations of the ancients we have our own experience, which if we will use and apply, we have better means to pronounce. It is true they opened the gates, and made the way that went before us, but as guides, not commanders: *Non domini nostri sed duces fuere.* Truth lies open to all; it is no man's several.

Ibid. p. 66:

Nothing is more ridiculous than to make an author a dictator, as the schools have done Aristotle. The damage is infinite knowledge received by it; for to many things a man should owe but a temporary belief, and a suspicion of his own judgment, not an absolute resignation of himself, or a perpetual captivity. Let Aristotle and others have their dues; but if we can make farther discoveries of truth and fitness than they, why are we envied? Let us beware, while we strive to add, we do not diminish or deface.

Of course, the influence of Francis Bacon is unmistakable here. Bacon, to be sure, is the subject of the paragraph from which this is taken.

Jonson's attitude toward the ancients, then, is one of respectful and sympathetic independence. This is further illustrated in the induction to *Every Man out of His Humor*:

Mitis. You have seen his play, Cordatus: pray you, how is't?

Cord. Faith, sir, I must refrain to judge; only this I can say of it: 'tis strange, and of a particular kind by itself, somewhat like *vetus comoedia;* a work that bounteously pleased me; how it will answer the general expectation, I know not.

Mit. Does he observe all the laws of comedy in it?

Cord. What laws mean you?

Mit. Why, the equal division of it into acts and scenes, according to the Terentian manner; his true number of actors; the furnishing of the scene with Grex or Chorus, and that the whole argument fall within compass of a day's business.

Cord. O no, these are too nice observations.

Mit. They are such as must be received, by your favor, or it cannot be authentic.

Cord. Troth, I can discern no such necessity.

Mit. No?

Cord. No, I assure you, signior. If those laws you speak of had been delivered us *ab initio,* and in their present virtue and perfection, there had been some reason of obeying their powers; but 'tis extant that that which we call comoedia, was at first nothing but a simple and continued song, sung by one only person, till Susario invented a second; after him, Epicharmus a third. Phormus and Chionides devised to have four actors, with a Prologue and Chorus; to which Cratinus (long after) added a fifth and sixth; Eupolis more; Aristophanes more than they. Every man in the dignity of his spirit and judgment supplied something. And though that in him this kind of poem appeared absolute, and fully perfected, yet how is the face of it changed since, in Menander, Philemon, Cecilius, Plautus, and the rest! who have utterly excluded the Chorus, altered the property of the persons, their names, and natures, and augmented it with all liberty, according to the elegancy and disposition of those times wherein they wrote. I see not then, but we should enjoy the same license, or free power, to illustrate and heighten our invention as they did; and not be tied to those strict and regular forms which the niceness of a few (who are nothing but form) would thrust upon us.

The "few" referred to are the continental perverters of Aristotle.[1] Despite his protestation, however, he was not as much of a non-conformist as he seemed to think he was. He did practice the five-act division, "according to the Terentian manner," as he had learned "in the third form at Westminster"; he did aim to have "the whole argument fall within compass of a day's business"; he even aimed to approximate the restriction of the action to a single place, concerning which Aristotle says nothing—which was merely one of "those strict and regular forms which the nice-

---

[1] The matter of sources and relations of Elizabethan dramatic conceptions is definitively treated in Professor T. W. Baldwin's *Shakespeare's Five-Act Structure.*

ness of a few" would thrust upon him. By his own enumeration he departed only in the matter of the number of actors, the choice of characters, and the inclusion of a chorus (though in this play he included what he nostalgically labeled *Grex*) reluctantly so far as the last is concerned, as indicated by his address to the readers of *Sejanus*:

> If it be objected that what I publish is no true poem, in the strict laws of time, I confess it: as also in the want of a proper chorus; whose habits and moods are such and so difficult, as not any that I have seen, since the ancients, no, not they who have most presently affected laws, have yet come in the way of. Nor is it needful, or almost possible in these our times, and to such auditors as commonly things are presented, to observe the old state and splendor of dramatic poems, with preservation of any popular delight. But of this I shall take more seasonable cause to speak, in my observations upon Horace his Art of Poetry, which, with the text translated, I intend shortly to publish.

The translation was published, but not the observations; these having been lost in the fire that broke out in his home. He concedes, then, that departure from ancient practice has spelled the deterioration of the drama, but is rendered compulsory by the inferior quality of his audience.

In the continuation of the address he points out that he has "discharged the other offices of a tragic writer," in that he has paid attention to "truth of argument, dignity of persons, gravity and height of elocution, fullness and frequency of sentence."

In the prologue to his next play, *The Fox*, he emphatically reaffirms his adherence to "the Laws of Time, Place, Persons"; but he cautiously adds: "From no needful rule he swerveth."

His position on the so-called Unity of Place is revealed in a passage in the induction to *Every Man out of His Humor* immediately following his expression of displeasure with "the niceness of a few:"

> *Mitis.* . . . what's his scene?
> *Cordatus. Insula Fortunata,* sir.
> *Mit.* O, The Fortunate Island? mass, he has bound himself to a strict law there.
> *Cor.* Why so?

Mit. He cannot lightly alter the scene without crossing the seas.

Cor. He needs not, having a whole island to run through, I think.

Mit. No? How comes it then that in some one play we see so many seas, countries, and kingdoms passed over with such admirable dexterity?

Cor. O, that but shows how well the authors can travel in their vocation, and outrun the apprehension of their auditory.

If he was willing to include the limits of England and Scotland, one would imagine that he would not have caviled about the comparatively narrow Dover Strait. But it illustrates the ridiculous predicaments into which playwrights of the Jonson type forced themselves.

Sad Shepherd. Prol.:

Hear what his sorrows are; and if they wound
Your gentle breasts, so that the end crown all
Which in the scope of one day's chance may fall . . .

It appears then that the reason why Jonson was antagonistic to the romantic dramatists was that they shot beyond the apprehension of the audience. In other words, he minimized the function of the imagination in art. Yet how much he, in spite of himself, had in common with his romantic contemporaries is illustrated by the interludes in *Every Man out of His Humor,* wherein he repeatedly urges his public to exert its imagination, in order to be carried from scene to scene. A striking instance, reminding one specifically of Shakespeare, follows Act IV:

Cor. To help your longing, signior, let your imagination be swifter than a pair of oars: and by this, suppose Puntarvolo, Brisk, Fungoso, and the dog arrived at the gate, and going up to the great chamber.

He gets involved, likewise, in a contradiction in the following passage in *Discoveries* (p. 85):

Now in every action it behooves the poet to know which is his utmost bound, how far with fitness and a necessary proportion he may produce and determine it. . . . For as a body without proportion cannot be goodly, no more can the action, either in comedy or tragedy, without his fit bounds. And every bound, for the nature of the subject, is esteemed the best that is largest, till it can increase no more; so it behooves the action in tragedy or comedy to be let grow till the necessity ask a conclusion; wherein two things are to be considered; first, that it exceed not the compass of one day; next, that there be place left for digression and art. For the episodes and digressions in a fable are the same that household stuff and other furniture are in a house.

We are told, then, that the larger the action of a play the more satisfying; and in the same breath we are commanded not to violate the sacred Unity of Time, which, not Aristotle, but those same despised "few," made into a law. Aristotle merely reported a contemporary practice. Jonson the classicist could not divorce himself from Jonson the Elizabethan.

More significant, perhaps, is the second part of the proviso; namely, "that there be place left for digression and art." Is not this an unclassical suggestion? That describes Shakespeare's practice, with the result that his plays are instinct with life. In voicing this penetrative opinion Jonson anticipated by three centuries, the man who has been spoken of as his modern counterpart, Bernard Shaw, who, in an interview with playwright Paul Green, (*New York Times Book Review,* Nov. 28, 1954) expressed himself thus:

This is the great trouble with the modern playwrights. It's become the style to cramp down everything, make every line tell, every sentence have some plot point, hurrying on toward the inevitable dénouement, straight as an arrow in its flight. What is the result? Something dry and dead. Consider the lilies of the field—that's it, that's what was meant—the flowers, the greenery, the luxuriant foliage of life.

What is particularly interesting about this pronouncement of Jonson's is that it departs radically from Aristotle, whom Jonson has been paraphrasing. Aristotle's statement is:

. . . the plot, which is an imitation of an action, must represent an action that is organically unified, the structural order of the incidents being such that transposing or removing any one of them will dislocate and disorganize the whole. Every part must be necessary, and in its place; for a thing whose presence or absence makes no perceptible difference is not an organic part of the whole.

An example of the shifts to which Jonson had to resort to keep the action within the time limit is proudly presented in the interlude following the third act of *The Magnetic Lady*:

> *Damplay.* This was a pitiful poor shift o' your poet, boy, to make his prime woman with child, and fall in labor, just to compose a quarrel.
> *Boy.* . . . the quarrel . . . hastened on the discovery of it, in occasioning her affright, which made her fall into her throes presently, and within that compass of time allowed to the comedy; wherein the poet expresses his prime artifice, rather than any error.

In *Bartholomew Fair,* IV ii, Jonson (like Shakespeare in *The Comedy of Errors* and *The Tempest*) keeps the audience apprised of the fact that the action of the plot coincides with the duration of performance:

> *Grace.* Sure you think me a woman of an extreme levity, gentlemen, . . . that, meeting you by chance in such a place as this, . . . and not yet of two hours' acquaintance, . . . I should so forsake my modesty. . .

In the interlude following Act III Scene ii, of *Every Man out of His Humor,* the authority of Plautus is appealed to to settle a question of type restriction:

> *Mitis.* . . . your author hath largely outstript my expectation in this scene, I will liberally confess it. For, when I saw Sordido so desperately intended, I thought I had had a hand of him then.
> *Cordatus.* What? you supposed he should have hung himself indeed?
> *Mit.* I did, and had framed my objection to it ready, which may yet be very fitly urged, and with some necessity: for though his purposed violence lost th' effect, and extended not to death, yet the intent and horror of the object was more than the nature of a comedy will in any sort admit.

Cor. Ay? what think you of Plautus, in his comedy called *Cistellaria?* there where he brings in Alcesimarchus with a drawn sword ready to kill himself, and as he is e'n fixing his breast upon it, to be restrained from his resolved outrage by Silenium and the bawd? Is not his authority of power to give our scene approbation?

Mit. Sir, I have this only evasion left me, to say: I think it be so indeed. Your memory is better than mine.

Apparently, there was a degree of self-delusion in his eloquent denial of the control of the ancients. They were to be looked upon as "guides, not commanders"—but he followed those guides in nearly all their tenets and practices, and expressed regret that his audience would not permit him to follow in others. His conservatism intensified with time. In the induction to *The Magnetic Lady,* his last play but one, he proclaims the inviolability of the ancient practice of presenting the action outdoors, what happens within to be published by report. This practice he had not followed in his earlier plays.

Regarding non-dramatic poetry, to be sure, his position was unqualified. That was to be a product of the times, regardless of classic example. Drummond reports:

His censure on my verses was: that they were all good . . . save that they smelled too much of the schools, and were not after the fancy of the time; for a child (says he) may write after the fashion of the Greek and Latin verses in running.

PLAY-MAKING

As we have seen, Jonson believed that literary creation called for the possession of a natural gift, plus art; the term art meaning, as explained by Puttenham, "a certain order of rules prescribed by reason, and gathered by experience." Without a knowledge of these rules, Jonson declares in the induction to *The Magnetic Lady,* playwrights "but grope in the dark, and feel or fumble" for the right thing to do. If they only wrote enough they might "happen on something that is good and great, but very seldom." (Disc., p. 26). In his old age, addressing Richard Brome, he pronounced himself to have been the first to teach his age how to write comedies.

Underwoods, XXVIII:

I had you for a servant once, Dick Brome,
And you performed a servant's faithful part;
Now you are got into a nearer room
Of fellowship, professing my old arts.
And you do do them well, with good applause,
Which you have justly gained from the stage,
By observation of those comic laws
Which I, your master, first did teach the age.
You learnt it well, and for it serv'd your time,
A prenticeship, which few do nowadays:
Now each court hobby-horse will wince in rhyme;
Both learned and unlearned, all write plays.

Writing plays, then, is a craft; hence, as in any other craft, a special apprenticeship must be served if one would become a master in it.

A. SELECTION OF MATERIAL

A basic principle in the aesthetics of Jonson the classicist is that art must make its appeal to the reason, not to the imagination. In the *Discoveries* (p. 82) he expresses disgust with the romantically conditioned Elizabethan public. He calls it "the beast, the multitude." "They love nothing that is right and proper," he complains. "The farther it runs from reason or possibility with them the better it is." In the prologue to *Every Man in His Humor* he proclaimed where he stood in the matter of choice of material for dramatic purposes:

> Though need make many poets, and some such
> As art, and nature have not bettered much;
> Yet ours for want hath not so lov'd the stage,
> As he dare serve th'ill customs of the age,
> Or purchase your delight at such a rate,
> As, for it, he himself must justly hate.
> To make a child, now was addled, to proceed
> Man, and then shoot up, in one beard, and weed,
> Past threescore years; or with three rusty swords,
> And help of some few foot-and-half-foot words,
> Fight over York and Lancaster's long jars,
> And in the tyring-house bring wounds to scars.
> He rather prays you would be pleas'd to see
> One such today as other plays should be;
> Where neither chorus wafts you o'er the seas,
> Nor creaking throne comes down, the boys to please;
> Nor nimble squib is seen, to make afeard
> The gentlewomen; nor roll'd bullet heard
> To say, it thunders; nor tempestuous drum
> Rumbles, to tell you when the storm doth come;
> But deeds, and language, such as men do use:
> And persons, such as comedy would choose,
> When she would show an image of the times,
> And sport with human follies, not with crimes.
> Except we make them such, by loving still
> Our popular errors, when we know they're ill.
> I mean such errors, as you'll all confess
> By laughing at them, they deserve no less:
> Which when you heartily do, there's hope left then,
> You, that have so grac'd monsters, may like men.

This assault upon romanticism first appeared in the 1616 folio. It therefore represents Jonson's matured attitude.

As if to emphasize the thought with which he closes he placed upon the title-page of *Sejanus* the following quotation from Martial:

Non his centaures, non gorgonas, harpiasque
Invenies: hominem pagina nostra sapit.

We surely are treated here to some of the subjects of the Jonson-Shakespeare debates at the Mermaid. Analogously, Leoncavallo, in reference to Wagner, scornfully averred that he was concerned with men, not dragons.

Alchemist. Prol.:

Our scene is London, 'cause we would make known,
No country's mirth is better than our own:
No clime breeds better matter for your whore,
Bawd, squire, imposter, many persons more,
Whose manners, now call'd humors, feed the stage,
And which have still been subject for the rage
Or spleen of comic writers.

Even when he wrote a pastoral, which by its nature has a romantic quality, he boasted of his homespun material.

Sad Shepherd. Prol.:

And though he now present you with such wool
As from mere English flocks his Muse can pull,
He hopes that when it is made up into cloth,
Not the most curious head here will be loth
To wear a hood of it; it being a fleece
To match or those of Sicily or Greece.

The older types of plays were the butt of his satire. This, like his denial of unlimited acceptance of ancient authority, shows in him an appreciation of the necessity of progress. In the induction to *Bartholomew Fair* he begs his audience not "to look back to the sword and buckler age." In *The Case is Altered* (I i) Antony Balladino, in whose person Jonson satirizes Anthony Munday, is made to say:

Why, look you, sir, I write so plain, and keep that old decorum, that you must of necessity like it. Marry, you shall have some now, (as, for example, in plays) that will have every day new tricks, and write you nothing but humors. Indeed, this pleases the gentlemen, but the common sort they care not for it; they know not what to make on't; they look for good matter, they, and are not edified with such toys.

Staple of News. Intermean after the second act:

Mirth. How like you the Vice i' the play?
Expectation. Which is he?
Mirth. Three or four: old Covetousness, the sordid Penny-boy, the money-bawd, who is a flesh-bawd too, they say—
Tattle. But here is never a fiend to carry him away. Besides, he has never a wooden dagger! I'ld not give a rush for a Vice that has not a wooden dagger to snap at every body he meets.
Mirth. That was the old way, gossip, when iniquity came in like Hokos Pokos, in a juggler's jerkin, with false skirts, like the Knave of Clubs! but now they are attired like men and women o' the time, the Vices male and female: Prodigality like a young heir, and his mistress Money (whose favors he scatters like counters) pranked up like a prime lady, the Infanta of the mines.

Cynth. Rev. Ind.:

3 Child. . . . they say the *umbrae,* or ghosts, of some three or four plays departed a dozen years since, have been seen walking on your stage here. Take heed, boy; if your house be haunted with such hobgoblins 'twill fright away all your spectators quickly.

Ibid.:

2 Child. A third great-bellied juggler talks of twenty years since, . . . and would enforce all wits to be of that fashion, because his doublet is still so.

E. M. in H. H. I iv:

Bobadill. What new book have you there? What, *Go By, Hieronimo?*

Mathew. Ay; did you ever see it acted? is't not well penned?

Bob. Well penned? I would fain see all the poets of these times pen such another play as that was! They'll prate and swagger, and keep a stir of art and devices, when, as I am a gentleman, read 'hem, they are the most shallow, pitiful, barren fellows that live upon the face of the earth.

Cynth. Rev. Ind.:

2 Child. Another whom it hath pleased nature to furnish with more beard than brain, prunes his mustaccio, lisps, and, with some score of affected oaths, swears down all that sit about him, that the old *Hieronimo* as it was first acted, [that is, before Jonson's additions] was the only best, and judiciously penned play of Europe.

Barth. Fair. Ind.:

He that will swear *Jeronimo* or *Andronicus* are the best plays yet, shall pass unexcepted at here, as a man whose judgment shows it is constant, and hath stood still these five and twenty or thirty years. Though it be an ignorance it is a virtuous and staid ignorance.

Again the reference to Shakespeare. Evidently Shakespeare weighed heavy on his mind. We might go along with him part of the way regarding *Henry VI* and *Titus Andronicus;* but in the prologue to *Every Man in His Humor* he speaks of the former in the same breath with *The Tempest,* and in the Induction to *Bartholomew Fair* just quoted his reference to *Titus Andronicus* is presently followed up with illustrations based on *The Tempest.* So far as he was concerned they belonged to the same category. Is there not a measure of malevolence in this allusion:

If there be never a servant-monster i' the fair, who can help it, he says, nor a nest of antiques? He is loth to make nature afraid in his plays, like drolleries, to mix his head with other men's heels.

In the following quotation from *Bartholomew Fair* we have a list of subjects for puppet plays (V i) :

Leatherhead. O, the motions that I have given light to in my time . . . ! *Jerusalem* was a stately thing; and so was *Nineveh,* and the *City of Norwich,* and *Sodom and Gomorrah,* with the rising o' the prentices, and pulling down the bawdy houses there upon Shrove-Tuesday. But the *Gunpowder-plot,* there was a get-penny! I have presented that to an eighteen or twenty pence audience nine times in an afternoon. Your home-born projects prove ever the best; they are so easy and familiar. They put too much learning in their things now o' days.

In the opening of the induction to *The Magnetic Lady* Jonson lists a string of items that might be drafted into the making of a comedy:

Boy. What do you lack, gentlemen? What is't you lack? Any fine fancies, figures, humors, characters, ideas, definitions of lords and ladies? waiting-women, parasites, knights, captains, courtiers, lawyers? What do you lack?

The subject chosen must have suitable dimension: it must not be too vast, nor too petty. In developing this idea Jonson merely paraphrases Aristotle (*Discoveries,* p. 84):

As to a tragedy or a comedy, the action may be convenient and perfect that would not fit an epic poem in magnitude. . . . in every action which is the subject of a just work, there is required a certain proportionable greatness, neither too vast nor too minute. . . . I look upon a monstrous giant, as Tityus, whose body covered nine acres of land, and mine eye sticks upon every part; the whole that consists of those parts will never be taken in at one entire view. So in a fable, if the action be too great, we can never comprehend the whole together in our imagination. Again, if it be too little, there ariseth no pleasure out of the object; it affords the view no stay.

Toward the end of his dramatic career, in the interlude following the first act of *The Magnetic Lady,* he issued a final feeble shot at the romantic drama. He could do no better than virtually to repeat what he had said in the prologue to *Every Man in His Humor*:

Boy. . . . if a child could be born in a play, and grow up to a man i' the first scene, before he went off the stage; and then after to come forth a squire, and be made a knight; and that knight to travel between the acts, and do wonders i' the Holy Land or elsewhere; kill paynims, wild boars, dun cows, and other monsters; beget him a reputation, and marry an emperor's daughter for his mistress; convert her father's country; and at last come home, lame, and all-to-be-laden with miracles.

In *The Devil Is an Ass* (II i) Jonson contributes an amusing item to the discussion over the use of history as source material:

> *Fitzdottrel.*   Thomas of Woodstock,
> I'm sure was Duke, and he was made away
> At Calais, as Duke Humphrey was at Bury:
> And Richard the Third, you know what end he came to.
> *Meercraft.* By m' faith, you are cunning i' the Chronicle, sir.
> And think they 're more authentic.
> *Ingine.* That's sure, sir.

We see that even as late as 1616 Jonson had not been able to get Shakespeare's cavalier treatment of history out of his scholarly head.

In *Bartholomew Fair* (V iii) there is an interesting discussion of the question of adaptation of material:

> *Leatherhead.* And here is young Leander, is as proper an actor of his inches . . .
> *Cokes.* But do you play it according to the printed book? I have read that.
> *Leath.* By no means, sir.
> *Cokes.* No! how then?
> *Leath.* A better way, sir; that is too learned and poetical for our audience. What do they know what *Hellespont* is, *guilty of true love's blood?* or what *Abydos* is? or *the other, Sestos hight?*
> *Cokes.* Tho' art i' the right; I do not know myself.
> *Leath.* No, I have entreated Master Littlewit to take a little pains to reduce it to a more familiar strain for our people.
> *Cokes.* How, I pray thee, good Master Littlewit?
> *Lit.* It pleases him to make a matter of it, sir; but there is no such matter, I assure you; I have only made it a little easy, and modern for the times, sir, that's all. As for the *Hellespont*, I imagine our *Thames* here; and then *Leander* I make a dyer's son about Puddle-wharf; and *Hero* a wench o' the Bankside, who going

over one morning to Old Fishstreet, *Leander* spies her land at Trigs-Stairs, and falls in love with her. Now do I introduce *Cupid,* having metamorphos'd himself into a drawer, and he strikes Hero in love with a pint of sherry; and other pretty passages there are of the friendship, that will delight you, sir, and please you of judgment.

B. TECHNIQUE

Jonson analyzes the structure of his plays in a number of discussions distributed through them. The most inclusive is found in the Chorus following Act I of *The Magnetic Lady* (1633):

> *Boy.* Now, gentlemen, what censure you of our *Protasis,* or first *Act?*
> *Probee.* Well, Boy. It is a fair presentment of your actors, and a handsome promise of somewhat to come hereafter.
> *Damplay.* But there is nothing done in it, or concluded: therefore I say, no Act.
> *Boy.* A fine piece of logic! Do you look, Master Damplay, for conclusions in a *Protasis?* I thought the Law of Comedy had reserv'd [those] to the *Catastrophe:* and that the *Epitasis,* (as we are taught) and the *Catastasis,* had been intervening parts, to have been expected. But you would have all come together it seems: the clock should strike five at once, with the Acts.

If we compare this with Heywood's statement of the formula (p. 131) we find that Jonson has added a fourth term (not counting *Prologue*): *Catastasis.* This term was coined late in the history of Renaissance criticism by Scaliger to represent an extension of the *Epitasis,* and was ignored in England. Professor Baldwin found no reference to it earlier than 1614, and Jonson makes no mention of it in discussions antedating *The Magnetic Lady.*

"As we are taught"—that was in the third form at Grammar School, where Jonson and his contemporaries (including Shakespeare) were nourished on Terence and his commentators.

At the end of the Chorus following Act II Probee remarks:

> Let us mind what you come for, the play, which will draw on to the *Epitasis* now.

Protasis, Epitasis, Catastrophe corresponded to Aristotle's *Beginning, Middle* and *End*. There was little question about the propriety of the five-act structure[1]—that had been emphatically enjoined by Horace—but the apportionment of three parts in five divisions created a problem. We see that Jonson spread his Protasis over two acts. He does the same in *The New Inn,* as he informs us in the Argument, or summary of the play, prefixed to the text:

Here begins, at the third act, the Epitasis, or business of the play.

Similarly in *Every Man out of His Humor*: after the second scene of the third act Cordatus says:

. . . lose not yourself, for now the *Epitasis,* or busy part of our subject, is in act.

The summary of the fifth act begins:

The fifth and last act is the Catastrophe, or knitting up of all.

Concerning the fifth Act we read the following dialogue in the Chorus preceding Act V of *The Magnetic Lady*:

Damplay. Why, here his play might have ended, if he would ha' let it, and have spar'd us the vexation of a fifth Act yet to come, which every one here knows the issue of already, or may in part conjecture.

Boy. That conjecture is a kind of figure-flinging, or throwing the dice, for a meaning was never in the poet's purpose perhaps. Stay, and see his last Act, his *Catastrophe,* how he will perplex that, or spring some fresh cheat, to entertain the spectators with a convenient delight, till some unexpected and new encounter break out to rectify all, and make good the conclusion.

Probee. Which, ending here, would have shown dull, flat, and unpointed, without any shape, or sharpness, brother Damplay.

---

[1] There were proponents of a four-act structure. We must not overlook the fact that the leader in the glorious procession of Elizabethan dramas, *The Spanish Tragedy,* was written in four acts.

Jonson's last act technique, we see, fits into Freytag's formula, which calls for a "moment of final suspense."

So far as composition goes there is no difference between comedy and tragedy, Jonson tells us in the *Discoveries* (p. 81):

> The parts of a comedy are the same with a tragedy, and the end is partly the same, for they both delight and teach; the comics are called διδάσκαλοι of the Greeks no less than the tragics.

The last act should be the best. Webster, Fletcher, and the author of *Cromwell* had expressed the same opinion. (Cf. p. 149.) (*New Inn* V i):

> *Host.* . . . I had thought to have sacrificed
> To merriment tonight in my Light Heart, Fly,
> And like a noble poet, to have had
> My last act best; but all fails in the plot.

The "full scene," or what Shakespeare called "the swelling act," was considered a desideratum by Jonson.

E. M. out of H. H. After II i:

> *Cordatus.* . . . is it not an object of more state to bring the scene full, and reliev'd with variety of speakers to the end, than to see a vast empty stage, and the actors come in, one by one, as if they were dropt down with a feather into the eye of the spectators?

As Jonson carried his Apotasis through the fourth act, the Catastrophe had to be a quick and sudden one in the fifth act. By means of an analogy he illustrated the desirability of such a procedure.

Ibid. After Act IV:

> *Cordatus.* . . . you will almost have wonder to think how 'tis possible the current of their dispositions shall receive so quick and strong an alteration.
> *Mitis.* Ay, marry, sir, this is that on which my expectation has dwelt all this while: for I must tell you, signior, . . . I made it a question in mine own private discourse how he should properly

call it *Every Man out of His Humor,* when I saw all his actors so strongly pursue and continue their humors.

Cor. Why, therein his art appears most full of luster, and approacheth nearest the life: especially, when in the flame and height of their humors they are laid flat, it fills the eye better and with more contentment. How tedious a sight were it to behold a proud exalted tree lopt, and cut down by degrees, when it might be feld in a moment? and to set the ax to it before it came to that pride and fulness, were as not to have it grow.

Jonson's construction, then, is in reality a three act construction. Acts I and II are structurally the first act, Acts III and IV the second. Thus simply has Jonson resolved the difficulty of apportioning three logical parts among five artificial divisions.

When one thinks of the pains Jonson took, by means of interludes that went by various names, such as Grex, Chorus, Intermean, to interpret the action of his play for the benefit of his audience,[1] one is taken aback when one hears him affirm, as he does at the end of the Induction to *The Magnetic Lady,*

that to be the most unlucky scene in a play which needs an interpreter.

In the same Induction he resorts to an analogy to describe what he considers a well constructed plot:

For I must tell you, a good play is like a skein of silk, which, if you take at the right end, you may wind off at pleasure on the bottom or card of your discourse; . . . but if you light on the wrong end, you will pull all into a knot, or elf-lock, which nothing but the shears, or a candle, will undo or separate.

Cartwright plainly borrowed from this passage for his lines in memory of Jonson quoted on page 148.

If Jonson digested the interpretation of the principle of unity of action contained in the following note in the *Discoveries* he

---

[1] It is worth observing that Jonson's device of interspersing discussions between the author and representatives of the public has been adopted in the current television dramatizations of O. Henry's stories.

should have given his whole-hearted approval to the double plot, like that of *King Lear,* for example:

Now that it should be one and entire. One is considerable two ways; either as it is only separate, and by itself, or as, being composed of many parts, it begins to be one as those parts grow or are wrought together. That it should be one the first way alone, and by itself, no man that has tasted letters ever would say, especially having required before a just magnitude and equal proportion of the parts in themselves. Neither of which can possibly be if the action be single and separate, not composed of parts which laid together in themselves with an equal and fitting proportion, tend to the same end; which thing out of antiquity itself hath deceived many, and more this day doth deceive.

Anticipation is a fundamental form of dramatic interest and an essential consideration in plot construction. Its exercise is condemned by Jonson, since it implies a demand upon the imagination.

E. M. out of H. H. After III ii:

Mitis. . . . I wonder what engine he will use to bring the rest out of their humors.
Cordatus. That will appear anon; never preoccupy your imagination withal. Let your mind keep company with the scene still.

The correct direction in the conception of a play is from the whole to the detail, not the reverse.

Fox. Prol.:

Nor made he his play for jests stolen from each sable,
But makes jests to fit his fable.

The length of a scene is to be determined by the amount of action it presents.

Every Man out of H. H. After I i:

> *Mitis.* . . . methinks Macilente went hence too soon; he might have been made to stay, and speak somewhat in reproof of *Sordido's* wretchedness now at the last.
>
> *Cordatus.* O, no; that had been extremely improper; besides, he had continued the scene too long with him, as 'twas, being in no action.

Cordatus goes on to prove that a prolongation of the scene would not have been in keeping with the characters of the persons.

A similar dialogue after II i:

> *Mitis.* Methinks, Cordatus, he dwelt somewhat too long on this scene; it hung i' the hand.
>
> *Cor.* I see not where he could have insisted less and t' have made the humors perspicuous enough.
>
> *Mitis.* True, as his subject lies; but he might have altered the shape of his argument, and explicated 'hem better in single scenes.
>
> *Cor.* That had been single indeed. Why, be they not the same persons in this as they would have been in those?

Character, then, is made a determining factor in construction.

C. MIXTURE OF TYPES

Jonson had nothing to say on the general question of types, nor on the propriety of mixing them. Encouraged perhaps by Sidney, who approved of mingling (cf. p. 201), he affirmed the propriety of introducing comic situations in a pastoral.

Sad Shepherd. Prol.:

> But here's an heresy of late let fall,
> That mirth by no means fits a pastoral.
> Such say so who can make none, he presumes:
> Else there's no scene more properly assumes
> The sock. For whence can sport in kind arise,
> But from the rural routs and families? . . .
> The wise and knowing critic will not say
> This worse or better is before he weigh

371

Whe'er every piece be perfect in the kind:
And then, though in themselves he difference find,
Yet if the place require it where they stood,
The equal fitting makes them equal good.
You shall have love, and hate, and jealousy,
As well as mirth, and rage, and melancholy:
Or whatever else may either move,
Or stir affections, and your likings prove.
But that no style for pastoral should go
Current, but what is stamp'd with Ah, and O,
Who judgeth so may singularly err.

It seems clear that he has paraphrased Sidney's statement: "If severed they be good, then conjunction cannot be hurtful."

He also wrote another, non-extant, pastoral entitled *The May Lord*. We know of it because it is mentioned by Drummond, who comments: "Contrary to all other pastorals, he bringeth the clowns making mirth and foolish sports." It was probably this work that evoked the criticism he refers to in the prologue just quoted.

Such mingling he of course would not have tolerated in a tragedy; but even in a comedy he could not endure the association of kings and clowns.

Case is Altered. I i:

> *Onion.* You are in the right; I'll not give a half-penny to see a thousand of them. I was at one the last term; but an ever I see a more roguish thing I am a piece of cheese, and no Onion; nothing but kings and princes in it; the fool came not out a jot.

Staple. Intermean after Act I:

> *Mirth.* But they ha' no fool i' this play, I am afraid, Gossip . . .
> *Expectation.* They are all fools, the rather, in that.

Ibid. Intermean after Act II:

> *Censure.* Why, this is duller and duller! intolerable! scurvy! neither devil nor fool in this play!

His attitude toward farcical elements in any play would be reinforced by a theory he held concerning laughter. It is found expressed in *Discoveries* (p. 81):

Nor is the moving of laughter always the end of comedy; that is rather a fowling for the people's delight, or their fooling. For, as Aristotle says rightly, the moving of laughter is a fault in comedy, a kind of turpitude that depraves some part of a man's nature without a disease. As a wry face without pain moves laughter, or a deformed vizard, or a rude clown dressed in a lady's habit and using her actions. We dislike and scorn such representations; which made the ancient philosophers ever think laughter unfitting in a wise man.

Two of the illustrations are suggested by Aristotle; but for the general statement Jonson is probably indebted to Sidney. He proceeds:

And this induced Plato to esteem of Homer as a sacrilegious person, because he presented the gods sometimes laughing. As also it is divinely said of Aristotle that to seem ridiculous is a part of dishonesty, and foolish. So that what either in the words or sense of an author, or in the language or actions of men, is awry or depraved doth strangely stir mean affections, and provokes for the most part to laughter. And therefore it was clear that all insolent and obscene speeches, jests upon the best men, injuries to particular persons, perverse and sinister sayings, and the rather unexpected in the old comedy did move laughter, especially where it did imitate any dishonesty; and scurrility came forth in the place of wit, which, who understands the nature and genius of laughter cannot but perfectly know.
Of which Aristophanes affords an ample harvest, having not only outgone Plautus or any other in that kind, but expressed all the moods and figures of what is ridiculous oddly.

With a calm inconsistency he proceeds to find fault with the multitude for not laughing:

In short, as vinegar is not accounted good until the wine is corrupted so jests that are true and natural seldom raise laughter with the beast, the multitude.

Inconsistent with his theory, too, is his practice. He did aim to raise laughter. He even attributed to it therapeutic value.

Mag. Lady. After Act I:

A source of ridiculous matter may break forth anon that shall steep their temples, and bathe their brains in laughter, to the fomenting of stupidity itself, and the awaking any velvet lethargy in the house.

Fox. Prol.:

All gall and copperas from his ink he draineth;
Only a little salt remaineth,
Wherewith he'll rub your cheeks, till (red with laughter)
They shall look fresh a week after.

Sad Shep. Prol.:

Safe on this ground, then, we not fear today
To tempt your laughter by our rustic play.

Apparently he believed that if clownage, or what he would consider such, is to be presented in a play, it should occupy the stage exclusively. On that principle he wrote *A Tale of a Tub*, the prologue of which promises:

No state affairs, no politic club,
Pretend we in our tale here of a tub:
But acts of clowns and constables today
Stuff out the scenes of our ridiculous play:
A cooper's wit, or some such busy spark,
Illumining the High Constable and his clerk,
And all the neighborhood; from old records,
Of antique proverbs, drawn from Whitson-Lords,
And their authorities at wakes and ales,
With country precedents, and old wives' tales,
We bring you now, to show what different things
The cotes of clowns are from the courts of kings.

In two instances he felt not quite blameless in the matter of type. In *Every Man out of His Humor* Sordido contemplates suicide, and actually takes a step toward consummating it. Such violation seemed heinous enough to call for justification before the world. Jonson's defense is that Plautus provided a precedent. The passage is quoted on page 358.

The other instance is connected with *The Fox,* whose Catastrophe did not appear to be in keeping with "the strict rigor of the comic law." The play does not have a happy ending. Jonson's explanation is presented in the dedication to "The two Famous Universities:"

And though my Catastrophe may, in the strict rigor of comic law, meet with censure, as turning back to my promise, I desire the learned and charitable critic to have so much faith in me to think it was done of industry. For with what ease I could have varied it, nearer his scale (but that I fear to boast my own faculty) I could here insert. But my special aim being to put the snaffle in their mouths that cry out we never punish vice in our enterludes, &c., I took the more liberty; though not without some lines of example, drawn even in the ancients themselves; the goings out of whose comedies are not always joyful; but oft-times the bawds, the servants, the rivals, yea, and the masters are mulcted.

D. STOCK DEVICES

He satirizes the employment of situations that have become conventional stock in trade of the stage.

Fox. Prol.:

Yet thus much I can give you as a token
Of his play's worth: no eggs are broken,
Nor quaking custards with fierce teeth affrighted,
Wherewith your rout are so delighted;
Nor hales he in a gull, old ends reciting,
To stop gaps in his loose writing;
With such a deal of monstrous and forc'd action,
As might make Beth'lem a faction.

Barth. Fair. Ind.:

Stage-keeper. . . . and yet I kept the stage in Master Tarleton's time, I thank my stars. Ho! and that man had liv'd to have play'd in *Bartholomew Fair,* you should ha' seen him ha' come in, and ha' been cozened i' the cloth-quarter so finely! And Adams, the rogue, ha' leap'd and caper'd upon him, and ha' dealt his vermin about, as though they had cost him nothing. And then a substantial watch to ha' stolen in upon 'em, and taken 'em away, with mistaking words, as the fashion is in the stage practice.

A clear allusion to Dogberry and Verges.

Cynth. Rev. Ind.:

3. By the way Cupid meets with Mercury, (as that 's a thing to be noted: take any of our play-books without a Cupid or a Mercury in it, and burn it for an heretic in poetry).

E. CHARACTER

We saw that Jonson considered character a determining factor in the making of a play (p. 370). Several of his plays he prefaced with an elaborate description of each of the *dramatis personae.* In *Every Man out of His Humor,* when he gets to Mitis his comment is: "Mitis is a person of no action, and therefore we have reason to afford him no character." In his treatment of character he accepted the traditional principle of decorum. Several times in the *Conversations with Drummond* he shows annoyance with important authors for violating the principle.

Sidney did not keep decorum in making every one speak as well as himself.
Guarini, in his *Pastor Fido,* kept not decorum, in making shepards speak as well as himself could.
Lucan, Sidney, Guarini, make every man speak as well as themselves, forgetting decorum, for Dametus sometimes speaks grave sentences.

An amusing example of Jonsonian egoism is afforded by a passage in *Every Man out of His Humor* (II i). Mitis asks: "Is't possible there should be any such humorist?" The reply of Cordatus, who represents Jonson, is: "Very easily possible, sir; you see there is." Thus Jonson's play not merely depicts life—it *is* life.

There is a pertinent comment on the exposition of character in the description of *The Masque of Queens*:

> At this, the Dame enter'd to them, . . . and she spake, uttering, by way of question, the end wherefore they came: which, if it had been done either before, or otherwise, had not been so natural. For, to have made themselves their own decipherers, and each one to have told upon their entrance what they were, and whether they would, had been a most piteous hearing, and utterly unworthy any quality of a poem.

QUALITIES

In his address to the readers of *Sejanus,* Jonson enumerates the essential qualities of a good tragedy: "truth of argument, dignity of persons, gravity and height of elocution, fulness and frequency of sentence." This of course describes the ideal of the Senecan play. The idea that a tragedy might possess a different set of desirable characteristics could not penetrate his classical mind. Nothing more faithfully reveals his instinctive reaction to the romantic drama than the fact that when he decided to devote himself to tragedy, he turned to Seneca for a model, despite the fact that Shakespeare had offered him the example of *Romeo and Juliet* and *Julius Caesar.* We happen to know in what a critical mood he was when he witnessed a performance of the latter. And when he ventured a second time he had the whole array of Shakespeare's immortal creations before him. Nevertheless he did the same thing, despite his original failure. The interim had taught him nothing.

Two qualities he demanded of any type of play: avoidance of vulgarity, and originality.

A. PROPRIETY

Cynth. Rev. Ind.:

It is in the general behalf of this fair society here that I am to speak; at least the more judicious part of it, which seems much distasted with the immodest and obscene writing of many of their plays.

Poet. III i:

Tucca. And what new matters have we now afoot, sirrah, ha? I would fain come with my cockatrice one day, and see a play; if I knew when there were a good bawdy one; but they say you ha' nothing but Humors, *Revels, and Satires,* that gird and fart at the time, you slave.

Histrio. No, I assure you, captain, not we. They are on the other side of Tiber: we have as much ribaldry in our plays as can be, as you would wish, captain. All the sinners i' the suburbs come and applaud our action daily.

Fox. Ded.:

. . . now, especially in dramatic, or (as they term it) stage-poetry, nothing but ribaldry, profanation, blasphemy, all licence of offence to God and man is practis'd . . . For my particular, I can (and from a most clear conscience) affirm that I have ever trembled to think toward the least profaneness; have loathed the use of such foul and unwash'd bawdry as is now made the food of the scene . . . The increase of which lust in liberty, together with the present trade of the stage in all their masc'line enterludes, what learned or liberal soul doth not already abhor? where nothing but the filth of the time is utter'd, and that with such impropriety of phrase, such plenty of solecisms, such dearth of sense, so bold prolepses, so rack'd with metaphors, with brothelry, able to violate the ear of a pagan, and blasphemy, to turn the blood of a Christian to water.

B. ORIGINALITY

Jonson's references to plagiarism are numerous. A selection will suffice.

Cynth. Rev. Ind.:

3. *Child.* . . . they (*i.e.* the judicious public) could wish your poets would leave to be promoters of other men's jests, and to waylay all the stale apothegms, or old books, they can hear of (in print, or otherwise) to farce their scenes withal. That they would not so penuriously glean wit from every laundress or hackney-man, or derive their best grace (with servile imitation) from common stages, or observation of the company they converse with; as if their invention liv'd wholly upon another man's trencher.

He was exercised over the plagiarists because they plagiarized *him*. His prologue to *Eastward Hoe* begins:

Not out of envy, for there's no effect
Where there's no cause; nor out of imitation,
For we have evermore been imitated.

Epigram LVI. On Poet-Ape:

Poor Poet-Ape, that would be thought our chief,
Whose works are e'en the frippery of wit,
From brokage is become so bold a thief,
As we, the rob'd, leave rage, and pity it.
At first he made low shifts, would pick and glean,
Buy the reversion of old plays; now grown
To a little wealth, and credit in the scene,
He takes up all, makes each man's wit his own.
And, told of this, he slights it. Tut, such crimes
The sluggish gaping auditor devours;
He marks not whose 'twas first: and after-times
May judge it to be his, as well as ours.
Fool, as if half eyes will not know a fleece
From locks of wool, or shreds from the whole piece.

The resemblance this bears to Greene's attack on Shakespeare is apparent; and Chalmers and Gifford believe that Shakespeare is meant—a tempting assumption, but unlikely. Whom can he refer to in Epigram CXII, *To a Weak Gamester in Poetry?*

With thy small stock why art thou vent'ring still,
At this so subtle sport: and play'st so ill?
Think'st thou it is mere fortune that can win?
Or thy rank setting? that thou dar'st put in
Thy all, at all: and whatsoe'er I do,
Art still at that, and think'st to blow me up too?
I cannot for the stage a drama lay,
Tragic, or comic, but thou writ'st the play.
I leave thee there, and giving way, entend
An epic poem; thou hast the same end.
I modestly quit that, and think to write,
Next morn, an ode; thou mak'st a song ere night.

I pass to elegies; thou meet'st me there:
To satires; and thou dost pursue me. Where,
Where shall I 'scape thee? in an epigram?
O, (thou cry'st out) that is thy proper game.

Epigram C:

Playwright, by chance, hearing some toys I had writ,
Cried to my face, they were the elixir of wit:
And I must now believe him: for today,
Five of my jests, then stolen, past him a play.

In the prologue to *Epicœne* he tells us that the jokes that are cracked over tables at ordinaries are stolen from his plays. In the prologue to *Cynthia's Revels* he declares that he scorns to follow or imitate:

In this alone his muse her sweetness hath:
She shuns the print of any beaten path,
And proves new ways to come to learned ears.

Jonson realized, however, that there was a type of imitation that was eminently desirable. He explains himself carefully in *Discoveries* (p. 77):

The third requisite in our poet or maker is imitation, *imitatio,* to be able to convert the substance or riches of another poet to his own use. To make choice of one excellent man above the rest, and so to follow him till he grow very he, or so like him as the copy may be mistaken for the principal. Not as a creature that swallows what it takes in, crude, raw, or undigested; but that feeds with an appetite, and hath a stomach to concoct, divide, and turn all into nourishment. Not to imitate servilely as Horace saith, and catch at vices for virtue, but to draw forth out of the best and choicest flowers, with the bee, and turn all into honey, work it into one relish and savor; make our imitation sweet; observe how the best writers have imitated, and follow them: how Virgil and Statius have imitated Homer; how Horace, Archilochus; how Alcaeus, and the other lyrics; and so of the rest.

By his own estimate, then, Jonson should have had a great admiration for Shakespeare.

THE TITLE

That the name of the play possessed significance in the mind of Jonson is indicated by the following extracts:

Eastward Hoe. Prol.:

And for the title, if it seem affected,
We might as well have call'd it *God You Good Even*,
Only that eastward westwards still exceeds—
Honor the fair sun's rising, not his setting.
Nor is our title utterly enforc'd
As by the points we touch at you shall see.

Mag. Lady. Ind.:

Damplay. And what is the title of your play here, *The Magnetic Lady?*
Boy. Yes, sir; an attractive title the author has given it.
Probee. A magnet, I warrant you.

STANDARD OF JUDGMENT

Jonson felt quite sufficient unto himself. No man ever affirmed more confidently that he was the measure of all things—all things dramatic, at any rate.

E. M. out of H. H. Ind.:

I do not this to beg your patience,
Or servilely to fawn on your applause,
Like some dry brain, despairing in his merit.
Let me be censured by the austerest brow
Where I want art, or judgment; tax me freely:
Let envious censors, with their broadest eyes,
Look through and through me; I pursue no favor.
Only vouchsafe me your attentions,
And I will give you music worth your ears.

Ibid.:

If we fail,
We must impute it to this only chance:
"Art hath an enemy call'd ignorance."

Cynth. Rev. Epil.:

Stiffly to stand on this, and proudly approve
The play, might tax the maker of self-love.
I'll only speak what I have heard him say:
"By—, 'tis good, and if you like't you may."

Ibid. V ii:

Mercury. Then let the truth of these things strengthen thee
In thy exempt and only man-like course:
Like it the more, the less it is respected.

Staple of News. Intermean after the first act:

Tattle. He is an errant learn'd man that made it (i.e. *The Devil is an Ass*), and can write, they say; and I am foully deceived but he can read too.

Ibid. Prol.:

> Mark but his ways,
> What flight he makes, how new: and then, he says
> If that not like you that he sends tonight,
> 'Tis you have left to judge, not he to write.
> . . . a well-erected confidence
> Can fright their pride, and laugh their folly hence.
> Here now, put case, our author should, once more,
> Swear that his play were good, he doth implore
> You would not argue him of arrogance;
> Howe'er that common spawn of ignorance,
> Our fry of writers, may beslime his fame,
> And give his action that adulterate name.
> Such full-blown vanity he more doth loath
> Than base dejection. There's a mean 'twixt both,
> Which, with a constant firmness, he pursues,
> As one that knows the strength of his own muse.
> And this he hopes all free souls will allow;
> Others, that take it with a rugged brow,
> Their moods he rather pities than envies:
> His mind it is above their injuries.

To what degree he lacked the gift to see himself!

Cynth. Rev. Vii:

> *Crites* [Jonson]. Phoebus Apollo, if with ancient rites,
> And due devotions, I have ever hung
> Elaborate paeans on thy golden shrine,
> Or sung thy triumphs in a lofty strain,
> Fit for a theater of gods to hear; . .

New Inn. Prol.:

If any thing be set to a wrong taste,
'T is not the meat there, but the mouth's displaced;
Remove but that sick palate, all is well . . .
Beware to bring such appetites to the stage;
They do confess a weak, sick, queasy age,
And a shrewd grudging too of ignorance . . .
Hear for your health, then, but at any hand,
Before you judge, vouchsafe to understand,
Concoct, digest; if then it do not hit,
Some are in a consumption of wit,
Deep, he dares say.

Description of the Masque at the Lord Viscount Haddington's Marriage:

I adventure to give that abroad which in my first conception I intended honorably fit: and (though it hath labor'd since under censure) I, that know truth to be always of one stature, and so like a rule, as who bends it the least way must do an injury to the right, cannot but smile at their tyrannous ignorance, that will offer to slight me (in these things being an artificer) and give themselves a peremptory license to judge, who have never touch'd so much as to the bark, or utter shell of any knowledge. But, their daring dwell with them. They have found a place to pour out their follies, and I a seat to sleep out the passage.

Hymenæi:

After them, the musicians with this song, of which, then, only one staff was sung; but because I made it both in form and matter to emulate that kind of poem which was call'd Epithalamium, and (by the ancients) us'd to be sung when the bride was led into her chamber, I have here set it down whole: and do heartily forgive their ignorance whom it chanceth not to please.

The reason why only the first stave had been sung at the wedding was that the rest was considered too bawdy.

The Forest. XII:

. . . to notes I then shall sing
Will prove old Orpheus' act no tale to be;
For I shall move stocks, stones, no less than he.

Epic. First Prol.:

Nor is it only while you keep your seat
Here, that his feast will last; but you shall eat
A week at ordinaries on his broken meat.

Sejanus. To the Readers:

But that I should plant my felicity in your general saying good, or
well, &c. were a weakness which the better sort of you might
worthily contemn, if not absolutely hate, me for.

Under the circumstances it is amusing to hear Jonson recom-
mending humility to others; as he does near the end of *The Poetaster*, where Virgil advises Crispinus (i.e. Marston) :

And henceforth, learn
To bear yourself more humbly; not to swell,
Or breathe your insolent and idle spite
On him whose laughter can your worst affright.

Him means, of course, Jonson. A little farther on Tibullus enjoins
Crispinus and Demetrius (Marston and Dekker):

Neither shall you at any time, ambitiously affecting the title of the
Untrussers or Whippers of the age . . .

That title had been preëmpted by Jonson who had promised to
use a whip of steel to scourge the follies of the time (cf. p. 341).

In the *Apologetical Dialogue* appended to *The Poetaster* he
declares that the preference which the multitude showed the
rubbish of his rivals would be enough to impel him to destroy
his own creations, the product of toil and travail, were it not for
his consciousness of his own superior merit:

Polyposus.   . . . they say you are slow,
And scarce bring forth a play a year.
    Author.   'Tis true.
I would they could not say I did that.
There's all the joy I take i' their trade,
Unless such scribes as they might be proscrib'd
Th' abused theaters . . .
But, that these base and beggarly conceits
Should carry it, by the multitude of voices,
Against the most abstracted work opposed
To the stuff'd nostrils of the drunken rout!
O, this would make a learn'd and liberal soul
To rive his stained quill, up to the back,
And damn his long-watch'd labors to the fire;
Things that were born when none but the still night
And his dumb candle saw his pinching throes:
Were not his own free merit a more crown
Unto his travails than their reeling claps.

Jonson's arrogance evoked, from no less a man than Chapman,
a vituperative invective,[1] one hundred and ninety-seven lines long,
from which I quote:

Great, learned, witty Ben, be pleas'd to light
The world with that three-forked fire; nor fright
All us, thy sub-learn'd, with luciferous boast
That thou art most great, most learn'd, witty most.

If we compare this with what Chapman says of Jonson in his lines
on *Sejanus,* we get an idea of the value to be attached to the commendatory verses with which the age was flooded:

So thy chaste muse, by virtuous self-mistrust,
Which is a true mark of truest merit . . .

Another example is Jonson's own exaggerated self-deprecation
in his address to Beaumont:

How do I fear myself, that am not worth
The least indulgent thought thy pen drops forth! . . .

----
[1] Apparently he finally decided not to publish it.

What art is thine, that so thy friend deceives,
When even there where thou most praisest me
For writing better, I must envy thee!

In the *Discoveries* (pp. 21ff.) Jonson urges at some length the incapability of the public to pass judgment, winding up with the insistence that what he says applies to all classes of society:

Nor think this only to be true in the sordid multitude, but the neater sort of our gallants; for all are the multitude, only they dif-fer in cloths, not in judgment or understanding.

He found support for his opinion in Horace. In his own translation the passage reads:

For, alas, what knew
The idiot keeping holiday, or drudge,
Clown, townsman, base and noble mix'd, to judge?

This opinion is reiterated (*Cynth. Rev.,* Ind.) :

As some one civet-wit among you, that knows no other learning than the price of satin and velvets; no other perfection than the wearing of a neat suit; and yet will censure as desperately as the most professed critic in the house, presuming his clothes should bear him out in't.

Mag. Lady. Ind.:

Probee.   We are sent unto you, indeed, from the people.
Boy.   The people! which side of the people?
Pro.   . . . Not the feces, or grounds, of your people, that sit in the oblique caves and wedges of your house, your sinful sixpenny mechanics—
Damplay.   But the better and braver sort of your people, plush and velvet outsides! that stick your house round like so many eminences—
Boy.   Of clothes, not understandings!

Ibid. Chorus after II:

Damplay. Who should teach us the right at a play?

Boy. If your own science cannot do it, or the love of modesty and truth, all other intreaties or attempts are vain. You are fitter spectators for the bears than us—or the puppets. This is a popular ignorance indeed, somewhat better apparel'd in you than the people; but a hard-handed and stiff ignorance, worthy a trowel, or hammerman.

The following quotation is specially significant in that it comes from the preface to a masque—*Hymenæi*—a work intended solely for a courtly audience:

And however some may squeamishly cry out that all endeavor of learning and sharpness in these transitory devices, especially where it steps beyond their little, or (let me not wrong 'em) no brain at all, is superfluous, I am contented these fastidious stomachs should leave my full tables, and enjoy at home their clean empty trenchers, fittest for such airy tastes; where perhaps a few Italian herbs, pick'd up and made into a salad, may find sweeter acceptance than all the most nourishing and sound meats of the world. For these men's palates let me not answer, O Muses. It is not my fault if I fill them out nectar and they run to metheglin.

One section of the audience, named Curiosity, is primarily interested in the clothes worn by the actors.

Staple. Ind.:

Prologue. O, Curiosity! You come to see who wears the new suit today; whose clothes are best penn'd, whatever the part be; which actor has the best leg and foot; what king plays without cuffs, and his queen without gloves; who rides post in stockings, and dances in boots.

Censure. Yes, and which amorous prince makes love in drink, or does overact prodigiously in beaten satin.

Perhaps the bitterest of his outpourings against the pitiful public that sits in judgment over works of art, is found in Scene i of Act IV of *The Staple of News.* The speaker is watching a crowd dancing:

Look, look, how all their eyes
Dance i' their heads (observe) scatter'd with lust,
At sight o' their brave idol! how they are tickl'd
With a light air! the bawdy saraband!
They are a kind of dancing engines all,
And set by nature thus to run alone
To every sound! All things within, without them,
Move, but their brain, and that stands still! mere monsters
Here, in a chamber, of most subtil feet,
And make their legs in tune, passing the streets!
These are the gallant spirits o' the age!
The miracles o' the time! that can cry up
And down men's wits, and set what rate on things
Their half-brain'd fancies please! Now pox upon 'em!

Verses on *The Faithful Shepherdess*:

The wise and many-headed bench, that sits
Upon the life and death of plays, and wits,
Composed of gamester, captain, knight, knight's man,
Lady, or pucelle, that wears mask or fan,
Velvet or taffeta cap rank'd in the dark
With the shop's foreman, or some such brave spark,
That may judge for his sixpence . .

Jonson liked to play with the notion involved in the preceding quotation, that the price of admission covered the privilege to find fault.

Mag. Lady. Chorus after II:

Damplay. This were a strange empire, or rather a tyranny, you would entitle your poet to, over gentlemen, that they should come to hear and see plays, and say nothing for their money.

Boy. O, yes, say what you will so it be to purpose and in place.

Dam. Can any thing be out of purpose at a play? I see no reason, if I come here, and give my eighteen pence, or two shillings, for my seat, but I should take it out in censure on the stage.

Boy. Your two shilling worth is allow'd you: but you will take your ten shilling worth, your twenty shilling worth, and more.

Barth. Fair. Ind.:

It is further agreed that every person here have his or their free-will of censure, to like or dislike at their own charge, the author having now departed with his right; it shall be lawful for any man to judge his six pen'orth, his twelve pen'orth, so to his eighteen pence, two shillings, half a crown, to the value of his place; provided always his place get not above his wit. And if he pay for half a dozen, he may censure for all them too, so that he will undertake that they shall be silent. He shall put in for censures here as they do for lots at the lottery; marry, if he drop but six pence at the door and will censure a crown's worth, it is thought there is no conscience or justice in that.

In the same Articles of Agreement he takes a rap at the gallants, on the stage and off, who deliberately assumed an ostentatiously hostile manner to influence the rest of the audience:

It is also agreed that every man here exercise his own judgment, and not censure by contagion, or upon trust from another's voice or face, that sits by him, be he never so first in the commission of wit; as also, that he be fixt and settled in his censure, that what he approves or not approves today, he will do the same tomorrow; and if tomorrow, the next day, and so the next week, if need be; and not be brought about by any that sits on the bench with him, though they indite and arraign plays daily.[1]

Likewise in Scene iv of Act II of *The Case Is Altered:*

Valentine. . . . there are two sorts of persons that most commonly are infectious to a whole auditory.
Balthasar. What be they?
Val. Marry, one is the rude barbarous crew, a people that have no brains, and yet grounded judgments; these will hiss any thing that mounts above their grounded capacities; but the other are worth the observation, i'faith.
Omnes. What be they, what be they?
Val. Faith, a few capricious gallants. And they have taken such a habit of dislike in all things, that they will approve nothing, be it never so conceited or elaborate; but sit dispersed, making faces, and spitting, wagging their upright ears, and cry, "Filthy, filthy,"

---

[1] Much of this was quoted with slight modification by the editors of the First Folio.

simply uttering their own condition and using their wryed countenances instead of a vice, to turn the good aspects of all that shall sit near them, from what they behold.[1]

How unhappy the dramatists had reason to be because of such behavior we learn from the prologue to Chapman's *All Fools*. That the audience was of a kind to be influenced by such behavior is indicated by Jonson's plea, in the Articles of Agreement just quoted, that the spectator make up his mind and maintain some degree of constancy in his opinion. A graphic picture of his audience is presented in Act II, Scene iv of *The Case is Altered*:

> *Val.* But the sport is at a new play, to observe the sway and variety of opinion that passeth it. A man shall have such a confused mixture of judgment poured out in the throng there, as ridiculous as laughter itself. One says he likes not the writing, another likes not the plot, another the playing; and sometimes a fellow that comes not there past once in five years, at a parliament time, or so, will be as deep mired in censuring as the best, and swear by God's foot he would never stir his foot to see a hundred such as that is.
> *Sebastian.* Why, but methinks such rooks as these should be ashamed to judge.
> *Val.* Not a whit; the rankest stinkard of them all will take upon him as peremptory as if he had writ himself *in artibus magister*.

Yet the possession of a university degree would not have satisfied Jonson as a qualifying determinant: witness the scornful address *To the Reader in Ordinary* prefixed to *Catiline*:

> The muses forbid that I should restrain your meddling, whom I see already busy with the title, and tricking over the leaves: it is your own. I departed with my right when I let it first abroad, and now, so secure an interpreter I am of my chance, that neither praise nor dispraise from you can affect me. Though you commend the first two acts, with the people, because they are the worst, and dislike the oration of Cicero, in regard you read some pieces of it at school, and understand them not yet, I shall find the way to

---

[1] Dekker's advice to the gallant, of course, comes to mind.

forgive you. . . . Would I had deserved but half so well of it in translation as that ought to deserve of you in judgment, if you have any. I know you will pretend, whosoever you are, to have that, and more: but all pretensions are not just claims. The commendation of good things may fall within a many, the approbation but in a few; for the most commend out of affection, self-tickling, an easiness, or imitation: but men judge only out of knowledge. That is the trying faculty; and to those works that will bear a judge, nothing is more dangerous than a foolish praise. You will say I shall not have yours therefore, but rather the contrary, all vexation of censure. If I were not above such molestations now, I had great cause to think unworthily of my studies, or they had so of me.

This becomes positively insulting when followed, as it is, by an address To the Reader Extraordinary:

You I would understand to be the better man, though places in court go otherwise; to you I submit myself and work.

Both of these addresses were omitted in later editions.

Less venomous is a passage in the quarto ending of *Every Man out of His Humor*:

The cates that you have tasted were not season'd
For every vulgar palate, but prepar'd
To banquet pure and apprehensive ears;
Let then their voices speak for our desert;
Be their applause the trumpet to proclaim
Defiance to rebelling ignorance,
And the green spirits of some tainted few,
That, spite of pity, betray themselves
To scorn and laughter.

The later ending reads:

Marry, I will not do as Plautus in his *Amphytrio*, for all this, *Summi Jovis causa plaudite;* beg a plaudite for God's sake . . . *Non ego ventosae plebis suffragia venor.*

Cynth. Rev. Prol.:

393

To other weaker beams his labors close,
As loth to prostitute their virgin strain
To ev'ry vulgar and adult'rate brain . . .
Pied ignorance (his muse) neither loves nor fears.
Nor hunts she after popular applause,
Or foamy praise that drops from common jaws:
The garland that she wears, their hands must twine
Who can both censure, understand, define
What merit is.

Epigram XCVI. To John Donne:

>   Those that for claps do write,
> Let pui'nes', porters', players', praise delight,
> And till they burst their back, like asses load;
> A man should seek great glory and not broad.

Apologetical Dialogue appended to *The Poetaster*:

>   And, since the Comic Muse
> Hath prov'd so ominous to me, I will try
> If Tragedy have a more kind aspect;
> Her favors in my next I will pursue,
> Where, if I prove the pleasure but of one,
> So he judicious be, he shall b'alone
> A theater unto me.

Disc. p. 21:

Nothing in our age, I have observed, is more preposterous than
the running judgments upon poetry and poets; when we shall hear
those things commended and cried up for the best writings which
a man would scarce vouchsafe to wrap any wholesome drug in:
he would never light his tobacco with them. And those men
almost named for miracles, who yet are so vile that if a man
should go about to examine and correct them, he must make all
they have done but one blot. . . . Yet their vices have not hurt
them; nay, a great many they have profited, for they have been
loved for nothing else. And this false opinion grows strong against
the best men, if once it take root with the ignorant. Cestius, in
his time, was preferred to Cicero. They learned him without book,
and had him often in their mouths. But a man cannot imagine
that thing so foolish or rude but will find and enjoy an admirer;

at least a reader or spectator. The puppets are seen now in despite of the players; Heath's epigrams and the Sculler's poems have their applause. There are never wanting that dare prefer the worst preachers, the worst pleaders, the worst poets; not that the better have left to write or speak better, but that they that hear them judge worse; *Non illi pejus dicunt, sed hi corruptius judicant.* If it were put to the question of the water-rhymer's works against Spenser's, I doubt not but they would find more suffrages; because the most favor common vices, out of a prerogative the vulgar have to lose their judgments and like that which is nought.

Perhaps his bitterest outburst was evoked by the dismal failure of *The New Inn*:

Come, leave the lothed stage,
And the more lothsome age;
Where pride and impudence, in faction knit,
Usurp the chair of wit!
Indicting and arraigning every day
Something they call a play.
Let their fastidious, vain
Commission of the brain
Run on and rage, swear, censure, and condemn:
They were not made for thee, less thou for them.

Say that thou pour'st them wheat,
And they will acorns eat;
'Twere simple fury still thyself to waste
On such as have no taste;
To offer them a surfeit of pure bread,
Whose appetites are dead!
No, give them grains their fill,
Husks, draff to drink, and swill.
If they love lees, and leave the lusty wine,
Envy them not; their palate's with the swine.

No doubt some moldy tale,
Like *Pericles,* and stale
As the sheriff's crusts, and nasty as his fish—
Scraps, out of every dish
Thrown forth, and rak'd into the common tub,
May keep up the Play-Club:

There sweepings do as well
As the best order'd meal;
For who the relish of these guests will fit,
Needs set them but the alms-basket of wit.

He had to get in, somehow, another dig at Shakespeare!

In the *Discoveries* (p. 80) he makes the following radical assertion:

> To judge of poets is only the faculty of poets—and not of all poets, but the best.

In the light of this conviction, and in view of his opinion of his contemporaries, how can we take seriously his concession that he was willing to accept the verdict of those whom he vaguely refers to as "judicious" and "understanding?" By a process of elimination he would probably be the one left competent to pass judgment.

If he had no respect for "the better and braver sort," he could have nothing but scorn for the masses. They were the "stinkards," "the feces, or grounds of your people," "your sinful sixpenny mechanics," "the rude barbarous crew, a people that have no brains, and yet grounded judgments; these will miss anything that mounts above their grounded capacities." (*Case Is Altered,* II iv).

Barth. Fair. Ind.:

> *Stage-keeper.* . . . the understanding gentlemen o'the ground here ask'd my judgment.
> *Book holder.* Your judgment, rascal? for what? sweeping the stage? or gathering up the broken apples for the bears within? Away, rogue; it's come to a fine degree in these spectacles, when such a youth as you pretend to a judgment. And yet he may, i'the most o'this matter, i'faith: for the author hath writ it just to his meridian, and the scale of the grounded judgments here, his play-fellows in wit.

After he ceased writing for the public theater, the scene of his early successes, he could ungraciously brag (*Poet.* I i):

396

I am not known unto the open stage,
Nor do I traffic in their theaters.

At an earlier date he had spoken quite approvingly of the open stage (*Case Is Altered*, II iv) :

> *Valentine.* Marry, first they are brought to the public theater.
> *Juniper.* What, have they theaters there?
> *Val.* Theaters! ay, and plays too, both tragedy and comedy, and set forth with as much state as can be imagined.
> *Sebastian.* And how are their plays? as ours are, extemporal?
> *Val.* O no; all premeditated things, and some of them very good, i'faith; my master used to visit them often when he was there.
> *Balthasar.* Why how? are they in a place where any man may see them?
> *Val.* Ay, in the common theaters, I tell you.

In the induction to *Bartholomew Fair*, quoted above, Jonson informs us that he had written down to the level of the crowd. Well, if he had, or thought he had, the result should have suggested to him that it was a good way to write a good play. But in interpreting his declaration we must take into account the fact that earlier in the same induction the stage-keeper picks the play to pieces; and it was "just to his meridian" that the play was supposed to have been written. However, this was not the first time that Jonson expressed the idea of author-audience relationship. In the discussion concerning the theater in *The Case Is Altered*, part of which I have just quoted, there is this passage:

> *Sebastian.* And do they stand to a popular censure for any thing they present?
> *Valentine.* Ay, ever, ever: and the people generally are very acceptive, and apt to applaud any meritable work.

The mood exhibited here would indicate that it was written after the successful production of *Every Man in His Humor*. The divergence, then, from his later prevailing attitude would present no difficulty. More puzzling is the prologue to *Epicœne*:

> Truth says, of old the art of making plays
> Was to content the people; and their praise

Was to the poet money, wine, and bays.
But in this age a sect of writers are
That only for particular likings care,
And will taste nothing that is popular.
With such we mingle neither brains nor breasts;
Our wishes, like to those make public feasts,
Are not to please the cook's taste, but the guests'.

Nothing could be more direct; therefore it is the more difficult to explain. Perhaps the key to the puzzle lies in the realization which he later expressed in the induction to *The Magnetic Lady*:

Boy. . . . he will not be intreated by us to give it a prologue. He has lost too much that way already, he says.

Anyway, he later dropped this prologue, and substituted another. Less emphatic and less difficult to explain is the conciliatory attitude toward the common reader in the address prefixed to *The New Inn*. On the stage the play had been a pronounced failure, having been relentlessly abused by the dandies. It was therefore only through a weak effort to bite back, and to promote the sale of his book, that he told his reader:

. . . if thou canst but spell, and join my sense, there is more hope of thee than of a hundred fastidious impertinents who were there present the first day, yet never made piece of their prospects the right way. What did they come for then? thou wilt ask me. I will as punctually answer: to see, and to be seen; to make a general muster of themselves in their clothes of credit; and possess the stage against the play; to dislike all, but mark nothing. And by their confidence of rising between the acts in oblique lines, make affidavit to the whole house of their not understanding one scene. Arm'd with this prejudice, as stage-furniture, or arras-cloths, they were there; as spectators, away. For the faces in the hangings and they beheld alike. So I wish they may do ever; and do trust myself and my book rather to thy rustic candor than all the pomp of their pride, and solemn ignorance to boot.

This contrasts forcibly with the prologue (quoted above) with which the play had been provided, in which he told the spectators that if they found anything wrong with the play the trouble was with them, not with the play. However, his frank submission to rustic candor did not improve the reputation of the play; so perhaps the passage quoted above from *The Magnetic Lady,* in which he, in the following year, again condemns the popular judgment, declaring that "he will not woo the gentile ignorance so much," may be looked upon as the hasty recantation of a repentant sinner.

The type of spectator described in the address is introduced in the Chorus of *The Magnetic Lady.* In the Chorus following the third act he speaks:

> *Damplay.* I care not for marking the play. I'll damn it, talk, and do that I come for. I will not have gentlemen lose their privilege, nor I myself my prerogative, for ne'er an overgrown or superannuated poet of 'em all. He shall not give me the law. I will censure, and be witty, and take my tobacco, and enjoy my *Magna Carta* of reprehension, as my predecessors have done before me.

The claims of the audience are also presented, in an amusing figure, in the masque, *Neptune's Triumph:*

> *Cook.* Were you ever a cook?
> *Poet.* A cook! no, surely.
> *Cook.* Then you can be no good poet; for a good poet differs nothing at all from a master-cook. Either's art is the wisdom of the mind.
> *Poet.* As how, sir?
> *Cook.* Expect. I am by my place to know how to please the palates of the guests; so you are to know the palates of the times; study the several tastes, what every nation, the Spaniard, the Dutch, the French, the Walloon, the Neapolitan, the Briton, the Sicilian can expect from you.
> *Poet.* That were a heavy and hard task to satisfy Expectation, who is so severe an exactress of duties; ever a tyrannous mistress, and most times a pressing enemy.
> *Cook.* She is a powerful great lady, sir, at all times, and must be satisfied.

The same parallel we saw hinted at in the prologue to *Epicœne.*

Of course, his dedicatees are extolled as competent judges, but no value can be attached to such utterances.

A sample of the taste of the crowd is supplied in the intermeans (as Jonson calls them) of *The Staple of News*, where selected types discuss the play, each contributing his idea of how the play should have been written. Jonson protested against this practice in the chorus following the fourth act of *The Magnetic Lady*:

> *Damplay.* . . . it is almost pucker'd, and pull'd into that knot by our poet, which I cannot easily, with all the strength of my imagination, untie.
>
> *Boy.* Like enough; nor is it in your office to be puzzled or perplexed with it, but to sit still, and expect. The more your imagination busies itself the more it is intangled, especially if you happen on the wrong end.
>
> *Probee.* He hath said sufficient, brother Damplay. Our parts that are the spectators, or should hear a comedy, are to await the process and events of things, as the poet presents them, not as we would corruptly fashion them. We come here to behold plays, and censure them as they are made and fitted for us; not to beslave our own thoughts, with censorious spittle tempering the poet's clay, as we were to mold every scene anew. That were a mere plastic, or potter's ambition, most unbecoming the name of a gentleman. No, let us mark, and not lose the business on foot by talking. Follow the right thread, or find it.

The stupidity of the crowd he illustrated in the intermean following the first act of *The Staple of News*:

> *Mirth.* But there was one Smug, a smith, would have made a horse laugh, and broke his halter, as they say.
>
> *Tattle.* O, but the poor man had got a shrewd mischance one day.
>
> *Expectation.* How, gossip?
>
> *Tat.* He had drest a roguy jade i' the morning, that had the staggers, and had got such a spice of 'em himself by noon, as they would not away all the play-time, do what he could for his heart.
>
> *Mirth.* 'Twas his part, gossip; he was to be drunk by his part.
>
> *Tattle.* Say you so? I understood not so much.[1]

---

[1] The play referred to is *The Merry Devil of Edmonton*.

Jonson lacked modesty, but not sincerity. Few would be unwilling to subscribe to the following self-appraisal, from the chorus at the end of Act II of *The Magnetic Lady*:

> But his clothes shall never be the best thing about him though; he will have somewhat besides, either of humane letters, or severe honesty, shall speak him a man though he went naked.

We, who have been conditioned to think in terms of democracy, are apt to react antagonistically to Jonson's outspoken assertion of himself versus the public. On the question of art values his position was not a democratic one. Neither was Shakespeare's. Let us consider with ourselves: if Jonson today, in a world of infinitely wider educational opportunities, were to take a good look at our media of entertainment, should he not feel called upon to repeat himself? And might he not even experience a sardonic delight in applying the newly acquired picturesque term, "the dictatorship of the proletariat?"

In his old age he apparently tried to delude himself into the belief that he had at last succeeded in raising the public to the level of his standard. Witness the friendly opening of the prologue to *The Sad Shepherd*:

> He that hath feasted you these forty years,
> And fitted fables for your finer ears,
> Although at first he scarcely hit the bore,
> Yet you, with patience harkening more and more,
> At length have grown up to him, and made known
> The working of his pen is now your own:
> He prays you would vouchsafe, for your own sake,
> To hear him this once more; but sit awake.

The final admonition makes one suspect that he was not quite settled in his optimistic belief.

Jonson's arrogance may be condoned, for he did possess a critical perception of a high order. The startlingly prophetic judgment he passed upon John Donne, as reported by Drummond, is alone sufficient proof of that:

> He esteemeth John Donne the first poet in the world in some things . . . That Donne himself for not being understood, would perish.

ACTOR AND ACTING

Jonson offers several references to acting that are worth quoting. *In Every Man in His Humor* (III ii) the consummate acting of one of the characters is lauded:

> *Well-bred.* . . . but was't possible thou shouldst not know him?
> *E. Kno'well.* 'Fore God, not I . . . He had written himself into the habit of one of your poor infantry, your decayed, ruinous, worm-eaten gentlemen of the round, such as have . . . translated begging out of the old hackney pace to a fine easy amble and made it run as smooth off the tongue as a shove-groat shilling. Into the likeness of one of the reformados had he moulded himself so perfectly, observing every trick of their action, as, varying the accent, swearing with an emphasis indeed all with so special and exquisite a grace, that, hadst thou seen him thou wouldst have sworn he might have been sergeant-major if not lieutenant-colonel to the regiment.
> *Wel.* Why, Brain-worm, who would have thought thou hadst been such an artificer?
> *E. Kn.* An artificer? an architect! Except a man had studied begging all his life time, and been a weaver of language from his infancy, for the clothing of it, I never saw his rival.

This was a high compliment to the actor who played the part. Was it Burbage?

In *The Devil Is an Ass* Jonson dilates on the skill of Richard Robinson (II iii):

> *Ingine.* Why, sir, your best will be one of the players!
> *Meercraft.* No, there's no trusting them: they'll talk on't, And tell their poets.

Ing.   What if they do? the jest
Will brook the stage. But there be some of them
Are very honest lads. There's Dick Robinson,
A very pretty fellow, and comes often
To a gentleman's chamber, a friend of mine. We had
The merriest supper there one night:
The gentleman's landlady invited him
To a gossips' feast. Now he, sir, brought Dick Robinson,
Drest like a lawyer's wife, amongst 'em all;
(I lent him clothes). But to see him behave it,
And lay the law, and carve, and drink unto 'em;
And then talk bawdy, and send frolics! O!
It would have burst your buttons, or not left you
A seam.
   Meer.   They say he's an ingenious youth.
   Ing.   O sir! and dresses himself the best! beyond
Forty o' your very ladies! Did you ne'er see him?
   Meer. No, I seldom see those toys.

In a sonnet exemplifying the conventional eternizing theme, Jonson pays tribute to Alleyn.

Epigram LXXXIX. To Edward Allen.

If Rome so great, and in her wisest age,
Fear'd not to boast the glories of her stage,
As skilful Roscius, and grave Æsop, men,
Yet crown'd with honors, as with riches then;
Who had no less a trumpet of their name
Than Cicero, whose every breath was fame:
How can so great example die in me,
That, Allen, I should pause to publish thee?
Who both their graces in thyself hast more
Outstript, than they did all that went before:
And present worth in all dost so contract,
As others speak, but only thou dost act.
Wear this renown. 'Tis just that who did give
So many poets life, by one should live.

Salathiel Pavy, one of the Children of the Chapel, played the roles of old men so naturally, he tells us, that the Fates mistook him for one, and cut his thread of life.

Epigram CXX:

Years he numbred scarce thirteen
    When Fates turn'd cruel;
Yet three fill'd zodiacs had he been
    The stage's jewel,
And did act (what now we moan)
    Old men so duly,
As, sooth, the Parcae thought him one,
    He play'd so truly.

The weight of Jonson's testimony is clearly not on the side of formal acting.

The acting of an unidentified comedian is described in the following quotation from *The Poetaster* (III i):

Tucca. . . . let him not beg rapiers or scarfs in his overfamiliar playing face, nor roar out his barren bold jests with a tormenting laughter, between drunk and dry. Do you hear, Stiff-toe? Give him warning, admonition, to forsake his saucy glavering grace, and his goggle eye; it does not become him, sirrah; tell him so.

CASTING. *Barth. Fair.* III i:

Quarlous. How now, Numps! almost tired in your protectorship? overparted, overparted?

The actor who played the part of Leatherhead in *Bartholomew Fair* is described as an irresistible mimic (III i):

Trash. But put him atop o' the table, where his place is, and he'll do you forty fine things. He has not been sent for, and sought out, for nothing, at your great city-suppers, to put down Coriat and Cokeley, and been laught at for his labor. He'll play you all the puppets i' the town over, and the players, every company, and his own company too; he spares nobody.

Ibid. V iii:

Cokes. Which is your Burbage now?

> *Leatherhead.* What mean you by that, sir?
> *Cokes.* Your best actor, your Field?

In the "short characterism of the chief actors" prefixed to *The New Inn* the actors who played the parts of Goodstock and Lovel are singled out as having played well.

In the open-air theater the voice had to be raised above what was required in the indoor theater.

Poetaster. IV ii:

> *Lupus.* Speak lower; you are not now i' your theater, stager.

Disapproval of overacting is voiced in the Induction to *The Staple of News*:

> You come to see . . . which amorous prince makes love in drink, or does overact prodigiously in beaten satin.

Likewise in his comment on *Tamburlaine* in the same work:

> . . . all the Tamerlanes and Tamer-chams of the late age, which had nothing in them but the scenical strutting and furious vociferation to warrant them to the ignorant gapers.

In the following quotation from *Bartholomew Fair* the moronic Cokes is being introduced to the puppets (V iii):

> *Cokes.* These be players minors indeed. Do you call these play-ers?
> *Leath.* They are actors, sir, and as good as any, none disprais'd, for dumb shows. Indeed, I am the mouth of 'em all . . .
> *Cokes.* Do they play perfect? Are they never fluster'd?
> *Leath.* No, sir, I thank my industry and policy for it. They are as well govern'd a company, though I say it . . .

Cynth. Rev. III i:

> *Amorphus.* . . . you must not sink under the first disaster. It is with your young grammatical courtier as with your neophyte player, a thing usual to be daunted at the first presence.

The comments of the "ignorant critic" are burlesqued in the Induction to *Cynthia's Revels*:

> *3. Child.* . . . I wonder that any man is so mad to come to see these rascally tits play here. They do act like so many wrens, or pismires—not the fifth part of a good face amongst them all. And then their music is abominable, able to stretch a man's ears worse than ten pillories; and their ditties lamentable things, like the pitiful fellows that make them—poets. By this vapor, an 'twere not for tobacco, I think the very stench of 'em would poison me; I should not dare to come in at their gates. A man were better visit fifteen jails, or a dozen or two of hospitals, than once adventure to come near them.

In *The Poetaster* (III i) the picturesque Tucca gives us in his inimitable manner a picture of the actor as viewed by his enemies:

> I have stood up and defended you, I, to gent'men, when you have been said to prey upon pu'nes and honest citizens for socks or buskins; or when they ha' call'd you usurers, or brokers; or said you were able to help to a piece of flesh—I have sworn I did not think so; nor that you were the common retreats for punks decay'd i' their practice: I cannot believe it of you.

Cokes, in *Bartholomew Fair,* V iii, remarking on the puppets, says:

> Well, they are a civil company; I like 'em for that; they offer not to fleer, nor jeer, nor break jests, as the great players do. And then, there goes not so much charge to the feasting of 'em, or making 'em drunk, as to the other, by reason of their littleness.

Jonson here contributes his testimony to the practice of petting the actor. (Cf. p. 241).

E. M. out of H. H. "Characterism" of Clove and Orange:

> An inseparable case of coxcombs . . . Their glory is to invite players, and make suppers.

The popular gibe at the prosperity of the actor:
Poet. III i:

Tucca. Do you hear? you, player, rogue, stalker, come back here! No respect to men of worship, you slave? What, you are proud, you rascal, are you proud, ha? You grow rich, do you? and purchase, you two-penny tear-mouth? You have Fortune, and the good year on your side, you stinkard? You have? you have?

Barth. Fair. I i:

Littlewit. I do feel conceits coming upon me, more than I am able to turn tongue to. A pox o' these pretenders to wit! your Three Cranes, Miter, and Mermaid men! not a corn of true salt, not a grain of right mustard, amongst them all. They may stand for places, or so, again the next wit-fall, and pay two pence in a quart more for their canary than other men. But gi' me the man can start up a Justice of Wit out of six shillings beer, and give the law to all the poets and poet-suckers i' town, because they are players' gossips. 'Slid, other men have wives as fine as the players, and as well drest.

Not only were the players feasted by the men, they were also favored by the women. *Cynth. Rev.* II i:

Cupid. A nymph of a most wandering and giddy disposition, humorous as the air; she'll run from gallant to gallant . . . She loves a player well, and a lawyer infinitely.

Ibid. IV i:

Moria. . . . I would tell you which madam lov'd a monsieur, which a player, which a page.

Inducements offered by a bawd (*Barth. Fair,* IV iii):

Whit. . . . dou shalt live like a lady, . . . and ride to Ware and Rumford i' dy coach, shee te players, be in love vit 'em . . .

Ibid. V iii:

Leath. This is he, that acts Leander, sir: he is extremely belov'd of the womenkind.

Nevertheless, the actor's status was such that Tucca (*Poetaster,* V i) could declare, as the ultimate of repulsion: "I'll turn stager first."

407

BALLAD, Etc.

In the *Conversations with Drummond* we read:

> Spenser's stanzas pleased him not, nor his matter.

"Him" was Jonson the classicist. Jonson the Elizabethan had a different opinion. In *The Discoveries* (p. 57) we read:

> Spenser, in affecting the ancients, writ no language; yet
> I would have him read for his matter.

And again, at page 22, the already quoted passage:

> Nay, if it were put to the question of the water-rimer's works,
> against Spenser's, I doubt not but they would find more suffrages;
> because the most favor common vices.

Thus he felt Spenser to be a great poet, but as a devout classicist he could not give his critical approval to work which was born of the romantic product of the Middle Ages—the "Gothic" Ages. I suppose the psychiatrist would see here the operation of "tensions," as in his contradictory attitude toward dramatic theory and practice. In *An Execration upon Vulcan,* concerning the burning of his library, he complains:

> Had I compiled from Amadis de Gaul,
> The Esplanadians, Arthurs, Palmerins, and all
> The learned library of Don Quixote,
> And so some goodlier monster had begot: . . .
> Thou then hadst had some color for thy flames . . .
> Had I foreknown of this thy least desire
> T' have held a triumph, or a feast, of fire,

Especially in paper, . . . many a ream,
To redeem mine, I had sent in; Enough!
Thou shouldst have cry'd, and all been prpoer stuff:
The Talmud, and the Alcoran had come,
With pieces of the Legend; the whole sum
Of errant knighthood, with the dames, and dwarfs,
The charmed boats, and the inchanted wharfs,
The Tristrams, Lanc'lots, Turpins, and the peers,
All the mad Rolands, and sweet Olivers;
To Merlin's marvels, and his cabal's loss,
With the chimera of the Rosie-cross,
Their seals, their characters, hermetic rings,
Their gem of riches, and bright stone that brings
Invisibility, and strength, and tongues.

He hasn't left out much of the medieval stock in trade, has he?
Nevertheless the Elizabethan in him forced him, in spite of himself, to accept Spenser.

But his tolerance did not extend to other forms of popular
literature. For the ballad he had the same special contempt as
his fellows. He could not express the scorn he felt for Anthony
Munday more emphatically than by the name he assigned to him
in *The Case Is Altered*: Antonio Balladino.

Neptune's Triumph:

Stay till the abortive and extemporal din
Of balladry were understood a sin,
Minerva cried.

Underwoods XLI:

What though the greedy fry
Be taken with false baits
Of worded balladry,
And think it poesy?
They die with their conceits,
And only piteous scorn upon their folly waits.

E. M. in H. H. I ii:

E. Kn. Well, if he read this with patience I'll be gelt, and trool ballads for Master John Trundle yonder, the rest of my mortality.

Epic. II ii:

Dauphine. Then this is a ballad of procreation?
Clerimont. A madrigal of procreation; you mistake.

The madrigal was esteemed by music-loving England.

The dumb show and the puppet play shared his contempt.

Onion. . . . you are in print already for the best plotter.
Antonio Balladino. Ay; I might as well have been put in for a dumb show too.

Disc. (p. 22) :

. . . but a man cannot imagine that thing so foolish or rude but will find and enjoy an admirer; at least a reader or spectator. The puppets are seen now in despite of the players.

V. GENERAL CONSIDERATIONS

It now remains to take up some general questions such as would arise in reflecting on the material as a whole without any attempt to determine the special characteristics of the parts. Our subject matter presents a peculiar difficulty, for we are trying to treat as a unit what is in fact a composite. Not what one man deliberately and methodically developed is the topic of our investigation, but what many men at various times and independently of each other gave utterance to. Hence we are confronted by contradiction and disproportion. Formal completeness is out of the question. Yet the task of establishing some sort of unity in our material is not by any means a hopeless one. The material was produced within a certain period, and the mental product of any age finds an integrating factor in the spirit of that age. The spirit of the Elizabethan age was the spirit of the Renaissance, a rebellious spirit that demanded the freedom of the individual. Such a spirit in literature we characterize as romantic, and under its influence the shackles of the past are shaken off and something new is created. The criticism under consideration revealed its romantic nature by accomplishing both these things—it denied the authority of rules which had been handed down and asserted the validity of new truths which had been learned by experience. Among these new truths two are of profound significance in the history of criticism: first, that freedom is essential to art; second, that reason is subordinate to imagination in the sphere of art. It must be remembered that we are dealing with what is only the second genuine contribution to a theory of poetics, the first being Aristotle's treatise. Practically all that had been done in between was a paraphrase of the latter. There can be no doubt that Aristotle would have granted willing recognition to the dictum that freedom is essential to art. This is such a self-evident proposition. He did not state it himself because the opportunity was lacking to formulate it. He attempted to discover the intrinsic laws of the drama by an examination of the drama of his country. Now this had been produced under the free guidance of an artistic impulse. The Greek dramatists inherited no material dogmas to obey or to violate.

It was quite otherwise with the Elizabethan playwright. He was introduced to a model and a code of rules. The model was the comedy of Terence and the tragedy of the pseudo-Seneca; the code was a perversion of Aristotle's *Poetics*. Both of these were contrary to his own Renaissance instinct and national heredity, and instinct won the day. He refused to submit to uncongenial directions, and this conscious rebellion naturally developed, in self justification, the conception of the invalidity of external authority. Aristotle clearly expressed the idea that an art form at any given time may be in a state of progressive evolution. He says: "Whether tragedy has as yet perfected its proper types or not, and whether it is to be judged in itself, or in relation also to the audience,—this raises another question." This is a profound perception. In other words, a play that is good for an ancient Greek might not be so good for an Elizabethan. The observation was made after the Greek theater had borne its best fruit and had entered upon a process of degeneration, yet Aristotle realized that the best that had been done was not necessarily patterned after the best possible model that might have been evolved or might still be evolved. The implication of course is that any laws that might be educed from a literary product cannot be set up as an inviolable canon for future generations. Aristotle did not explicitly state the fact, because there could be no denial of laws before any laws had been formulated.

If Aristotle came close to the conception of the first of the new truths listed as the Elizabethan dramatist's contribution to a poetic theory, he did not and could not conceive the second. No Greek could. It was not in keeping with the Greek *Weltanschauung*. The difference between the Greek view of art and the modern view is the difference between the Greek worship of the rational, the finite, the perfect, and the modern apotheosis of the mystical, the infinite, the imperfect. Greek ideals rose little above the world of fact, hence their representation could be controlled by the reason; on the other hand, today the world of fact is such a small part of the vast universe in which we pass our conscious existence, that the reason which governs sensuous experience is inadequate as a guide for the imagination which soars aloft into the region of our ideals and bodies them forth in the perduring forms of art. Hence the principle of the supremacy of the imagination in the sphere of artistic creation is the natural outgrowth of modern life.

What was the relation between the theory we have been studying and the practice of its exponents? In the main there is harmony between the two. Both are, in general, romantic. Further, literary history justifies the *a priori* inference that the practice preceded the theory; and this inference is confirmed by an examination of the chronology of our material. Where the practice was not in the romantic spirit—as in the case of Jonson—the theory came first. Occasionally, also, in the romantic practice some change would be effected through conscious dissatisfaction with an existing fashion; as, for example, when Marlowe made blank verse the medium for tragedy.

Did the theory, on the whole, have any effect on the practice? If the playwrights had never drawn any generalizations from their work, would the drama have been visibly different? Probably not. Is literature ever really influenced by theory in a creative period? From what we know of human nature, however, we may conclude that the conscious belief that he had the law on his side must have acted as a stimulus to the dramatist.

The question may be asked whether the Elizabethan dramatists were not indebted to some extent for the development of their critical consciousness to the regular criticism of the past and of their own time. The answer must undoubtedly be in the affirmative. As to contemporary criticism, the hostility of the Puritans put the playwrights on the defensive; so they had to discover reasons for their craft. As to the numerous treatises based on Aristotle's *Poetics*, these certainly were more or less known among the playwrights. Aside from Jonson, whose familiarity with them is well known and so much of whose theory was vitally influenced by them, we have definite knowledge that Thomas Heywood, Chapman, and Fletcher were acquainted with them, and there is more than slight evidence that Shakespeare and Webster were not ignorant of them. In one of the epistles prefaced to his *Apology for Actors,* Heywood has a passage bearing on the point: "We may as freely answer as they object, instancing myself by famous Scaliger, learned Doctor Gager, Doctor Gentiles, and others, whose opinions and approved arguments on our part I have in my brief discourse altogether omitted, because I am loath to be taxed in borrowing from others; and besides, their works, being extant to the world, offer themselves freely to every man's perusal." If these works offered themselves freely to every man's perusal we have no right to believe that a knowledge of them was confined to those whom we can actually prove to have read them. Granting, therefore, that the Elizabethan dramatists were more or less acquainted with classical criticism, in what way did this acquaintance affect their own theoretical reflection? It served as a stimulus to bring their ideas to a focus. Here were definitely stated doctrines—their own ideas could therefore be formulated in answer to them.

Did the romantic theory thus informally formulated have any bearing on the future of literary history? The fact that the task of investigating its emergence has been reserved to this late day is sufficient answer to the question. It did not. It passed away with the passing of those who applied it. A new spirit crept into life, a spirit not congenial to romantic theories. Hence a new critical canon established itself and held its position for over a century. It is possible of course that the views of Ben Jonson had some connection with the establishment of the new canon. The Tribe of Ben served as a bridge connecting two separate generations. Surely if Jonson's work on Horace had not been destroyed it would have had its influence. When, toward the end of the eighteenth century, the new critical philosophy was forced to give way, the same literature which had given birth to the forgotten doctrine gave birth anew to a criticism which closely resembled her first-born, by inspiring such men as Schlegel and Coleridge. It is just possible that these had their attention called to the significance of some of the important passages quoted in this compilation, but there is no evidence for the hypothesis. Modern romantic criticism must be regarded as an independent growth.

The present volume embodies what I consider the only dramatic criticism of any value to which the period under consideration gave birth. In defense of my position I cannot do better than quote what Spingarn, whose authority in this matter is unquestioned, has to say about that Elizabethan dramatic criticism which is not included in the present study. He says: "Dramatic criticism in England began with Sir Philip Sidney. Casual references to the drama can be found in critical writings anterior to the *Defense of Poesy*; but to Sidney belongs the credit of having first formulated, in a more or less systematic manner, the general principles of dramatic art. Those principles, it need hardly be said, are those which, for half a century or more, had been undergoing discussion and modification in Italy and France, and of which the ultimate source was the *Poetics* of Aristotle." We learn, therefore, that the regular criticism in England was an echo of continental criticism, having no relation to the actual English drama. Is it not hard to see what appreciable value can be accredited to criticism that is but an echo; particularly if it is an echo of a criticism which is itself only a scholastic elaboration of some other criticism? As criticism it has no value at all.

In itself the continental criticism was but a hair-splitting differentiation of terms without reference to things connoted, and hence running into empty speculations and silly trivialities. For example, Maggi asks: "If in a tragedy we should send a messenger to Egypt, and he would return in an hour, would not the spectator regard this as ridiculous?" And again, Robortelli is certain that when Aristotle limited the action of tragedy to a single revolution of the sun he meant to exclude the night; "for as tragedy can contain only one single and continuous action, and as people are accustomed to sleep in the night, it follows that the tragic action cannot be continued beyond one artificial day." "Nay," interrupts Segni, "he must have included the night, since things dealt with in a tragedy are more likely to happen at night." "But," persists the obstinate Robortelli, "night is naturally the time for repose." "Yes," retorts the undaunted Segni, "but unjust people act contrary to the laws of nature."

Such puerility is typical of what the mysterious human consciousness is capable of evolving out of itself when it is not inclined to accept the assistance of empirical investigation. Of course any theory is of value only insofar as it is generalization from fact. It is this truth which gives value to the criticism embodied in the present volume. Thus, the doctrines enunciated by the dramatists are superior to those preached by the professional critics, both practically and theoretically: practically, because they are an outgrowth of actual problems presented by the English theater of the time; and theoretically, because, *being* an outgrowth of new conditions, they constitute a new contribution to analytic thought.

But I must quote Spingarn further: "Dramatic criticism in England was thus, from its birth, both Aristotelian and classical, and it remained so for two centuries. The beginnings of the Elizabethan drama were almost contemporary with the composition of the *Defense of Poesy,* and the decay of the drama with Jonson's *Discoveries.* Yet throughout this period the romantic drama never received literary exposition. The great Spanish drama had its critical champions and defenders, the English drama had none. It was, perhaps, found to be a simpler task to echo the doctrines of others, than to formulate the principles of a novel dramatic form."

The material collected within the covers of this volume constitutes the contemporary literary exposition of the romantic drama.

NOTE. In the current issue of *Renaissance News* (XV, 3, 1962, p. 217), I find welcome confirmation of my position: "If it were required," wrote De Quincy in 1828, "to assign the two bodies of writers who have exhibited the human understanding in the most abject poverty, and whose works by no possibility emit a casual scintillation of wit, fancy, just thinking, or good writing, we should certainly fix upon Greek rhetoricians and Italian critics. Amongst the whole mass there is not a page that any judicious friend to literature would wish to reprieve from destruction."

INDEX

417